MASTER DYERS TO THE WORLD

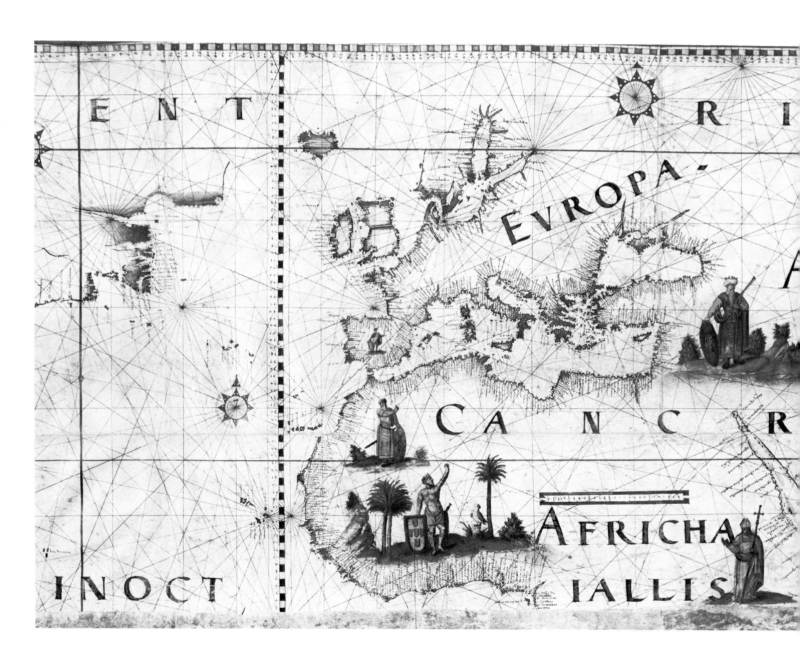

Master Dyers to the World

Technique and Trade in Early Indian Dyed Cotton Textiles

Mattiebelle Gittinger

The Textile Museum, Washington, D.C.

This volume is published in conjunction with the exhibition "Master Dyers to the World" held at the Textile Museum, Washington, D.C.; the Field Museum of Natural History, Chicago; and the Asia Society Gallery, New York.

Editor   Caroline Kastle McEuen
Designer   Susan Lehmann
Printed by Garamond Pridemark Press, Baltimore

Cover   Seventeenth century Indian hanging, detail of Figure 108.
Pages 2-3   Anonymous planisphere of ca. 1545. Österreichische Nationalbibliothek, Vienna.

Library of Congress Cataloging in Publication Data

Gittinger, Mattiebelle.
Master dyers to the world.

Bibliography
1. Cotton fabrics—India—Exhibitions. I. Title.
TS1557.U62W373   1982   667'.3'09540740153   82-10695
ISBN 0-87405-020-0

Contents

7 Foreword
by *Marion Stirling Pugh*

9 Preface

13 **INTRODUCTION**

19 **MASTER DYER'S SKILLS**

31 **MASTER DYERS IN ANTIQUITY: FOSTAT**

59 **MASTER DYERS TO INDIA**
with contributions by *Nina Gwatkin*

137 **MASTER DYERS TO THE EAST**

175 **MASTER DYERS TO THE WEST**

192 Pictorial Supplement

197 Glossary

200 Bibliography

Foreword

Major General John Ramsey Pugh, the founder's son-in-law, remembers that George Hewitt Myers' favorite collections were antique Oriental rugs and Pre-Columbian textiles. These were his specialties, for which The Textile Museum is best known. Nevertheless, he appreciated any beautiful and unusual textile, and until his death in 1957 he purchased ancient Coptic pieces, numerous Indonesian fabrics, special Greek Island embroideries, and antique Indian textiles—the last of these, of course, being the subject of this publication and exhibition.

Thanks to the foresight of George Hewitt Myers, The Textile Museum possesses an extensive collection of Indian trade textiles dating from the fifteenth to eighteenth centuries that were recovered from surface finds and excavations at Fostat, the site of the ancient Egyptian capital.

After Dr. Mattiebelle Gittinger was appointed Research Associate for Southeast Asian Textiles in December 1975, she used the Museum's collection as a nucleus to research and organize an exhibition of Indonesian textiles and, in 1979, published *Splendid Symbols: Textiles and Tradition in Indonesia*. This was one of the Museum's most popular publications and was reprinted.

The Director and Trustees were delighted with Dr. Gittinger's scholarly approach and its success and were pleased to encourage her when she suggested that her next research project be the study and published documentation of Indian textiles, again using the Museum's collection as a nucleus. Thirty-five examples of the Fostat textiles are included in the exhibition, and they provide a bridge to antiquity. In addition to her research during the years she has been associated with us, Dr. Gittinger has assisted the Museum in innumerable other ways: she has written articles for the *Journal*; lectured; taught educational classes; organized exhibitions; hosted the 1978 Roundtable; and raised funds.

We thank the Indo-U.S. Subcommission on Education and Culture for their pivotal role in making the exhibition possible. They initiated agreements with the Indian government, financed research by The Textile Museum's staff in India, and gave invaluable assistance in facilitating the loan of textiles from museums throughout India. We would have been unable to present the exhibition without their help.

In India many institutions cooperated with this project; we are particularly grateful for the assistance of the National Museum, the Crafts Museum, and the Indian Council for Cultural Relations in New Delhi.

A grant from the National Endowment for the Arts provided funds for the project and furnished the initial endorsements that buoyed the effort when additional funds needed to be sought elsewhere.

We also gratefully acknowledge the financial support of the Smithsonian Institution's Special Foreign Currency Program in regard to this proj-

1 *A bandhani worker in Bagru, Rajasthan, displays her wares. Some of the small ties that serve to resist penetration of the dye remain on the textile. The woman wears a similarly worked textile over her head. (Mattiebelle Gittinger, Washington, D.C.)*

7

This detail of an early nineteenth century palm leaf manuscript from Orissa depicts a nobleman inspecting his wardrobe. Such garments were patterned by dye techniques, embroidery, or by supplementary yarns applied while weaving.

ect and the assistance given by the U.S. International Communication Agency.

The exhibition catalogue has been supported by P. Kaufmann, Inc., in collaboration with Sheila Hicks. Sheila Hicks came to the aid of the Museum when efforts to secure the additional funding for the project appeared to be failing, and it was through her personal intervention and commitment that success was assured. The Indian League of America and Nobuko Kajitani also responded to our search for funds, and we appreciate their confidence.

We also acknowledge the contribution of Air India in transporting participants for educational programs.

The staff of The Textile Museum contributed cheerfully in many ways. While Director, Andrew Oliver, Jr., supervised the project; after January 1982, Acting Director Patricia Fiske gave administrative support. Mary Lee Berger-Hughes arranged shipping and insurance. Mary Burgess conducted energetic fund-raising activities and handled public relations. Blenda Femenias contributed advice about European costume history; Katherine Freshley arranged interlibrary loan agreements; Lilo Markrich drafted letters in German; and Clarissa Palmai and Jane Merrit prepared textiles for exhibition.

Richard Timpson and Sollie Lee Barnes installed the exhibit.

We also join Dr. Gittinger in thanking the many other organizations and individuals whom she credits in the preface.

After opening in The Textile Museum in the fall of 1982, the exhibition will travel to the Field Museum of Natural History in Chicago and to the Asia Society Gallery in New York City.

This publication is a tangible justification of the Trustees' confidence in Dr. Gittinger's talents.

MARION STIRLING PUGH
Vice President, Board of Trustees
The Textile Museum

Preface

When the Indo-U.S. Subcommission on Education and Culture first suggested the possibility of an exhibition of Indian textiles to The Textile Museum, our response was a delighted "yes." We were then confronted by the need to impose a tyranny of choice on the vast array of possibilities that India presents in the textile arts. We early felt that the topic of the exhibition should center on cotton, yet this was scarcely a limiting criterion within the Indian context. Cotton would, however, show Indian accomplishment in textiles to singular advantage, for India's skill in dyeing and patterning cotton with brilliant, fast colors was achieved early and was unique; no other people had mastered such skills. So evident was this mastery that Indian textiles, mostly of cotton, had become a major item of trade to much of the world by the seventeenth and eighteenth centuries.

The problem we finally addressed was the documentation of this exceptional versatility and skill, and the exhibition presents some of the finest examples of Indian patterned and dyed cottons that remain to us of this art—from modest trade goods of the thirteenth and fifteenth centuries to masterpieces of the early eighteenth. In the brilliance of their colors and the startling range of forms, I hope the examples will also communicate my own delight and awe at the Indian artisans' skills.

A Note on Measurements

In the period represented there was also diversity in the measures and currencies with which to contend. At one point I tried to recast all measures into the metric system, but that seemed to deny the historical records that carried listings in yards, fractions of yards, or inches. Later records introduced centimeters and combined these with *hasta*. In the end, I decided to keep yards and inches when that seemed in accord with trade records and to convert the remainder to the metric system. It is also customary when dealing with textiles to list the warp dimension first, then the weft. On many fragments we had no selvage, or the textile was mounted in such a manner as to conceal the selvage so we could not determine the warp direction. Where a determination could be made, the warp and weft are listed in the catalogue entry; otherwise the dimensions alone are given.

Acknowledgments

From the moment we as an institution, and I personally, agreed to do the exhibition, we began to accrue a sizable debt of gratitude to a list of people and institutions that would eventually encompass the globe.

Of primary importance to this project, and to any understanding of this Indian accomplishment, is the scholarship of John Irwin and Alfred Bühler. We have drawn extensively on the works of Irwin for an understanding of the Indian mordant-patterned and dyed cottons and their trade to Europe. Bühler's great studies of resist patterning in both India and Southeast Asia have been called upon repeatedly. The work of both of these scholars is critical to all study in this field.

The scope of the exhibition, and its historical character, meant that we had to seek out examples residing in many institutional and private collections. There have been, I confess, fleeting moments when I would have welcomed a less extensive trade history to illustrate. Many individuals have contributed to the exhibition; in particular, the following deserve my very real appreciation.

In India, Martand Singh, director of the Calico Museum of Textiles at Ahmedabad, welcomed me to his museum and allowed me access to study the collection for a month. In Benares, I thank Devaki Ahivasi, of the Bharat Kala Bhavan, and also Anand Krishna, who discussed many topics with me and introduced me to his home and his city. In Bombay, Sadashiv V. Gorakshar and N.P. Joshi of the Prince of Wales Museum were most hospitable. In Hyderabad, Jagdish and Kamla Mittal welcomed me to their home and shared their holdings from the Jagdish and Kamla Mittal Museum of Indian Art. In Jaipur, Chandramani Singh, of the Maharaja Sawai Man Singh II Museum, introduced me to her museum's holdings and accompanied me on visits to nearby dyers. In New Delhi, Chhaya Bhattacharya, Krishna Lal, Nilima Roy, and G.K. Sharotri received me at the National Museum; Nilima Baxi of the Crafts Museum was instrumental in arranging the shipment of textiles to this country. There were others in New Delhi who assisted this project at various stages: Pupul Jayakar, All India Handicrafts Board; Usha Malik, Indian Council for Cultural Relations; Kapila Vatsyayan, Joint Educational Advisor, Department of Culture; and Theodore Riccardi, Cultural Affairs Officer, International Communication Agency, to name a few.

In Europe, colleagues have been most gracious on numerous occasions, and I especially thank the following people. In Amsterdam, Rita Bolland of the Tropenmuseum has shared her knowledge with me for many years, C.A. Burgers of the Rijksmuseum worked on a Saturday to introduce me to the museum's holdings, and Tine Cramer shared her home. In The Hague, Ebeltje Hartkamp-Jonxis made valuable suggestions regarding textiles in the Netherlands. In Hindeloopen, Gabriel Groenewoud of the Gemeentemuseum de Hidde Nijland Stichting was most helpful. In Leeuwarden, C. Boschma and Sytske Wille-Engelsma of the Fries Museum shared their fine collection. In London, Veronica Murphy, Robert Skelton, and Betty Tyres, principals of the India Section of the Victoria and Albert Museum, contributed repeated and gracious assistance, even when they were burdened with their own deadlines. I acknowledge them with special gratitude. I also thank Henry Ginsburg, of the British Library in London, who both loaned to the exhibition and helped with translations. In Wales, the Earl of Powis and the trustees of his estate through the help of P.L. Marriott generously made available an extraordinary tent wall. We thank Christopher Rowell for his aid in arranging the details.

In Paris, Krishna Riboud provided me a home, contributed photographs and slides, and graciously shared extremely important textiles from her collections in Paris and New York.

In Japan, Gai Nishimura in Kyoto agreed to share six examples from his private holdings and was extremely kind in arranging the necessary photography. In Tokyo, Yōzō Nomura was generous with the loan of an exceptional textile. I am particularly grateful to Nobuko Kajitani of The Metropolitan Museum of Art for extensive assistance in handling the many communications with individuals in Japan.

On this continent, a long list of institutions and individuals helped in many ways: Catherine K. Hunter, Museum of Fine Arts, Boston; Carolyn Shine, Cincinnati Museum of Art; Louise Cort, Freer Gallery of Art, Washington, D.C.; Peggy Gilfoy, Indianapolis Museum of Art; Amy Poster, The Brooklyn Museum; Milton Sonday and Lucy Commoner, Cooper-Hewitt Museum, The Smithsonian Institution's National Museum of Design, New York; Jean Mailey and Nobuko Kajitani, The Metropolitan Museum of Art, New York; Betsy Johnson, Philadelphia Museum of Art; and Louise Mackie and John Vollmer, Royal Ontario Museum, Toronto.

I deeply appreciate the support of the Indo-U.S. Subcommission on Education and Culture, particularly its Museum Committee, in the planning and preparation of this exhibition, including their sponsorship of my study in India. Particular thanks go to Ted Tanen, American Executive Director; to Linda Spencer Murchison, who acted as coordinator; and to Patrice Fusillo. Loan arrangements always require labor, but to handle the logistics half a world away presents an entire set of unfamiliar problems. The Subcommission repeatedly found solutions to the problems as they arose.

Others who deserve and receive our gratitude are Lora Redford, for her encouragement; Cynthia C. Cort, who escorted the textiles from India; Manuella Fuller, who helped in fundraising; and Nancy Selden, who arranged the labels.

I am, of course, also grateful for the cooperation of my colleagues at The Textile Museum and would like to mention each for the many kindnesses shown me. Quite special attention, however, is due to Mary Burgess and Nina Gwatkin. When the present economic situation threatened to cancel this exhibition, Mary's creative thinking and energy saved the project. She initiated new fund-raising ideas and worked tirelessly to make the project go forward. The necessity to seek funds caused great delay in the actual work on the project, and Nina's help made meeting deadlines possible. She did research on many aspects, sought out photographs, helped arrange source material, and patiently suffered telephone calls at all hours. She has written several essays regarding major textiles in the exhibition, for which she is credited by the entry. Her willingness to share her ideas has enriched other areas of the catalogue as well.

My gratitude to the trustees of The Textile Museum is implicit. I thank them, in particular Mrs. Marion Stirling Pugh, for their support.

MATTIEBELLE GITTINGER

Introduction

At the beginning of the seventeenth century, the French traveler François Pyrard could write from Goa on the Indian west coast, "... the principal riches consist chiefly of silk and cotton stuffs, wherewith everyone from Cape of Good Hope to China, man and woman, is clothed from head to foot."[1]

While there may be an element of exaggeration in Pyrard's statement, it is only one of degree. Before the arrival of Europeans, Indian and Arab traders had made Indian piece goods a major trade item in the Middle East, in the Mediterranean, and on the coast of Africa and a principal currency in the spice trade of the East Indies and other parts of Asia.

Indeed, the record of trade of Indian textiles to Southeast Asia reaches back as early as the fifth century, to documents that record an Indonesian diplomatic mission to China that carried textiles from India and Gandhara.[2] This early report suggests not just the availability of Indian trade goods in the Southeast Asian archipelago, but also the high esteem accorded them. There is further proof of this high regard from the eleventh century when 500 Jewish families, on their way to settle in the Northern Sung capital of China, bought cotton goods in India to take as gifts.[3]

We have a description of some of the Southeast Asian trade in Malacca dating from about 1515. Tomé Pires, the famous Portuguese traveler, tells us that each year ships arrived from Gujarat on India's west coast worth fifteen, twenty, and thirty thousand cruzados, and from Cambay a ship put into port worth seventy to eighty thousand. "[The] merchandize they bring is cloth of thirty kinds, which are of value in these parts." He further tells us that Malacca received from Bengal "very rich bed canopies, with cut-cloth work in all colours and very beautiful; wall hangings like tapestry . . ."; from the Indian Coromandel Coast came ships worth eighty to ninety thousand cruzados, carrying cloth of thirty different sorts, ". . . rich cloths of great value."[4]

The Europeans who viewed this lively Asian commerce in the sixteenth and seventeenth centuries quickly realized that if they hoped to prosper, or even to survive economically, they must join in the commerce of Indian textiles. This trade did not confine itself to barter for spices; the textile goods attained a worth in their own right. First as novelties, then in ever broader ranges, the cotton textiles came to Northern Europe. How remarkable this fabric must

2 Gossypium arboreum *was the first variety of cotton thought to have been used in India. Edward Terry, who traveled there in the seventeenth century, leaves an interesting description of the plant: "The staple commodities of this kingdome are indico and cotton-wooll," he wrote. "For cotton-wooll they plant seedes which grow up into shrubs like unto our rose-bushes. It blowes first into a yellow blossome, which falling off, there remaynes a cod about the bigness of a man's thumb, in which the substance is moyst and yellow, but, as it ripens, it swels bigger till it break the covering, and so in short time becomes white as snow, and then they gather it. These shrubs bear three or foure yeares ere they supplant them."[1] (Kirtikar 1918 I:Pl. 139. Courtesy of Smithsonian Institution Libraries.)*

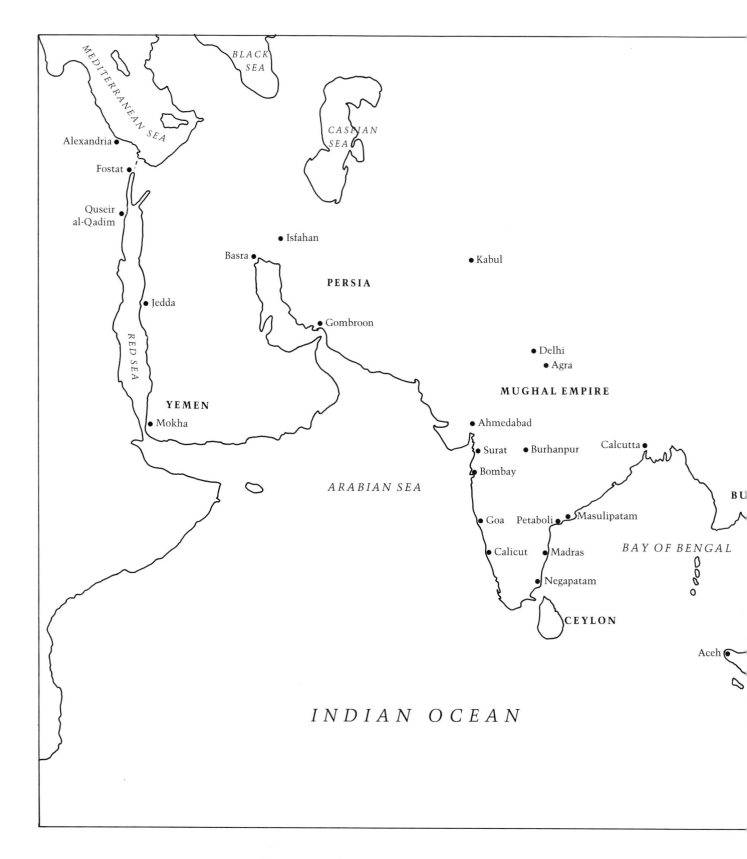

have seemed; it was light in weight, could be easily washed, and appeared in sparkling bright colors. In comparison with the ubiquitous European woolens and linens of this age before dry cleaning, cotton had obvious advantages. One historian of the period comments, "The adoption and rate of increase in the consumption of Indian textiles in the Western world during the seventeenth and eighteenth centuries was one of those astonishing processes of diffusion which is comparable to the discovery and spread of tobacco, potato, coffee [or] tea. . . ."[5] The availability of cotton textiles ultimately affected industry throughout much of Europe, al-

Map A

tered patterns of agriculture, and changed fashions and concepts of cleanliness.

By the mid-eighteenth century, how had the Indians come to this stage of virtually clothing the world? Essentially through the beneficence of nature and their own genius. Paramount was the Indian superiority in cultivating and processing cotton; second, their remarkable capacity for seemingly endless product differentiation—from sarongs for the East and turbans for the Middle East to high fashion for Europe.

By the most conservative estimate, India had more than two

millennia of experience in the growing, handling, and processing of cotton before any other areas of significant cotton cultivation developed in the Old World. The evolution of this mastery is shrouded in a time before that of the earliest known woven cotton—a sample found at Mohenjo Daro in the Indus Valley that dates to 1750 B.C. The fragment seems to have been of *Gossypium arboreum*,[6] the type of cotton cultivated in later classical times in India and possibly in parts of the Sudan and on Bahrein Island;[7] this was a perennial form that required an extensive growing period. The lack of annual varieties that would mature in a short growing season and the added demands of the perennial form for a warm climate and abundant water prevented early spread of this crop to more northern areas.[8] The variety that would significantly expand the range of cotton cultivation, the annual form *Gossypium herbaceum*, seems not to have appeared until the sixth or seventh century A.D. By the tenth century it had spread through the West, and by the thirteenth century through the Far East.[9] With its earlier experience in weaving the perennial form, India by this time clearly had mastered the difficulties of handling this plant fiber and had established markets abroad.

The processing included preparation of the fibers, spinning, weaving, bleaching, and dyeing; each of these became a craft specialty, even an art. Spinning alone required skills that were not easily imitated, and it was only with the invention of spinning and other textile machinery at the time of the Industrial Revolution in Britain that there arose a challenge to this Indian work. Next, there was the warping and mounting of the loom and final weaving, all of which required special skills. The very difficulties in performing these steps in the making of textiles with cotton may well have limited the spread of this fiber in many parts of the world.[10]

Above the proficiency in making cotton textiles, India's crowning textile accomplishment was the patterning of this cloth with brilliant fast dyes. This technology ranged from simply dyeing yarns for weaving to methods involving complex orchestration of a range of processes such as bleaching, pattern design, resist processes, application of mordants, the coordination of multiple carved stamps, mixing of complex dyes prepared for predictable effects, dyeing and painting of fine details, and, finally, careful dyeing, washing, and, occasionally, even the addition of tinsel.

These varied skills were based on empirical and hereditary knowledge that had its ancestry in the dye processes known at Mohenjo Daro. The dyeing involved the use of metallic salts called mordants to bind the dye to the cotton fibers. The Indians developed an expertise with the mordants for red and black and with all their variations. Together with indigo and a few other dye substances, these technologies provided a range of colors that could be used in their own right and in combination with other decorative techniques, such as resist patterning in the manner of batik. This particular work was done free-hand, by stamps, or by a combination of these two methods.

The mastery of the technical aspects of this craft allowed the dyer the freedom to respond to orders for different patterns and designs with assured success. He could meet the demands—in design and, usually, color preferences—of virtually any market. Dark maroons, blacks, and deep reds—patterned in grids with details worked with "nervous" white resist lines—went to Thailand. To Southeast Asia went hip wrappers with large saw-toothed borders and fields worked with geometric patterns or small flowers. To Armenia went Christian altar frontals. To Europe went bedhangings with great blossoming trees and dress goods patterned so that they could be cut and tailored into gowns, robes, or vests. From the European trade communiqués one can sense that this market became captive to the very ability of India to provide variation; as the "Indian craze" seized the fashion world at the end of the seventeenth century,[11] the companies' home offices requested ever more diversity and novelty. In 1697, for example, there is an order for "good brisk colours, the works of any sort of rambling fancyes of the country, but no English patterns."[12]

The ingenious and multifarious response of Indian dyers to these demands from different foreign markets and from domestic trade, primarily in the seventeenth and eighteenth centuries, is the topic of this exhibition. The spectrum of accomplishment is a full one, and the sample presented here only hints at the numbers, kinds, hues, variations, skills, and the rich artistic sensibilities that enliven the fabric of this art. Even so, it is enough to inspire the awe and respect that is its due.

Over the centuries, the lasting quality of this art has caused it to be revived, reinterpreted, and presented in a current guise. This has been particularly true for chintz, the name the English-speaking world adopted from Indian terms for the highly glazed, floral-patterned cottons. As recently as the summer of 1982, *The New York Times* illustrated current chintz interpretations from major textile design houses in New York and chronicled yet another revival. Said one designer, "Chintz represents the eternal summer day and produces an immediate atmosphere of memories."[13] This was the imagery India created for the West; there was other imagery created for the East, and still more for India itself, once the master dyer to the world.

NOTES TO TEXT

1. Pyrard de Laval 1887–89 II:247.
2. Wolters 1967:151.
3. Goodrich 1942–43:408.
4. Pires 1944: 269–70.
5. Chaudhuri 1978:277.
6. Watson 1977:359.
7. Ibid. and Forbes 1956:48.
8. Watson 1977:359.
9. Ibid.:360.
10. Ibid.
11. Slomann 1953:113.
12. Baker 1921:34.
13. Slesin 1982:Cl.

NOTES TO ILLUSTRATIONS

1. *Early Travels* 1968:301.

Master Dyer's Skills

Technical advances of the past two centuries create a scrim that obscures the magnitude of the Indian dyer's achievements in his own time. At the apogee of his skills in the seventeenth and eighteenth centuries, he had earned a fame based on both a spectrum of colors and a quality of fastness unmatched by dyers in other areas. Furthermore, he had perfected the manipulation of the dyes on the cloth surface to effect virtually every type of design from interlocking grids or diapers of small delicate flowers to intricate pictorial scenes—and all on cotton, one of the most difficult fibers to dye.

Unlike animal fibers such as silk and wool, which can accept most natural dyes with "comparative" ease, inherent properties of the cotton fiber reject a permanent bonding. An intermediary agent called a mordant must be used. The mordant unites with certain natural dyes to cause the coloring matter to be bound to the cotton fiber.[1] Technically, the mordant, a metallic oxide, combines with the dye to create an insoluble substance that coats the fiber. Different mordants will yield different colors in the same dye bath, and varying concentrations of a mordant can affect color density. The manipulation of the kinds of mordants, their purity and their density, is one of the secrets of the dyer's art.

The technology of mordants was known to the Indians in at least the second millennium B.C., as the few mordanted cotton yarns found in the Indus Valley site of Mohenjo Daro attest. It is not certain how these beginnings evolved into the elaborately colored textiles of the seventeenth century, which involved patterning with mordants in combination with wax resist, but the mordant process, at least at this stage of research, must be credited to Indian genius.[2] Some aspects of patterning with mordants, probably learned through trade with India, were known to the Egyptians in the first century A.D., but Pliny's report of this tells us neither the type of fabric used nor specific details about the patterning; he merely mentions several colors resulting from a single dye.[3] In Western and Middle Europe, use of mordants to pattern textiles was not significant until Indian textile imports of the seventeenth century began to excite industrial curiosity. At that time printed textiles in Europe were created by block printing a black pigment onto the cloth surface in a process more akin to painting than dyeing. Additional light colors might be applied to the surface

3 *At various stages in the dye process, the textiles are "cured" in the bright sun on the riverbank. Here two women near Deesa, Gujarat, return from the river, one carrying a great load of the partially worked textiles on her head. (Mattiebelle Gittinger, Washington, D.C.)*

4 Morinda citrifolia *is a member of a genus of small trees and creepers that carries the red coloring element alizarin. The roots, which contain the greatest concentrations, are called al, ail, saranguy, or chiranjee in various parts of India. While it served as a substitute for madder in India, it was the major source of red dye in Indonesia. (Kirtikar 1918 II:Pl. 506. Courtesy of Smithsonian Institution Libraries.)*

of the cloth, but none of this patterning could withstand washing.[4] The richly colored, patterned textiles of India must have been astonishing; that they were washable, miraculous.[5]

The two most elusive, but prized, colors at this period in European textiles were red and black. The Indian textiles excelled in capturing both of these colors by their use of alum and iron mordants. These elements, in conjunction with tannin, were the most important mordants in India. Alum in association with an alizarin dye could be controlled to produce reds to pinks. Iron, when steeped with a sour, acidic substance, yielded a mordant that would combine with tannin to create black. Violet resulted from a combination of the two mordants, while the addition of seemingly minor substances to the dye bath, such as pomegranate rinds or specific flowers, extended the color possibilities even further. An early Indian medical treatise lists forty-five shades that were the results of seventy-seven processes.[6]

5 Oldenlandia umbellata, *called* chayaver *and* chay, *provided a red dye superior to madder. It was known on the Coromandel Coast and parts of Ceylon. (Kirtikar 1918 II:Pl. 492. Courtesy of Smithsonian Institution Libraries.)*

The most complex of the Indian dye processes involved red dyeing. Although it is thought the original technique may have come from the Near East[7]—hence the name "Turkey red"—the Indians brought it to perfection in both the dyeing of yarns and in the patterning of cotton cloth. A critical step in the procedure requires treating the yarns or woven cloth with an oil or fatty substance and then an astringent. It is thought that this prevents the alum mordant from crystallizing while it is drying on the cloth and promotes a more complete depositing of aluminum oxide on the fibers.[8] After oiling and other preparatory steps, among them mordanting with alum, the cloth is dyed with an alizarin substance.

Alizarin is the coloring matter contained in the madder plant (*Rubia tinctorum*) and its relative *R. munjista*. Equally important for Indian dyers was its presence in several small trees and shrubs of the genus *Morinda*, and in a plant called *chay* (*Oldenlandia umbellata*). *Morinda citrifolia*, *M. tinctoria*, and *M. augustifolia* were important in western India where their roots, which bore the dye, carried the common name *aal* or *al*, *saranguy*, and in south India, *chiranjee*.[9]

Local al plants were supplemented by the importation from Armenia or Georgia by way of Persia of a root called *ronas*, probably a madder-like plant or even a *Morinda* species.[10] Ronas, or *runas*, from Persia was also imported in the east as a dye for the textiles made on the Coromandel Coast.[11] More important for these renowned textiles, however, was the regional chay root. That grown in certain parts of the Kistna delta was particularly famous because it yielded a bright, luminous red as a result of the calcium absorbed by the plant from the shell-rich flats of the delta. Empirical evidence showed that this chay yielded a superior color, but not until the eighteenth century did Europeans begin to suspect that calcium would perfect their own reds.[12] In the seventeenth century, foreign exporters of textiles working further south along the Indian east coast arranged for this chay to be used by the best of their own manufacturers, even though it was a more costly ingredient.[13] Demands for chay were great. Additional supplies were traded from northern Ceylon, the whole Madura region of south India, and the islands between Ceylon and the Indian coast; roots from these islands were considered particularly fine,[14] possibly because they, too, grew in calcium-rich soils.

Many of these plants with their inherent dye properties were not unique to India. Indeed, madder was grown in small quantities near Paris in the seventeenth century and had been used as a dye for wool in Europe by the sixteenth century.[15] The secrets of producing the brilliant fast reds on cotton and linen, however, eluded European investigators until well into the eighteenth century. In the Far East as well, the procedures associated with Turkey red dyeing were not known at an early date. The need was not great in China and Japan because silk, the primary fiber of concern, would more easily accept natural dyes, but even in Southeast Asia, where cotton was the primary fiber, the technique of red dyeing was not known at an early date. Because of its predominant distribution among coastal groups and those associated with courts

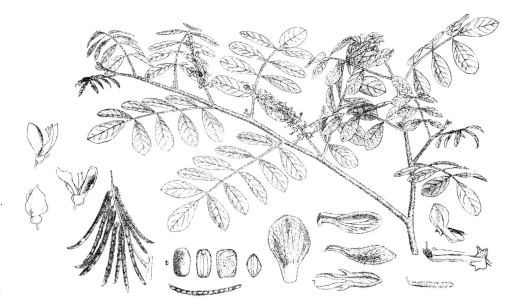

6 Indigofera tinctoria *was the predominant source of blue dye in India. The small shrubs were cultivated, and certain areas such as Sarkhej in Gujarat were once famous for this crop. In the seventeenth century it became a major export to Europe. (Kirtikar 1918 II: Pl. 299A. Courtesy of Smithsonian Institution Libraries.)*

and commercial centers, the suggestion has been made that Islamic traders carried the secrets of madder dyeing into the Southeast Asian area and were responsible for its spread in relatively recent times.[16]

The brilliant lasting reds were just one of the Indian dyer's important achievements. There were other colors and a range of sources.

It has been judged that there are nearly 300 dye-yielding plants in India.[17] Of these, none was both artistically and commercially more important than *Indigofera tinctoria,* indigo. This plant, along with at least fifty others, contains the basic blue dye agent indican, but it contains concentrations thirty times greater than the plants commonly used in the early western and far eastern world. The dye does not require a mordant, but it does require a processing with little tolerance for error. Methods of indigo dyeing were known throughout most of Asia, and these were practiced in varying degrees of complexity. The techniques used in India and Southeast Asia were the most complex. One difficulty in using indigo is that it is not soluble in water and must first be converted to an accessible form. This is done by treating the precipitate from the soaked leaves of the indigo plant with an alkaline solution to convert it to "indigo white." This serves as the dye, and after immersion in such a bath or vat, the cloth or yarns are exposed to the air where the so-called white indigo is oxidized and assumes its blue color. Repeating the cycle deepens the color. Some of the variations possible, alone or in combinations, include watery blue, greyish and sky blue, blue-black, dark blue, purple, lavender, mauve lilac, emerald blue, dark blue-green, sap green, and yellow green.[18] The greens were created by painting a yellow dye, usually tumeric, over dyed indigo. Because the yellow dyes were often fugitive, the green details in older textiles, such as the leaves and stems of plants, now appear blue, having lost the application of yellow.

Indigo is one of those fabled stuffs of history that carried a promise of fortunes to be made—at least for traders to the Levant and

Europe, where it did not grow naturally. So rare was it in Roman times that the little that was traded overland or by the Red Sea was used as a medicine and a valued pigment in paint.[19] This exclusive quality changed little as long as the commerce was dependent on overland routes. Only when sea navigation around the Cape of Good Hope became possible could indigo become available in quantities significant enough to remove it from the luxury category. The dye then became enmeshed in the realities of the European economy. Most formidable of the obstacles to its use was an existing blue dye industry based on woad (*Isatis tinctoria*), the European dye plant. Thousands of acres of woad were grown in southern France, Picardy, and north Germany, where it served not just an industrial need but was a tax base for the governments. To protect this structure, indigo was outlawed in much of northern Europe in the sixteenth century and was given such pejorative labels as "the devil's color."[20]

England, however, did not have a vested interest in the woad industry, and when its commercial representatives reached India in the early seventeenth century, they gave indigo "the place of honor among possible exports."[21] The Dutch, too, entered into this trade, and by the end of the seventeenth century the inevitable dominance of indigo was recognized in Europe. The ban on its use was finally lifted in France in 1737, although as late as 1810 Napoleon tried to reintroduce woad as a countermeasure to the British monopoly on the commerce of indigo.[22] The dependence on natural indigo dye continued until the beginning of the twentieth century, when a synthetic indigo was created by a German chemist after an industrial investment of 18 million marks and ten years of research.[23]

Although indigo grew throughout most of India, prime recognition went to that from Sarkhej, a town near Ahmedabad in Gujarat, and Biana, 50 miles southwest of Agra. Here the Dutch and English were not the only buyers in the seventeenth century; Persians, Mongols, and Armenians also sought a share of the limited supply. The competition was intense. Francisco Pelsaert, a buyer from Antwerp, gave in 1620 an amusing and obviously vexed description of his Armenian competitors' practice of buying:

> Goodness knows, the Armenians do quite enough of that, running and racing about like hungry folk, whose greedy eyes show that they are dissatisfied with the meal provided, who take a taste of every dish, [and] make the other guests hurry to secure their own portions but directly they have tasted each course, they are satisfied, and can hold no more. In the indigo market they behave just like that, making as if they would buy up the whole stock, raising prices, losing a little themselves, and causing great injury to us and to other buyers who have to purchase large quantities.[24]

In contrast to the quantities of indigo appearing on the manifests of ships headed west, those early cargoes east for which some records exist seem to have carried no indigo. This was undoubtedly because the similar climates of adjoining South and Southeast Asian countries supported indigenous cultivation of the plant. Whether these plants spread from an original point in India is not known,

7. Indian expertise in mordant patterning and dyeing was based on empirical evidence gained through more than two millennia of experience in the handling of cotton and dyes. Europeans in the seventeenth and eighteenth centuries sought to learn these skills to perfect their own dye technology. A 1734 report by the ship officer M. de Beaulieu is the most complete early description of the Indian process that remains to us today. Beaulieu followed the intricate process and cut off swatches of the textile as it was dyed to illustrate the effects of each step in the procedure. This manuscript and the accompanying textile segments, which record the process in Pondicherry on India's east coast, were eventually deposited in the Muséum National d'Histoire Naturelle, Paris, where they were rediscovered in the 1950s and published by P. R. Schwartz.[1] The eleven stages represented in the textile segments, each of which measures approximately 14.6 cm by 11.2 cm, follow. (Courtesy of Muséum National d'Histoire Naturelle, Paris)

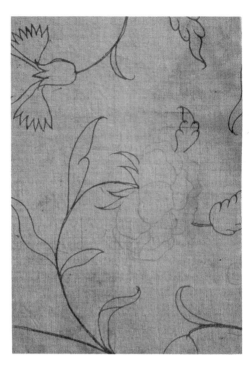

7a. The textile was prepared for dyeing by repeated soakings in a myrabolan solution; this gave the textile an ocher color. The design contours were applied in charcoal; those areas to be black were drawn with an iron mordant and those to have red outlines were worked with an alum mordant.

7b. The textile was boiled in a solution of chay root. The areas drawn with an iron mordant reacted with the myrabolan to yield a permanent black. The alum mordant reacted with the alizarin in the chay to yield red.

7c. The textile was bleached for several nights in a dung bath to lighten the ground and remove the myrabolan and mordants.

7d. Wax lines were applied for details that were to remain white in the areas of the design that would be blue and green.

7e. All areas not to be blue were covered with wax. The wax is blue because of prior use.

7f. *The textile was dyed in indigo and the wax was removed by immersing the textile in hot water. Bleaching in a dung bath followed.*

7g. *Alum mordant was applied in the details of the design a second time.*

7h. *Additional mordants and dyes were applied to create details in other colors.*

7i. *The textile was boiled and steeped in a chay root solution for more than four hours. Red, purple, yellow, and blue now became visible.*

7j. *The textile was bleached in dung baths and washed to lighten the background.*

7k. *Particular blue areas were painted with yellow to yield green. Because the yellow is fugitive it eventually rubbed off, leaving the blue underlayer as the color of leaves and stems.*

but indigo dyeing, with its requirements for a controlled vat, is thought to have derived originally from India.[25] This diffusion probably occurred at a very early date because the skill is known in extremely remote parts of Southeast Asia, and myth and ritual often surround the dye process as well as the dyed textiles.

Indian dyers were famous for their madder reds and indigo blues and a host of other colors. In their most complex works, the application of these dyes entailed a long and laborious series of steps that staggers the imagination. One of the most complete early records we have of the Indian dyer's work comes from observations made in Pondicherry in 1734 by a French naval man, M. de Beaulieu. His description of patterning a cotton has been studied and interpreted by the late French textile historian, P.R. Schwartz, who summarizes it as follows:

> The raw cloth is first of all half-bleached and prepared with a fatty aqueous solution containing an astringent. In this way, on the one hand, the mordants are prevented from running on the cloth and, on the other, the subsequent development of the colours they engender is assisted during the maddering operation.
>
> The iron mordant is prepared from a natural produce which contains the metal and which is immersed in palm wine which has turned sour. The alum represents the aluminium mordant. These two liquids are applied to the lines of the drawing which had first been pounced on the cloth with crushed charcoal. The iron mordant turns black on contact with the astringent with which the cloth was impregnated. The aluminium mordant, for its part, is lightly tinted red with a concoction of tinctorial wood, so that the workman can follow his work.
>
> The next step is the use of madder-dye, the function of which is to blacken the lines already black, and to develop the reds. Then the cloth is immersed in a dung-bath to remove the temporary red of the ground produced by the madder on parts where mordant had not been applied, and to remove the astringent harmful for the blue.
>
> The whole cloth is then covered with wax, except for the places which must be blue, and immersed in a vat of indigo, and after that the wax is removed in a bath of hot water. . . .
>
> The lines that are to remain white are traced on the flowers with molten wax and (without, it seems, using any more astringent) everything that is to be red is painted with red mordant, and the places where other colours are to be [are] painted with diluted mordants and mixtures of red mordant and Curcuma. A second dyeing follows, more concentrated than the first, which produces the final colours, and once again the reddish colour of the ground left by the dye is removed with dung.
>
> A yellow colour is next made from vegetable dye-stuffs. When painted on top of blue it produces green.
>
> The whole thing is washed again and the process is terminated.[26]

A summary by its nature obscures the tedious and numerous small stages that are the reality in creating a beautifully worked chintz.[27] Not the least of these steps was the controlled application of the mordants. On the east coast of India, artisans used a brush and a pen-like instrument made from split bamboo. The shaft of the pen had a ball of hair tied around it that acted as a reservoir for the mordant. Gentle pressure on the soaked ball fed liquid to the nib. The pen, or brush, permitted a creative interpretation of the design, even though the outlines were suggested by the pounced pattern. This was the method used on the Coromandel Coast during the great flowering of Indian dyeing in the seventeenth and eighteenth centuries. It was not, however, the predominant means of patterning cloth in the west of India. Here one or more carved wooden blocks were used to apply the mordant to the prepared cloth. The use of blocks eventually spread to the east coast, and they are used even today in many areas of India. This more mechanical but less time-consuming technique ultimately robbed the medium of its vitality, even though the artisans were clever in the variable spacing they often gave the block impressions.

An equally serious drawback to the use of wooden blocks or stamps was that the mordant had to be thickened with a resin or a similar substance to enable it to adhere to the wood surface. This thickener acted as a contaminant to the mordant and had to be washed out of the cloth before immersion in the dye, or the color would lack brilliance. The dull reddish brown of many of the fragments from Fostat in Egypt suggests that the carrying agent was not removed in some of the early trade pieces.

Carved wooden blocks and a modification of the pen described above were also used to apply resist substances such as molten wax to the cloth. The resist prevented the penetration of the mordant—or in the case of indigo, the dye—leaving the stamped or drawn area beneath it the color of the foundation fabric. Patterning with a resist substance is most commonly associated with indigo dyeing because traditionally the entire cloth had to be submerged in the dye vat to effect the proper blue. After achieving the desired color, the resist was washed or melted off. When used with a mordant-based dye, the resist was applied before the mordanting because the red dye bath is hot and would have melted the wax. Indian artisans used resists to outline forms; to create fine details, as within a dyed leaf or stem; or to pattern textiles with large, sweeping forms. The same kinds of constraints and capabilities that were evident in the application of mordants were true for the resist substances—the pen allowed free interpretations, but the stamp was mechanical. Stamped and freely drawn resist designs were used in conjunction with both blue and red dyeing in western India as early as the fifteenth century. At the time of early European trade the metal pen, or *kalam*, was used to apply wax resist in areas of western India, but we associate the use of the kalam in both wax resist and mordant application more with the Coromandel Coast than with western India.

As these patterned textiles entered the English trading world, they carried the terms *chint, chints, chites,* and the like—all from the Indian *chitta,* "spotted cloth."[28] This designation embraced both the mordant-painted and stamped textiles.[29] It remains with us today as "chintz," a word we have come to couple with images of industry's large floral prints on the highly glazed, cotton upholstery fabrics that were particularly in vogue two generations ago. The Portuguese used *pintado* to designate these textiles, and the Dutch *sits.* It is often unclear whether these terms strictly designated hand-applied mordants or if occasionally stamped work was also intended. The Persian word *kalamkari* best avoids this confusion; it means "pen work." The term *sarasa,* from the Gu-

Other Materials

In addition to the plants and materials described in detail in the text, the following were important to Indian dyers:

- The tumeric plant (*Curcuma domestica*), or *halda*, produces a rhizome carrying curcumin, a bright yellow coloring substance that dissolves readily in water. Its soluble properties mean that it is not fast to washing, and its main function in Indian textiles is as a dye in conjunction with other, more subtle dyes; as a fugitive dye substance for turbans; and as a top dye to create mixed colors such as green. It is interesting that one epithet for the god Vishnu is *Pitambara*, "clothed in yellow garments."[33] This appellation undoubtedly has a connection with ancient belief that held tumeric sacred, and the association suggests an explanation for the use of this dye on turbans.

- The safflower (*Carthamus tinctorius*) is thought to be one of the oldest dye plants. From its petals two fugitive dyes may be made, a safflower yellow and a red. The latter color is separated from the yellow by treatment with alkalis. Its unstable nature means that it must be treated with acid substances.[34]

- Sappan wood (*Caesalpinia sappan*), also called brazilwood, is used with mordants and yields a red dye that is not fast.

- Myrabolan, also myrobalan, also mirobolan, also called *cadoucai* in Tamil, is the fruit of several *Terminalia* species that provides tannin, which acts as a dye and a fixing agent with iron.

- Lac dye is made from the insect *Coccus lacca*, which lives on several species of trees in India, Burma, and Southern Asia. The insect attaches to a twig of the tree, and after about four months it becomes covered with a viscous coating. The dye is extracted from this coating with hot sodium carbonate. This solution is evaporated, and the residue is formed into cakes to be sold. This red coloring matter is laccaic acid.[35] It is expensive and most frequently associated with silk.

jarati "excellent, beautiful,"[30] appeared in the trade lists to describe certain patterned cotton garments, and it passed into the Japanese terminology to signify any textile that uses a mordanting and dyeing technique to effect a pattern—whether drawn, blocked, stenciled by hand, or printed by machine.[31]

The deft combination of indigo, mordant dyes, and resist patterning on cotton created the products that captured the admiration of most markets. But there were also additional means of dye patterning, and for specialized markets these were of equal or even greater importance. The most significant of these other techniques are two *bandhani* processes, which are generally referred to in English today by the Indonesian terms *ikat* and *plangi*.

In the ikat technique the designs are tied on the unwoven measured yarns before dyeing. After dyeing, these resists are cut away and the pattern remains in the color of the ground yarn. New combinations may be retied and different dyes applied. When woven, these reserved areas form the textile pattern. Ikat may be worked on the warp, the weft, or on both. Working both sets of yarns, an extremely complex process requiring precise synchronization, is the patterning technique used to create the *patolu* textiles of western India. This and other occurrences of ikat technique in India are discussed in relation to Indian costumes.

The other bandhani technique, plangi (*chunari*), has an ancient history in the subcontinent.[32] In this technique, areas of the woven textile are tied off in small circles or squares, which resist the dye. These resists may be large or very small, may be grouped to create fine, complex designs, or may be scattered at random in less organized patterns.

The Indian artisan's creative genius may not be assigned strictly to any one of the textile processes we have described. Rather, it was his orchestration of all of these, informed by a sympathetic understanding of what each technique could contribute to the work he envisioned, that made his textiles unique.

This catalogue focuses primarily on textiles patterned with the aid of the kalam—and less so on fabrics using stamped mordants, stamped resists, and stamped dyes. A few textiles designed by other processes are briefly discussed in reference to their importance to particular markets.

NOTES TO TEXT

1. Mordants eventually came to be used with wool and other animal fibers because they increased the colorfast properties (see Rawson 1915:233–35).
2. Bühler and Fischer 1972 1:27ff. and 321.
3. Plinius 1857 VI:282.
4. Brunello 1973:169, 210.
5. By 1672 an industry to imitate these textiles, called Indiennes, was begun in Marseille and, in 1678, in Holland. Because two Armenians were critical to the French factory and a Turk to the Dutch works, some question arises regarding the immediate source of seventeenth century processes used in Europe (Bühler and Fischer 1972 I:273).
6. Naqvi 1967:47.
7. Bühler 1941:1423.
8. Schwartz 1966:122 fn.1.
9. Schwartz 1969:22, fn. 39.
10. Ibid.:14–17.
11. Dam 1932:206.
12. Schaefer 1941:1399.
13. Schwartz 1966, 1969, records and interprets the earliest known reports by Westerners of the Indian dye materials and processes.
14. Dam 1932:206.
15. Schaefer 1941:1400.
16. Bühler 1941:1423–24.
17. *Natural Dyes of India* 1980:2.
18. Naqvi 1974:182–83.
19. Vetterli 1951:3067.

20. Ibid.:3068.
21. Moreland 1975:109.
22. Vetterli 1951:3070.
23. Brunello 1973:293.
24. Pelsaert 1925:16.
25. Bühler 1948:2504.
26. Schwartz 1966:87–88.
27. More extensive descriptions of this process are given in Irwin and Brett 1970:36ff.
28. Turner 1962:276.
29. Irwin 1959c:77.
30. Varadarajan 1981a.
31. Nobuko Kajitani 1982: personal communication.
32. Singh 1979:xxxvii.
33. Birdwood 1880:235.
34. Bühler 1948:2489.
35. Forbes 1956:104–5.

NOTES TO ILLUSTRATIONS

1. Schwartz 1956:5ff. and Schwartz in Irwin and Brett 1970:36ff. The description that follows here is adapted from Schwartz's interpretation of the Beaulieu manuscript. A much more detailed account may be found in the works cited.

Master Dyers in Antiquity: Fostat

The earliest examples of Indian textiles that remain (following the Mohenjo Daro fragments) come to us by way of Egypt. These are cotton fragments that were revealed during the course of excavations made in the search for the ruins of Egyptian Babylonia. At the time of this archaeological work in the late nineteenth century, however, there was scant interest in these apparently "late" textiles, and nothing was done at the site to correlate the textiles with other datable material. Later plundering of the area by treasure hunters brought forth more textiles, again under far from ideal archaeological circumstances.

In recent years controlled excavations at this and other sites in Egypt have recovered textiles within a datable context.[1] When these data are available in final form, it may be possible to assign more "secure" time periods to museum fragments such as those displayed here. In the meantime, preliminary reports of this material, both published and unpublished,[2] encourage a general dating of the fifteenth century for many of the Fostat examples. This time frame had previously been "comfortable" for many fragments, based on a comparison of the designs of the textiles and those in datable media,[3] but the excavated evidence is reassuring. It also permits an earlier dating, to the thirteenth century, for certain fragments and confirms the presence of two-color, blue and red patterned cottons in the fourteenth century. The dated material comes from Quseir al-Qadim, once a small port on the Red Sea that functioned in both Roman and Islamic times (1200–1500 A.D.). Much more prosperous and important in these same periods, however, was Fostat.

The site of Fostat, on the southern edge of present-day Cairo, became an important trading area in the first century A.D. when the Romans reopened a canal that linked the Nile to the Red Sea. This and other improved transportation ways, coupled with the new Roman knowledge of how the seasonal winds could be used in the Indian Ocean, opened a period of flourishing trade between the East and the Roman world.[4] Woven cottons, silks, and dyes were important in this commerce; equally stimulating must have been the sharing of technologies. It is possible that within this period the knowledge of the use of mordants in dyeing became familiar to the Egyptians. Known to Indian dyers since at least the

8 *The garment depicted in this fifteenth century western Indian miniature painting shows a mordant-stamped mythological animal called gajasinha. Similar figures may be seen on some of the Fostat fragments.*[1] *(Courtesy of the Royal Asiatic Society, London.)*

9 Fragment
India (found at Fostat), 18th century (?)
Cotton; stamped and drawn resist and
  painted mordants, dyed
Brick red, blue, black
41 cm x 32 cm
Textile Museum, Washington, D.C.
  6.152

*The fragment contains a segment of
an arc displaying large petal forms, a
broad border of formally arranged
leaves and flower heads, and a corner
interval filled with curious small,
comma-like elements.*

*This is technically one of the most
complex of the Fostat fragments; any
analyses of the procedure followed
must be highly speculative. It appears
that the resist outlines were stamped
and applied by a pen on the textile.
Blue was then applied by hand
within certain areas defined by the
wax. The mordants for red and black
were then painted in the appropriate
areas and the textile dyed in a dye
bath containing alizarin.*

*This, of course, presupposes the
ability to apply indigo by means
other than immersion in a vat. Theoretically, this technology was unknown in India before the mid-eighteenth century, when an orpiment vat
for printing and hand application of
indigo was developed in Europe.[2] Irwin suggests that the Indian dyers
did not trust the colorfastness of the
new commercial dyes. They further
processed all cloth so dyed—including the blues, which normally do not
require an alum mordant—in a final
bath of alum.[3] There may be a suggestion of that practice here. In the
lines of crenelations that border the
arc, segments of the blue have a
heavy black shading. If alum had
been applied over the blue and this
alum had been contaminated with
iron—as is common, for example, in
alum originating in the Kutch region—it would very probably have
produced this black shading in the
red dye bath. There are, however,
many difficult questions posed by
this textile, and additional analytical
work is required.*

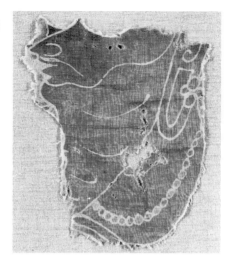

10 *Although not included in the exhibition, this Fostat fragment is of
extreme interest because the resist
has been drawn to depict the profile
and elongated ear of a person. The
relatively large scale of the head indicates that the original textile could
have been a didactic hanging or related piece. The style of drawing
characteristic of western Indian miniatures is reflected in the rendering, but
the style also has close affinity to
that of the wajang puppets of Indonesia. Exports such as these resist-
drawn textiles may have served to
communicate the style to Southeast
Asia. (Courtesy of the Cleveland Museum of Art, Cleveland 51.530. J. H.
Wade Fund.)*

second millennium B.C., this process was first reported in the
West only in the first century A.D.[5]

Although it suffered a loss of trade, Egyptian Babylonia remained
important after the decline of the Roman Empire and was a major
stronghold of the Byzantines—and thus a focus of attack for the
Arabs in their seventh century invasion of Egypt. After the fall of
the city's fortress, the Arabs settled the land of their original siege
camp, which gave the site its name *al fostat*, or "the camp." Fostat
merged with the city and became the capital of the Egyptians until
the move to Cairo a few kilometers to the north in the tenth
century. Egypt's geographical importance in East-West trade remained and even increased in the medieval period, its focus merely
shifting from Fostat to Cairo. The environs of the old site were
occupied by Jewish and Coptic peoples, but the Muslim cemetery
there remained sacred to the Arabs. From this tenth century period
onward, the ruins preserved remnants of the detritus of the ancient
scene, and it is this evidence that comes to us today in the form
of the so-called Fostat fragments.

At the time of the excavations, these lesser fragments were not
recognized as Indian. Only in 1938 did the work of R. Pfister trace
their origin to Gujarat.[6] The Indian material was later classified
by Irwin and Hall according to the technique by which the cotton
was patterned;[7] they assign two categories, block-printed and re-
sist-dyed. That this classification is somewhat ambiguous becomes apparent in examining a group of the textiles.

All of the textiles are a plain-weave cotton, which is relatively
coarsely spun and woven. They display a range of dye craftsmanship often lacking in care or precision and only occasionally showing exceptional skill. Inescapable is the sense that these were made
for a modest clientele and do not represent elements of a "luxury"
trade. They claim attention primarily as our only tangible link
with the early historical records.

The fragments are patterned in a number of ways. Some have
been stamped with a resist medium such as wax (or mud), Figure

continued on page 43

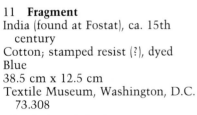

11 **Fragment**
India (found at Fostat), ca. 15th
  century
Cotton; stamped resist (?), dyed
Blue
38.5 cm x 12.5 cm
Textile Museum, Washington, D.C.
  73.308

*The design of the fragment suggests it
was once part of a large, rayed floral
pattern. The work is carefully done,
and a pleasing interest is added by
variation in the diameter of the dots
used to pattern certain areas. Stamps
or a stencil appear to have been used
to apply the resist.*

12 **Fragment**
India (found at Fostat), 15th
  century (?)
Cotton; stamped resist, dyed
Blue
Warp 23.5 cm, weft 17 cm
Textile Museum, Washington, D.C.
  6.264

*The Indian use of scrolling vines and
reverse scrolls with flowering heads
can be found in many media, but
none lent itself to the development of
this motif more readily than the textile worked with mordants or resists,
whether stamped or drawn. In this
example, swirling curves, tendrils,
and flower heads have been stamped
on the textile in a resist medium and
the textile dyed indigo.*

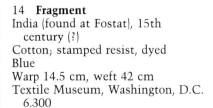

14 **Fragment**

India (found at Fostat), 15th
century (?)
Cotton; stamped resist, dyed
Blue
Warp 14.5 cm, weft 42 cm
Textile Museum, Washington, D.C.
6.300

*This fragment displays a series of
borders, or stripes, which carry either
a pattern of undulating, leaf-covered
vines or a simulated bandhani configuration, worked by a stamped resist, not by a tie-dye process. A resist
was stamped on the textile, which
was then dyed in indigo.*

13 **Fragment**

India (found at Fostat), 15th century (?)
Cotton; stamped resist, dyed
Blue
68 cm x 25 cm
Textile Museum, Washington, D.C.
6.116

*This mosaic-like interface of circles
and modified floral squares was a
common Indian textile patterning device; later it was made for export to
the East, Figure 141, and for internal
consumption, Figure 119f. The script
configurations in the border have
proven unintelligible to experts, but
they are said to be rendered in a mirror image.[4] Thus, the person who cut
the stamp was probably completely
unaware of the proper orientation.
The designs were stamped with a resist and the textile dyed in indigo.*

15 **Fragment**

India (found at Fostat), 15th
century (?)
Cotton; stamped resist, dyed
Blue
Warp 17 cm, weft 15 cm
Textile Museum, Washington, D.C.
73.205

*A long-legged bird set within a circle
marks the intersection of two lines of
rayed flower heads. The flower areas
are lined with thin stripes and a row
of large dots. The center region, now
badly damaged, seems to have a simple lattice grid. The designs were
stamped with a resist medium and
the textile dyed blue.*

16 Fragment
India (found at Fostat), 15th
   century (?)
Cotton; stamped resist, dyed
Blue
33 cm x 40 cm
Textile Museum, Washington, D.C.
   73.232

*The fragment shows two broad bor-
ders—one incorporating three bands,
the other, four—that seem at one
time to have flanked a field decorated with dotted clusters. The design
elements of the borders and field are
typical of the west Indian design vocabulary to be found in miniatures
and pierced screen work of the fourteenth and fifteenth centuries.
Stamps seem to have been used to
apply all the resist.*

17 Fragment
India (found at Fostat), 15th
   century (?)
Cotton; stamped resist, dyed
Blue
Warp 37.5 cm, weft 46 cm
Textile Museum, Washington, D.C.
   6.127

*An interlocking tangle of plants
twists and turns in harmony with a
simply patterned circle. A single
stamp, approximately 11 cm by 16
cm, was used to apply the resist
medium, probably wax, and afterward the textile was dyed in indigo.*

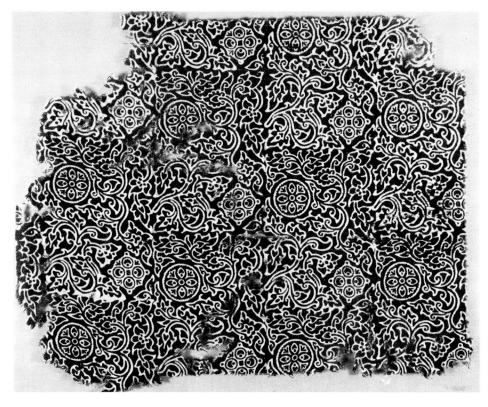

18   Fragment

India (found at Fostat), 15th century
Cotton; stamped and drawn resist, dyed
Dark blue
50.5 cm x 31 cm
Textile Museum, Washington, D.C.
   6.120

This textile was patterned with a resist (probably wax) and dyed in indigo. In the borders, stamps were used to apply the resist; elsewhere the elements were freely drawn. The recurved vine with leaf or floral cluster is common to architectural ornament in the fifteenth century in western India. The tendril of the guard stripes also appears on fragments from Quseir al-Qadim dated to the fourteenth or early fifteenth century.[5]

19 Fragment

India (found at Fostat), 15th
  century (?)
Cotton; stamped and drawn resist,
  dyed
Two blues
61 cm x 36 cm
Textile Museum, Washington, D.C.
  6.124

*This fragment has a subtle design
feature rarely found in the usually
modest textiles left at Fostat. The
original format included a heavily resist-worked white and blue field and
a blue end panel, or* pallava, *bounded
by three narrow white stripes. Within
the pallava is a dainty pattern, possibly representing clover leaves. The interesting feature is on the reverse face
of the pallava: additional resist, in
the pattern of a grid that overlays
and unites the clover leaves, was added after the initial blue dye bath.
Resist was also applied next to the
three framing white stripes. When
immersed in the indigo bath again,
these new resist-worked areas remained the light blue of the initial
dyeing, while the remainder of the
textile was colored a deep blue. Thus,
when worn, the textile would display
two patterns: white clover leaves on
a deep blue ground on one side, and
white clover leaves set on a light blue
grid with a dark ground on the reverse. The design effect of this juxtaposition is intriguing, although the
process was quite simple.*

*Only one step in the execution of
this design required precision: control
of the second resist. It was important
that it not permeate the other side of
the cloth, which would have caused a
mottling of the solid blue ground in
the second bath. In the center field
just the opposite effect was required
in application of the initial resist:
this resist was stamped and, because
it would not be worked on the reverse, it was desirable that it permeate the cloth to reserve the other
face. In more recent periods, this was
done by using wax and placing the
cloth in the sun to allow the wax to
melt slightly.*

20 Fragments
India (found at Fostat), ca. 13th
 century (?)
Cotton; stamped and drawn resist,
 dyed
Dark blue, light blue
47 cm x 56 cm; 33.5 cm x 19 cm
Textile Museum, Washington, D.C.
 6.88

*These fragments display two rows of
human figures separated by a band of
recurved, scrolled leaves. A grouping
of three figures, apparently two
women flanking a male, is the motif
repeated in the top row. Because the
male figure seems to carry a trident,
he has been thought to represent
Shiva. In the lower row, standing
women appear in niches created by a
scarf that flutters overhead or, perhaps, the form is an actual architectural niche.*

*The figures have been drawn or
stamped with a liquid resist substance in a bold, cursory manner.
Stamps or stencils may have been
used in parts of the textile, but resist
was also freely applied. An interesting variation was created in the top
row by alternating one group of light
blue figures with another in the
white of the ground cloth. This was*
*probably done by removing the resist
from the light blue group so that it
received part of the final indigo dye
bath.*

*The largest of the fragments was
created from two textiles sewn together before the resist patterning
and dyeing were done. Only one face
of the textile was worked.*

*The 1982 excavations of Quseir al-
Qadim revealed additional resist-patterned textile fragments that display
the same alternating pattern of light
blue and white (no. 945). Although
the designs are in no way similar, the
style of the resist work—in the gross-
ness of line and summary approach
to form—may suggest a common origin with the fragments displayed
here. It is currently thought that the
recently excavated Quseir al-Qadim
textiles, and thus our examples as
well, date to the thirteenth century.*

21 Fragment
India (found at Fostat), 15th
century (?)
Cotton: stamped mordant, dyed
Rust-brown
20 cm x 13 cm
Textile Museum, Washington, D.C.
6.151

*A random pattern of fanciful crea-
tures remains visible on this fragment. The only one that can be
clearly seen appears to be a winged
creature with a snake's head for a
tail. The other shapes also suggest bi-
ological forms, but they defy a closer
description. The small size of the
fragment and the lack of clear repeat
preclude a satisfying analysis of the
technique used. It is possible that
mordant was applied with a block to
create the background, leaving the
plain figures in relief. The designs are
clearly rendered on the reverse, however, which suggests that a wax or
similar resist may have been stamped
onto the surface in the form of the
figures and allowed to melt through
to the back. A mordant could then
have been applied to the intervals to
create the ground color.*

22 Fragment
India (found at Fostat), 15th century (?)
Cotton; stamped resist, dyed
Blue, deep blue
25 cm x 26 cm
Textile Museum, Washington, D.C.
73.511

*A regularly repeated pattern of rayed
flowers, squares containing a smaller
square with a cross, and a square
cluster of simple crosses decorate this
textile. The colors are the white of
the textile and deep blue on a sky-
blue ground. Resists were stamped on
the textile and the whole piece dyed
in indigo. Precisely what procedure
was followed to effect the deep blue
in the squares is unclear; possibly the
remainder of the textile was covered
with a resist and the textile redyed.*

24 Fragment
India (found at Fostat), 13th
  century (?)
Cotton; stamped mordant, dyed
Red-brown
69 cm x 30 cm
Textile Museum, Washington, D.C.
  6.142

*Large, scalloped rosettes alternate
with small, eight-rayed flower heads
on a ground regularly patterned with
smaller flower heads. The textile is
unusual in the size of the major ro-
sette—26.5 cm in diameter—and in
the dimension of the block used to
stamp the mordant (a slight misa-
lignment allows us to see that the
block was 15 cm by 29.3 cm). The
printing of the mordant was hastily
done and the blurred edges of the design suggest that the block was well
worn. The thirteenth century date is
tentative and is based on analogous,
but not identical, designs found at
Quseir al-Qadim; the unusual size of
the block used; and the unconven-
tional division of the circle in halves,
not quarters. These physical properties of the stamp are not common in
textile designs attributed to the fifteenth century.*

 23 Fragment
India (found at Fostat), ca. 15th
  century
Cotton; stamped mordant, dyed
Brick red
Warp 41 cm, weft 30.5 cm
Textile Museum, Washington, D.C.
  6.276

*The textile is patterned with forms
suggesting a Kufic script, but several
scholars who have attempted to read
the forms report that they are unintelligible. The block used to apply the
mordant in the center field was 26.5
cm by 20 cm.*

25. Fragment

India (found at Fostat), 15th century
Cotton; drawn and stamped resists,
  applied mordant, dyed
Red-brown
40.5 cm x 9 cm
Textile Museum, Washington D.C.
  6.165

*Large squares with eight-pointed
stars alternate with small squares
containing single, eight-petal flowers
to form the major elements of this
design. Intervals around the square
are filled with a rectangular grid of
dots and rayed flower forms. A majority of the resist lines (applied to
one side only) have been drawn, but
the dots and eight-petal flower configurations of the ground appear to
have been stamped. The script has
proven unintelligible.*

*There is a random variability in
the color, which suggests that the
mordant was applied by hand. The
color on the reverse face, however, is
as strong as the obverse, making it
unclear if the mordant was applied
by hand or the textile immersed in a
mordant solution.*

26 Fragment

India (found at Fostat), 15th century
Cotton; stamped mordant, dyed
Rose-brown
46 cm x 32 cm
Textile Museum, Washington, D.C.
  6.141

*A regularly repeated grid of geometric
forms fills this fragment. Eight-
pointed stars alternate on each cardi-
nal axis with flower-filled circles, and
on the diagonal with floral squares
having four attached lobes. These
were stamped with a single mordant.
A second, more corrosive mordant
may have been applied to the center
of the stars, because each center has
deteriorated. The cotton is coarse and
the work was done without precision.*

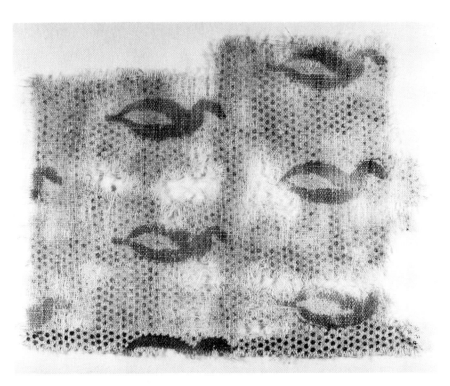

27 Fragment
India (found at Fostat), 15th
  century (?)
Cotton; stamped and painted (?)
  mordants, dyed
Red-brown, brown
23 cm x 18 cm
Textile Museum, Washington, D.C.
  73.405

The hamsa, or goose, of this fragment is probably one of the oldest, most enduring figures in Indian textile design. A person in a fifth century mural at Ajanta wears a tailored garment with a pattern almost identical to that seen in this fragment. This is not to suggest that the textile is of the same period; it merely represents a continuation of a favored theme. This is discussed further in relation to Figure 38.

In this textile, the bird rides on a dot-filled ground. Although the fragment is badly faded, it appears that the geese were mordant-painted, and an effort was made to reinforce the outline. The mordant of the dots in the ground seems to have been applied with stamps. The outline of the geese also may have been stamped.

continued from page 33

11, and in others the resist has been hand-drawn by an instrument, Figure 10. After dyeing, and the removal of the resist, the designs remain the color of the foundation cloth. This technique, now commonly called batik, occurs frequently in the Fostat fragments.

A second group of the textiles has been dyed with the aid of one or more mordants. When slightly thickened, as in today's custom of adding a resin, the mordant may be applied by a stamp to the surface of the cloth. This technique of stamped patterning, using one or possibly two mordants to produce a brown and a red, is another frequently used means, Figures 28–30. Other fragments show that an outline of a pattern was first stamped on the cloth in a resist medium, and the resulting intervals were painted with the desired mordants, Figure 38. After dyeing, the colored forms remained outlined in white, which was the color of the cotton, on a colored ground.

A third type of fragment shows a combination of indigo and mordant dyeing, Figures 41–43. The resist that outlines the design was applied, and the cloth was dyed in indigo; particular resists

28 Fragment
India (found at Fostat), 15th century
Cotton; stamped mordants, dyed
Red, brown
Warp 30 cm, weft 20.5 cm
Textile Museum, Washington, D.C.
6.303

Two different design complexes, each created by a pair of stamps, pattern the fragment. In one, a central lotus and framing square are set amid thick leafing branches. In the other, a central lobed medallion filled with dots rides in a tangle of thin tendrils and flower heads. This ground is now brown, but originally the dye may have been purple. The adjoining design complex is entirely red, as is the dotted medallion. Each of these "compositions" employs quarter medallions in the corners. Their lack of complementarity when used in this manner does not seem to have been critical.

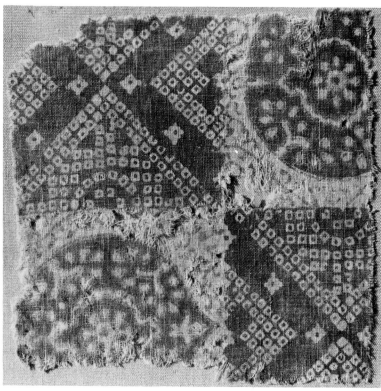

29 Fragment
India (found at Fostat), 15th
century (?)
Cotton; stamped mordants, dyed
Brick red, brown
19 cm x 18 cm
Textile Museum, Washington, D.C.
73.302

Three different design units, each created with a stamp, have been used to pattern the textile. One stamp imitates a bandhani pattern, a process that was usually done by tying off small areas of the cloth by hand to reserve them from the dye (Figure 1). Another stamp was used to create a flowered circle set in a square filled with twisting vines. The third design incorporated the same elements in an oval. The outlines of the circle, the oval, and the vines were first stamped in a mordant for brown; the red mordant was then stamped and the textile dyed.

The designs of the blocks are not complementary, which is apparently no accident. Fostat patterns frequently show this unusual practice of using disparate stamps together.

30 Fragment
India (found at Fostat), 15th
  century (?)
Cotton; stamped mordants, dyed
Brick red, brown
40.5 cm x 32 cm
Textile Museum, Washington, D.C.
  73.412

The predominant design of this fragment is striking evidence of market specialization practiced by Indians as early as the fifteenth century. The large, dotted, circular interlace configuration is a debased rendering of the interlaced designs common in the late Roman and Byzantine periods.[6] There seems little doubt that a design such as this was created for a Mediterranean market.

Adjoining this circular interlace is an unusually patterned square. Ordinarily one would expect such a brown outline to be filled with a stamped red device. On this textile, however, the red filling devices do not register in the outlines, or they are of an entirely different nature; they have no connection with the brown outlines. These disparate filling elements also interdict the straight edge of the background of the adjoining circular pattern. This disruption of the outline of the block lends to the design a freer, more subtle unity. This is a completely new manner of using stamps for the Indian artisan.

were then removed, and a mordant was applied to specific areas. These areas were then able to absorb the red dye, which, of course, did not affect the blue and other areas that had no mordant. There are additional variations in the procedures followed, and these are discussed in relation to the specific fragments.

Until recently, comparative design analysis has been virtually the only available means to date the Fostat fragments. Some of this work was done by Pfister,[8] and other comparative material has been suggested by Irwin and Hall.[9] These authors relate textile design elements to fifteenth century carved stone screens in Ahmedabad, India; sixteenth century Persian book cover designs; and seventeenth-century Italian silks. (Italian silks were available in western India even before the seventeenth century, and it is not surprising that the designs of this luxury commodity were translated into a cheaper medium.)

Fostat fragments containing human figures are rare; in the limited number existing, two types are evident. In one, Figure 39, the paired figures of symmetrically posed dancers rotate about a central hub. In technique and spatial arrangement this textile fragment resembles that of the geese in Figure 38. In these cloths the

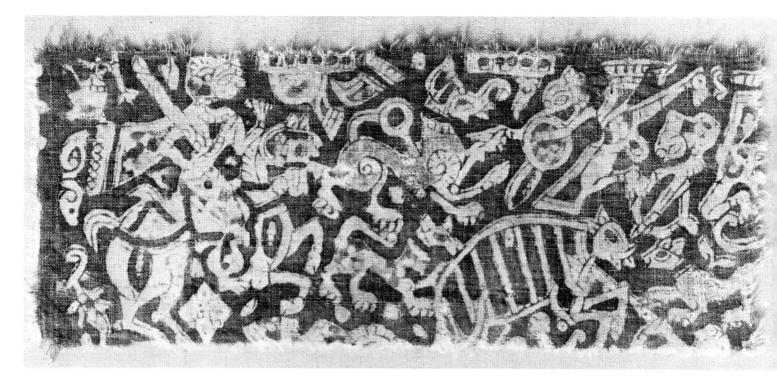

31 Fragment
India (found at Fostat), 15th to 17th
  century (?)
Cotton; stamped and painted
  mordants, dyed
Brick red, dark brown
32 cm x 13 cm
Textile Museum, Washington, D.C.
  6.119

*The scene depicts a horsewoman,
complete with sword and flowing
shoulder cloth, accompanied by a dog
and a long-snouted mythological
creature, the* gajasinha, *in an attack
upon a boar. Other people with javel-
ins or swords and bows and arrows
join in the attack. A bird carrying a
stalk in its beak appears in the upper
left, but other shapes remain enig-
matic.*

*This textile, quite exceptional in its
human representation, has been interpreted by Jain and Fischer "as representing an age-old Gujarati myth
concerning the mother goddess, Khodiar."[7] (For a further discussion of
this figure, see the text.) The figural*

*style was common in the painting of
western India from the twelfth into
the seventeenth centuries and could
have continued in use on a village
level afterward.*

*Outlines of the figures are stamped
with a mordant to effect a dark
brown. The background and select
details were painted with a mordant
for red. All colors show on the reverse, but the soft, blurred edges indicate that the reverse was neither
stamped nor painted.*

figures were stamped in a resist, and mordants were painted around
the resist. The second type of figured fragment—Figures 31–32—
differs in technique and arrangement. Here mordants have been
applied by stamps to create first the outline of the figures and then
the color of the background, leaving the figures in the color of the
cotton textile. In this type, there is also a larger range of design
elements: a horse and rider, a bird carrying an object in its beak,
dogs, a mythical animal (*gajasinha*), a boar, and figures armed with
bows and arrows. The action of a hunting scene, the implied narrative, and the lack of symmetrical design structure place this
example in striking contrast to most Fostat textiles. Yet there can
be no doubt of its Indian origin.

The figural style of both fragments is assuredly that of western
India. The three-quarter profile rendering of the human face with
its sharply pointed nose and eye projecting beyond the cheek, coupled with an abrupt linear rendering of the body, as well as the
style and kind of animals, are all found in illustrated manuscripts
of the fifteenth and sixteenth centuries that were painted in western India.[10] One expert even says this Gujarati style was fully developed in at least the latter half of the fourteenth century, with

32 Fragment
India (found at Fostat), early 15th
   century
Cotton; stamped and painted
   mordants, dyed
Brick red, dark brown
39 cm x 31 cm
Textile Museum, Washington D.C.
   73.522

Outlines of the figures were stamped
with a mordant that yielded a dark
brown. Intervals among the figures
and some of the details within were
then painted with a mordant for the
brick red.

The design appears to be a composite of several scenes. In the upper
zone, an elephant and a person flank
an ornate mound. In the middle
zone, to the left, one person stands
and another sits on a raised chair or
dais; in the center a horsewoman
with a dog and a mythological, long-
snouted creature are in conflict with
a boar (see Figure 31). In the lower
zone only the hind quarter of an elephant may be discerned.

We have little but supposition on
which to base an interpretation of
this textile. If, however, the interpretation given by Fischer and Jain for

Figure 31 is correct, we may conjec-
ture that each of the seemingly dis-
crete compositions in this textile depicts a mythological tale.

The mythological, long-snouted animal of this fragment appears as a
motif on clothing in fifteenth century
miniatures. This coincidence, as well
as the physical characteristics of the
cloth, which is coarse and loosely
woven, serve as the basis for the
early fifteenth century date given to
this fragment. That such textiles were
used as clothing and not just mne-
monic devices is also implied by the
miniatures.

33 Fragment

India (found at Fostat), 15th
  century (?)
Cotton; stamped mordants, dyed
Red-brown, brown
60 cm x 36 cm
Textile Museum, Washington, D.C.
  6.137

A mihrab *filled with two floral patterns is repeated to create the borders
of this textile. In the center field,
bold zigzags filled with tangent hexa-
gons or a blossoming vine alternate
with plain ground carrying a simple
square or branched grid. Two colors
remain, a faded maroon and brown;
the latter may originally have been
purple. Similar zigzag patterns appear
in textiles depicted on Indian painted
miniatures from the fifteenth century.*

34 Fragment

India (found at Fostat), 15th to 16th
  century (?)
Cotton; stamped resist, applied
  mordants, dyed
Brick red, dark brown
Warp 16 cm, weft 42.5 cm
Textile Museum, Washington, D.C.
  73.475

*Large spirals, formed by a line of
dots, once alternated with a rayed
floral head on this textile. The dots
and rays were created by reserving
the textile with a wax resist before
mordanting. A darker color sometimes appears within the spirals, suggesting that a second mordant may
have been used to accentuate the
form. The resist designs are very clear
on the reverse face.*

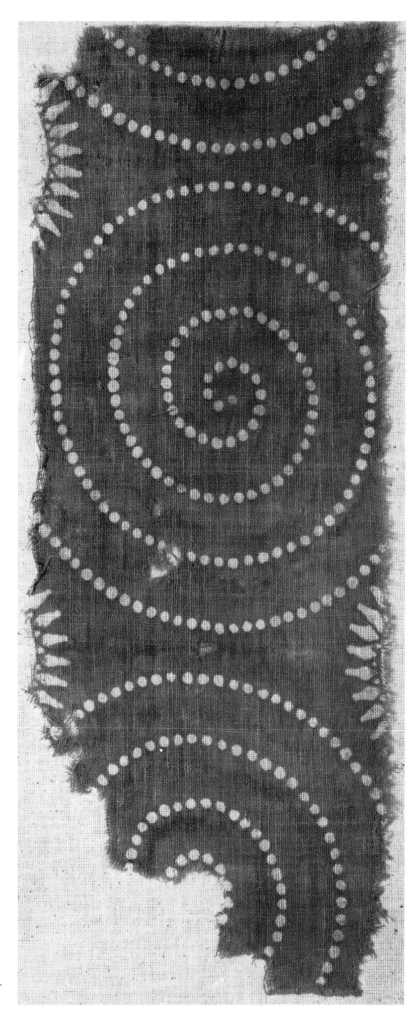

35 Fragment

India (found at Fostat), uncertain date
Cotton; stamped and painted
  mordants, dyed
Brick red, deep brown
Warp 24 cm, weft 21 cm
Textile Museum, Washington, D.C.
  73.408

Circles containing tendrils and eight-petal flowers fill the textile surface. Evenly spaced between the circles are four-rayed floral "stars." The work has been done with care, and the colors remain today a saturated red and brown.

A single stamp, whose four corners are the nucleus for the four circles, was used to stamp the mordant for the dark brown outlines and brown ground surrounding the tendrils. The mordant for red was subsequently applied by hand in the flower petals and intervals between the circles. After dyeing, the area not mordanted remained the ecru of the cotton. Only one side of the textile was worked.

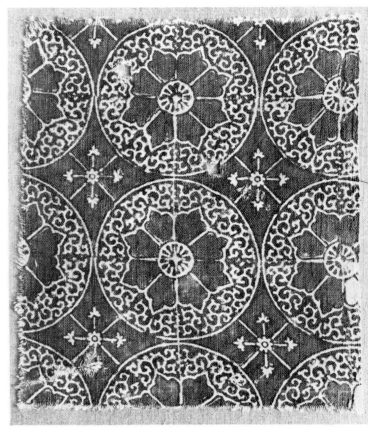

36 Fragment

India (found at Fostat), 15th
  century (?)
Cotton; stamped resist, applied
  mordants, dyed
Brick red, brown
41.5 cm x 27 cm
Textile Museum, Washington, D.C.
  73.298

An evenly spaced pattern of eight-pointed stars with red centers is aligned within a lattice of dots in this fragment. Contrary to what one might expect, the background does not appear to have been stamped with the mordant. Instead, the details seem to have been stamped in a wax resist and the surrounding areas filled with a mordant.

37 Fragment
India (found at Fostat), 15th
  century (?)
Cotton; stamped resist and mordants,
  dyed
Red-brown, brown
50 cm x 27 cm
Textile Museum, Washington, D.C.
  6.263

*Arched forms embracing a rayed
flower, all set on a background tracery of tree limbs, are the main decorative elements of this fragment.*

*Above and below are guard stripes
containing an assortment of round
floral renderings. Fragmentary remains beyond the two guard stripes
show that there was a field dotted
with small circles and squares on one
side and a pattern of irregular diagonal lines on the other, both created
by a resist. The segments of the fields
and background to the arched forms
are a purplish brown; the remaining
forms are brick red. Stamps were
used to apply the mordants and the
resist in the field.*

its significant characteristics traceable to the late tenth century.[11]
We cannot be sure when this style, especially in the folk traditions, ceased.

A possible interpretation for Figure 31 has been proposed by
Jyotindra Jain.[12] He believes that the scene relates to an ageless
Gujarati story of a boar being chased after having ruined a king's
garden. The theme reappears in the legend of the Gujarati mother
goddess Khodiar, and this textile motif may refer more specifically
to her.[13] There is no way to tell if the fragment was part of a
narrative scroll or other didactic device. More probably it was a
"popular" textile print similar to that seen in the miniature paintings of the fifteenth century that show the same mythical animal,
the gajasinha, on garments.

Whatever its inspiration, the inherent qualities of the Fostat
fragments of Figures 31–32 suggest that it was a very humble and
common commercial piece. The cotton is coarsely woven and the

38 Fragment

India (found at Fostat), 15th century
Cotton; stamped resist, painted
  mordants, dyed
Two shades of maroon, brown
33 cm x 28.5 cm
Textile Museum, Washington, D.C.
  6.134

*A delightful file of hamsa, or geese,
circle a lotus medallion in the center
of this fragment. Repetitions of the
motif are linked by an expanding floral bud. The textile was patterned by
stamping a wax resist to create the
outline of the figures. Mordants were
then painted within the wax boundaries and the cloth dyed.*

*The goose has been a favored motif
in India for centuries. Writing about
a Hamsa-Laksana sari in 1927, the
famous Indian art historian Coomaraswamy said that "the hamsa, or sacred goose, is both a real and a mythological animal; as the former, a
palace pet, a symbol of pure white-
ness (white as a hamsa the moonlight
fell on the earth, Kadambari), the living ornament of parks and lakes, the
image of a woman's gait, and a con-
stant motif in decorative art of all
kinds from the Mauryan periods on-
wards, and as the latter, the vehicle
of Brahma, a type of insight (inas-
much as it can drink only the milk
from a mixture of milk and water),
and a former incarnation of the Buddha in the* Hamsa Jataka. . . . *Several
literary references of textiles decorated with hamsa can be cited in the
Jaina* Antagada Dasao, *on the occasion of the hair-cutting ceremony,
'the mother of Prince Goyame received the ends of his hair in a precious swan-figured robe.' Here the
word translated 'swan-figured' is*
hamsa-lakkhana, *equivalent to Sanskrit hamsalaksana; the bird is really
a goose, and always represented as
such, but some translators render
'swan' as more picturesque."*[8]

40 **Fragment**

India (found at Fostat), 15th century
Cotton; drawn resist, painted
  mordants, dyed
Red-brown, dark brown
36 cm x 19 cm
Textile Museum, Washington, D.C.
  6.254

*Stepped squares and crosses outlined
with the ecru of the cotton textile
create a vibrant pattern on this fragment. The procedure followed is
somewhat puzzling. This is a pattern
that would lend itself easily to
stamping techniques; it seems, however, that a resist was drawn to create the outline of each design segment, and mordants were then
painted in and around these boundaries.*

*Patterns of interlocked, stepped
squares on textiles attributed to the
thirteenth and early fifteenth centuries have been found at Quseir al-
Qadim (study photo, fragment la-
beled no. 937, 574).*

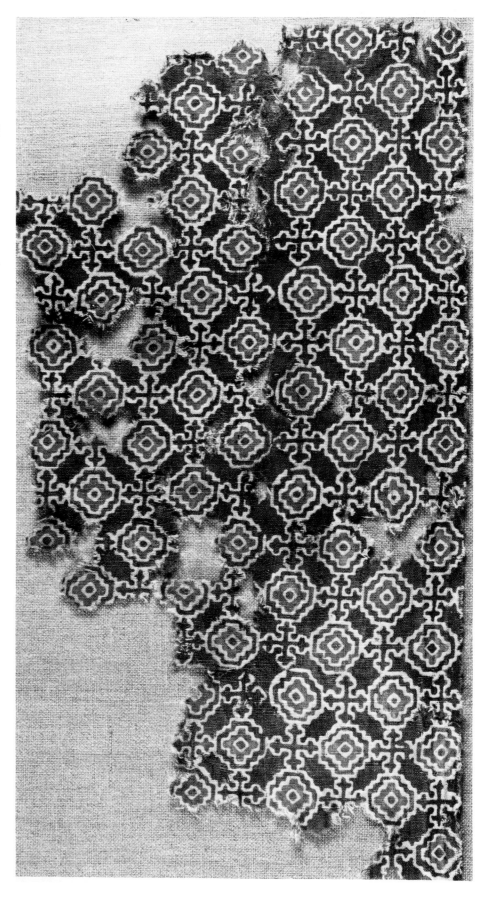

41 Fragment

India (found at Fostat), 15th
century (?)
Cotton; stamped resist, stamped and
painted mordant, dyed
Blue, red
Warp 40 cm, weft 16 cm
Textile Museum, Washington, D.C.
73.410

*Single leaves outlined with dots and
undulating vines bearing leaves and
carefully articulated nodes fill the
borders of this fragment. Originally,
the borders probably framed a field
of metrically arranged circles and
dots; only a small portion of this
field remains. The designs are a brick
red, and the background is blue. In
the blue area, many regions were
worked in small patches or in a network of veins with an alum mordant,
so that after dyeing, red darkened the
blue. The textile was first stamped
with a resist, dyed blue, and then, after the resist was removed, stamped
with the mordant for red. The mordants for the broad red stripes lining
the selvage and center field were applied with a brush or similar instrument.*

42 Fragment

India (found at Fostat), early 15th
century
Cotton; stamped resist, painted
mordant, dyed
Blue, red-brown
47 cm x 23.5 cm
Textile Museum, Washington, D.C.
73.200

*This fragment originally came from a
textile that displayed two distinctly
different designs. In the upper area,
two forms of stylized tree alternate.
Below, in the area bounded by a red-
brown stripe, fanciful leaves and decorative resist details form a swirling
pattern. To achieve this effect, the resist, probably wax, was first applied
with stamps and the textile dyed
blue. The resists were then removed
from select areas, and the mordant
for red-brown was applied with a
brush within the remaining wax outlines. This was done very carelessly—
the color often spilling beyond the
boundaries made by the wax resist,
so that as the cloth was dyed red, the
light blue of the ground turned a
deep blue.*

*The rayed outline of the tree also
appears in west Indian miniatures of
the fifteenth century; this has served
as the basis for placing the textile in
this period.*

43 Fragment

India (found at Fostat), 15th century
Cotton; stamped mordant and resist,
  dyed
Two blues, rose
17.5 x 29 cm
Textile Museum, Washington, D.C.
  6.253

*Large rose-colored leaf forms outlined
with rows of dots or rayed flower
clusters pattern this fragment. They
are set in a jungle of twisting stems
and leaves. The fragment was first
stamped with a resist and then dyed
in indigo. After the resist was removed, there were white areas left,
including the center of the leaves.
These areas were then stamped with
the mordant for red, and the textile
was dyed with a red coloring material. Blue was then added to the
small white areas of the textile
ground remaining in the leaf forms.*

*A group of Indian-made Quseir al-
Qadim fragments dating to the fifteenth century show similar shades
of blue and rose and a sequence of
patterning technology analogous to
that of this fragment.*[9]

44 Fragment
India (found at Fostat), date uncertain
Cotton; stamped mordant, dyed
Red-brown, light blue
44.5 cm x 35.5 cm
Textile Museum, Washington, D.C.
  73.239

This remarkably organic design is in striking contrast to the geometric character of most of the Fostat fragments. Its inspiration remains unknown. The colors of the textile are a single shade of red-brown, which was used for outlining, and a faint light blue, which fills the background dots, the dots in the wave-like configurations, and the floral core of the ovals. How the blue was applied is not clear.

The imprecise register of the stamp used to apply the mordant for red-brown clearly betrays the dimension of the block on this fragment.

stamping is crude and imprecise. This textile, with its human representations, would very probably not have been made for trade in an Islamic market. More likely, the cloth was available in a west Indian port and was carried back to Egypt by an individual, possibly a Coptic sailor. Coptic seamen were known to have served in great numbers in Arab ships, at least in earlier centuries, and that some may have carried such souvenirs home is conceivable.

Textiles patterned with geese, or *hamsa*, must be very ancient in India. As they appear in the Fostat remains they are of two styles: as a dark silhouette arranged in lines on a light ground, Figure 27, and as paired decorative designs placed in a regular circle about a lotus flower, Figure 38. The former rendering strongly recalls a textile, from the fifth century, shown in Cave 1 at Ajanta.[14] This is not to suggest dating the textile to that early period; rather it demonstrates the continuity of design in western Indian fabrics. Geese similar to the second fragment appear in fifteenth century paintings on women's skirts[15] and on fans and umbrellas and continue, according to miniatures, into the sixteenth century as a textile motif.[16] After that time, however, this type of hamsa ceases to be a popular motif in paintings.

The miniatures from these two centuries—the fifteenth and six-teenth—do show textile patterns similar to those in the Fostat fragments. There is a heavy reliance in the miniatures on geo-metric patterns arranged in grids, large circles, and recurved vine motifs. Some of these, or closely similar patterns, continue to be made in block prints in Gujarat today to meet the demands of a conservative market. In the mainstream of Indian fashion, how-ever, the regularly placed flower or flower cluster predominated in the seventeenth century, but these patterns evidently did not enter the trade to Egypt. Trade certainly continued to the Red Sea in this period, but it is probable that the "traditional" designs and textures were the products traded. Continued extensive archaeo-logical excavation at these sites in Egypt holds promise for a more precise dating of this Fostat material and the textile dye tech-niques represented from this era of the Indian dyer's art.

NOTES TO TEXT

1. Whitcomb and Johnson 1978, 1980, 1981. These excavations at Quseir al-Qadim have also revealed the first Indian Tamil inscription found in Egypt. Its context—within poorly constructed rooms and in association with an iron forge—may indicate "that Indian merchants, perhaps even iron workers, may have lived here."
2. Janet H. Johnson of The Oriental Institute, one of the scholars respon-sible for the Quseir al-Qadim excava-tions, has generously shared photo-graphs of some of the textile finds from that site.
3. Pfister 1938 and Irwin and Hall 1971:10–13.
4. Warmington 1974:231.
5. Plinius 1857 VI:282.
6. Pfister 1938:29.
7. Irwin and Hall 1971:4.
8. Pfister 1938:29ff.
9. Irwin and Hall 1971:4.
10. U.P. Shah 1976:1 and Khandalawala and Chandra 1969:30ff., Figs. 45–67.
11. U.P. Shah 1976:10.
12. Jain 1980:18.
13. See also Fischer 1981.
14. Yazdani 1930:xviii.
15. U.P. Shah 1976:Fig. 30.
16. Chandra and Shah 1975:Pl. VI.

NOTES TO ILLUSTRATIONS

1. Royal Asiatic Society, London, Tod. Ms. 34 fol. 17a.
2. Schwartz 1966:124 fn.1.
3. Irwin and Hall 1971:10.
4. The author thanks Henry Ginsburg and Katherine van der Vate of the British Library for their assistance in the translation of this and other in-scriptions.
5. Eastwood in Whitcomb 1980:292, Fig. 20.
6. My colleague James Trilling consid-erably enriched my thoughts about this motif.
7. Jain 1980 and Fischer 1981.
8. Coomaraswamy 1927:36–37.
9. Whitcomb 1978:Pl. 66n.

Lahore ● ★ ◆
PUNJAB
Sirhind ● ★ ◆
★
Samana ● ■ ◆
OUDH
Delhi ●
RAJASTHAN
Agra ●
● Jaipur
● Sanganer
▲ **Benares**
Patna ●
BIHAR ★
● Sironj ■
BENGAL
● Patan ▲ ■
■ ★
● **Ahmedabad** ▲ ■ ★
Dacca
● Cambay ★
GUJARAT
■ ◆ ★ **Calcutta** ●
Surat ★ ◆
● **Burhanpur** ★ ◆ ■
● Bombay
ORISSA
INDIA
ARABIAN SEA
● **Golconda**
● **Masulipatam**
Petaboli ★ ■
Goa
BAY OF BENGAL
COROMANDEL
● Pulicat
● **Madras** ■ ◆ ★
● St. Thome
Pondicherry ★ ◆
Cauvery
Tanjore ● **Negapatam** ★
Madura ●
INDIAN OCEAN
CEYLON

Major Textile Areas 1600-1750

★ Plain white
◆ Checks and stripes
■ Chintz
▲ Silk
– – Present Day Boundaries

Master Dyers to India

Although Indian textile printers, painters, and dyers did eventually serve much of the world, they had their own subcontinent to please as well. In addition to providing fabric for clothing, they patterned cloth for wall hangings for secular and religious purposes, floor spreads, table covers, cart or litter covers, animal trappings, tents, canopies, and a host of less familiar objects such as banners and bookcovers.

The delightful variety of textiles available for clothing in the Indian markets of the seventeenth century may be seen by examining the costumes depicted in the wall hanging of Figures 108–111. Both men and women wear textiles having light or colored grounds with patterns of small floral repeats, simple dots, lattice-work patterns both small and large of scale, or simple stripes. While some of the fabrics are surely silk, many of the patterns are those associated with cottons worked and dyed with the aid of mordants. The specialized skills and materials required for this work had been perfected over centuries. The major textile regions about the time this hanging was made (see Map B) existed in the west in Gujarat and the Sind; in the east in Bengal, Orissa, and the Ganges Valley; in the vicinity of Masulipatam; and in the south at Madras, Kumbakonam, and Negapatam. Expertise was also reported in locations northwest of Delhi at Samana, Sirhind, and at the more centrally located towns of Sironj and Burhanpur. Some of these are mentioned in reports by English traders, such as a letter by William Finch in 1605 in which he speaks of "Pintodoes of all sorts, especially the finest . . . for quilts and fine hangings . . . from a place called Brampore [Burhanpur]. . . ."[1] In 1630 communications speak of Sironj chintz as "next in goodness to those of Masulipatam,"[2] and in 1678 there were 400 houses of painters in Sironj.[3] In 1639 Armenians and Persians traded in Delhi for "chintz which are here made in good quantities, well coloured, in appearance little inferior to those of Mesulapatam. . . ."[4] The importance of these textile centers fluctuated with the happenstance of nature and history; a few disappeared in importance entirely, but most retained significance until the rise of mechanical fabrication and patterning in the nineteenth century effectively killed this intensive handwork.

Great famines were a recurring vicissitude that affected the history of these textile-producing regions, at times bringing all production to a halt. This was the case in 1630–31 when the rains

Map B (Adapted from Chaudhuri 1978:244)

59

failed, bringing disaster to agriculture. A merchant reported from Masulipatam in July 1630 that "the major part of both weavers and washers are dead, the country being almost ruinated."[5] In Gujarat "'the garden of the world' was turned into a wilderness with few or no cultivators or artisans; indigo was rotting on the ground for want of men to gather it; and places which had yielded fifteen bales of cloth in a day could now produce barely three bales in a month. A Dutch factor writing at the time saw no hope of trade for three years to come. . . ."[6] Ample rains restored the industry on India's east coast, and much of the trade that once sought supplies in Gujarat established new trading patterns to the Coromandel Coast and to the Sind and northern India. The death of senior craftsmen also meant that knowledge of the arts was not passed on to a new generation, and "the cotton goods of Gujarat suffered in reputation owing to this cause for many years."[7] Such calamities seemed always incipient, and by 1647 a similar fate befell the east. Fifteen thousand died in Pulicat, a similar number in St. Thomé, and the English reported of the area in the vicinity of Madras "that there is not above 1/3 of the weavers, painters and washers liveinge of what were formerly."[8]

Dislocation of craftsmen and a consequent shift in the locus of weaving, painting, and dyeing could also be the result of political factors. For instance, the defeat of the Vijayanagar Empire in 1565 dispersed its accomplished craftsmen. Irwin feels that the wars of Aurangzeb, and later the raids of the Marathas, caused many craftsmen of Gujarat to seek work in Rajasthan and other parts of northwest India.[9] In 1712 Maratha raiders disturbed the chintz printers near Broach, and in "1725 the printers fled from village to village carrying with them unfinished pieces of cloth in order to avoid the invading troops."[10] In 1741 Maratha raiders plundered both the south and east of India, causing weavers to move from the Madras region further southward and from parts of Bengal. In this latter area, where most of the silk goods were made, the Marathas burned many houses and with them the weavers' looms. In 1755 a Dutch factor estimated that 400,000 people were killed in Bengal and Bihar, among them weavers, silk dealers, and the like.[11]

Often as disastrous to textile production as war was the extortion by local rulers, tax collectors, or brokers who became so oppressive that whole villages would move away. The English reported that "the weavers when disgusted leave lighted Lamps in their Houses and remove to some other part of the Country, so that whole Towns are deserted in a Night."[12] Yet cloth was the major item of trade for certain areas, and a ruler jeopardized his source of wealth if his policies forced the weavers to flee. These craftsmen therefore retained some leverage, and some small fraction even earned moderate incomes.[13] Dyers were rarely singled out for description in this regard, but one might suppose that the very specific needs of their craft would not have allowed them to move easily nor very successfully, so that to some extent they may have been captive to locale. There are, however, instances when alternatives arose. Thus, when the Europeans established their own textile production centers, dyers readily moved to escape the oppression in Golconda,[14] but there is little doubt that, as a rule, dyers lived in economic and social poverty.

The organization of the dyers' trade is not well reported. It seems that middlemen "put out" textiles to the dyers. This at least was the custom reported for foreign export commodities in western India and sometimes on the Coromandel Coast. Other reports say that cash was advanced. Dyers worked on the basis of extended families, with different segments of the family group carrying out specific steps in the process. One notice from the 1680s says that in Palakollu there were four kinds of cloth painters. An order was allotted among these, who in turn subdivided the order to workers of lower rank.[15] One finds parallels to this system today in dyers' communities such as Deesa in Gujarat, where preparing the cloth with myrobalan, stamping the mordants and mud resists, dyeing, and so forth are done by different people who work on a piece-work basis.

Although it is uncertain how many contemporary practices are accurate representations of traditional custom, they are of interest. In Ahmedabad printers (chippas) currently may work for only one merchant, and the association between the merchant and the dyer's family may have been inherited over several generations. This middleman supplies all the materials—blocks for printing, dyes, fabrics, and so on—and specifies the kind of textile to be created. These are market-specific types of cloth and patterns. One study has also found that, because the dyes are such a critical component to the sale of the cloth, women in the merchants' households prepare the dyes for the dyers.[16] This practice was not completely unfamiliar in the past, for we know that on the Coromandel Coast northern chay, considered superior, was at least supplied (though not prepared) by commission agents for dyers further south.

Who actually made the designs is another issue. In the 1670s Carré reported that in Madras the designs and initial tracing of the first lines on the textile were the work of caste groups different from those who did the dyeing.[17] Today master craftsmen in Ka-lahasti draw designs on the cloth with charcoal and again with iron acetate, and others complete the work. It is interesting to find that this initial work is considered just slightly less than 50 percent of the entire production cost.[18] In Gujarat the wooden blocks used to print textiles are also designed and carved by special groups in no way directly connected with the dyeing process,[19] although a printer or merchant may suggest a design. A blockmaker customarily has a sample book of designs, and orders for blocks are selected from this source.

The design books contain selections of the components that contribute to the entire composition—that is, border elements, guard stripes, center field motifs, and the like. Certain conservative rural markets accept little variation in the way traditional elements are rendered, and there obviously are age-old combinations. Once carved, the block inherently restricts creativity. The brush and kalam are certainly more flexible tools; they allow relative degrees of interpretation even when working from designs supplied by brokers.

45 Fragment
Rajasthan, 19th century
Cotton; stamped resist and mordants,
dyed, stamped dyes
Purple, pink, brown, green, olive
green, black on beige ground
Warp 21 cm, weft 23 cm
Cooper-Hewitt Museum, The
Smithsonian Institution's National
Museum of Design, New York
1962-175-4. Gift of Nasli
Heeramaneck

46 Fragment
Rajasthan, 19th century
Cotton; stamped resist and mordants,
dyed, stamped dyes
Dark maroon, purple-brown, dark
green on brown ground
Warp 47 cm, weft 103 cm
Cooper-Hewitt Museum, The
Smithsonian Institution's National
Museum of Design, New York
1962-175-6. Gift of Nasli
Heeramaneck

The Fostat remains give ample proof that block printing of both mordants and resists was a long-established textile art in western India by the time these textiles were created. If this tradition has any direct descendants today, they exist in villages such as Deesa, north of Patan, where small printers still meet the demands of conservative rural markets. Metrically arranged floral heads or clusters, however, were not a part of the Fostat tradition. This seems to be an expression of a design convention that developed later, and it is certainly one associated with brocades and patterned muslin. Today this is also thought of in connection with the prints of Sanganer in Rajasthan, although this town, which received early mention as a place of fine dyes, does not seem to have adopted block printing until just before the opening of the eighteenth century.[1] According to tradition, King Sawai Jai Singh invited artists to settle at Jaipur. The historian Singh relates that printers from Gujarat were brought to Jaipur. She proposes, based on the style of design, that others came from Malwa.

The Jaipur area produced printed cottons for women's and men's clothing and for quilts and upholstery. It remains an active printing center today.

The examples shown here may come from Rajasthan or, possibly, sites in Gujarat. In the textile of Figure 45 a white fleabane or similar composite flower, with a purple center and green leaves, is accented with a pink center dot and pink buds. All are set on a yellow-cream ground. In Figure 46 repeated clusters of four flowers with heavy red details are arranged on an ocher-brown ground. In Figure 49 a composite, purple-rayed flower, accented with a red dot and arranged with green leaves and stems, patterns a yellow-green ground. In Figure 47 red poppies with nodding heads, green stems, and leaves outlined in black are set on a green ground. The border carries a vine, outlined in black, with a flower of purple, red, and white. In Figure 48 a large purple flower, accompanied by smaller purple and red varieties, is set on an ocher-brown ground. In addition to grid and diaper arrange-

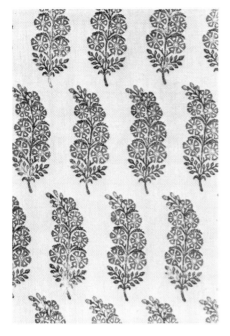

47 Fragment
Rajasthan, 19th century
Cotton; stamped resist and mordants,
  dyed, stamped dyes
Red, pink, green, dark green, black on
  pale green ground
Warp 48 cm, weft 62 cm
Cooper-Hewitt Museum, The
  Smithsonian Institution's National
  Museum of Design, New York
  1962-175-8. Gift of Nasli
  Heeramaneck

48 Fragment
Rajasthan, 19th century
Cotton; stamped resist and mordants,
  dyed, stamped dyes
Red, maroon, purple, dark green,
  black on brown ground
Warp 66 cm, weft 34 cm
Cooper-Hewitt Museum, The
  Smithsonian Institution's National
  Museum of Design, New York
  1962-175-10. Gift of Nasli
  Heeramaneck

49 Fragment
Rajasthan, 19th century
Cotton; stamped resist and mordants,
  dyed
Purple, pink, brown, olive green,
  black on green ground
Warp 32.5 cm, weft 47 cm
Cooper-Hewitt Museum, The
  Smithsonian Institution's National
  Museum of Design, New York
  1962-175-11. Gift of Nasli
  Heeramaneck

*ments, floral elements were aligned
in stripes as in Figure 50. Here a
flowering vine in green and maroon,
outlined in black, is flanked by maroon and tan guard stripes.*

*These examples tend to be more
generic renderings of flowers; others
are quite specific, including fine depictions of cockscomb, iris, tulip, and
the like. Nevertheless, one cannot but
marvel at the precision and intricate
nature of this work, in which the use
of five or six stamps was not unusual.*

50 Fragment
Rajasthan, 19th century
Cotton; stamped resist and mordants,
  dyed, stamped dyes
Maroon, light maroon, tan, green,
  olive green, black on beige ground
Warp 29 cm, weft 55 cm
Cooper-Hewitt Museum, The
  Smithsonian Institution's National
  Museum of Design, New York
  1962-175-5. Gift of Nasli
  Heeramaneck

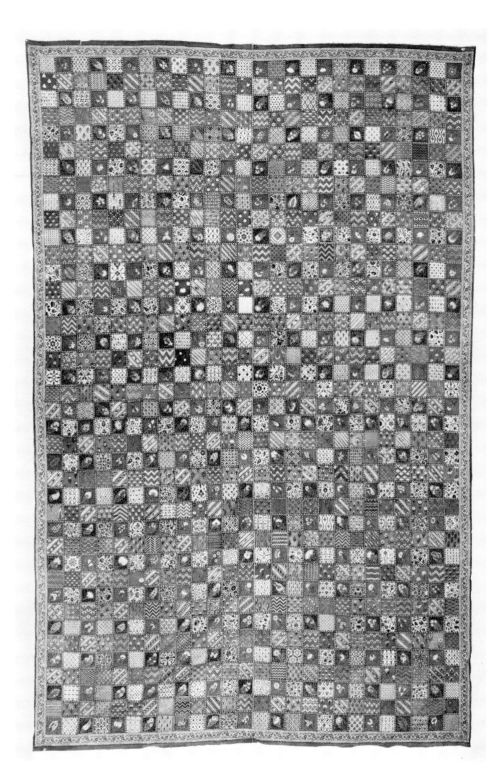

51–52 **Bedcover** (?)
Western India, precise area unknown,
  late 18th century
Cotton; stamped mordants, dyed
Reds, purple, pink, blue, yellow,
  green, black
Warp 273 cm, weft 177 cm (two
  lengths joined)
Textile Museum, Washington, D.C.
  6.140

This textile may be viewed as a sampler of the stamps available to a dyer of this period. Some who have seen the textile consider it to be exactly that. Its careful workmanship, large size, and complete framing border, however, suggest it was made for a specific purpose—possibly a bedcover or floor spread. In all, there are 1,040 squares; only two designs were used a second time. Two different cartouches containing Persian letters appear in the red outer border. One, which is reserved in the red ground, reads Aadil-Shah; the other, stamped four times in a dark red, has not been read. The two pieces joined to create the large spread were seamed before stamping and dyeing.

52

Gujarat and the Western Regions

Although each of the regions shown on Map B produced a diverse range of textiles for local consumption,[20] each also came to be associated with certain types of textiles. Gujarat and adjacent western regions are particularly renowned for their arts of printing and dyeing. As witnessed in early miniature paintings, such as Figure 8, early woodblock printing skills served a local market, as well as the market to the Middle East as discussed in relation to Fostat. In the fifteenth and early sixteenth century illustrations, textiles display a strong preference for geometric patterns—stripes, zigzags, spirals, and circles. There are other examples that show patterns of geese;[21] lattice works filled with geese, elephants, and horses; and others with floral and scroll patterns.[22] Such block-printed cottons are shown used as women's *dhoti*, in skirts (*ghaghara*), head shawls (*odhani*), the man's dhoti, and the wrap, *dupatta*. Printed cottons are also depicted in household objects such as floor spreads, table covers, pillows, fans, and umbrellas.

The textile designs seem to have been large in scale, or the conventions of the miniature painter ordained that he render patterns large so they could be readily understood as a known textile. In the mid-sixteenth century either the artistic conventions in these western Indian miniatures, or the textile patterns themselves, began to change. The geometric shapes became smaller in scale, and the broad design bands that had zoned many textile schemes became rare in textiles for costume but remained in upholstery fabrics. More popular in costume was a small design element repeated over the cloth with metrical regularity.[23] In some instances this patterning surely represents tie-dye work such as chunari (in which small dots are tied off in a woven cloth to resist penetration of the color in the dye bath); in others it may very well represent stamping of small designs. The progression to the metrically arranged floral repeat that prevails in the Mughal period is a predictable next stage in the history of these textile fashions.

The chunari type of tie-dye, Figure 1, while practiced all over India, is a specialty of the western regions. It is mentioned in sixth century literature,[24] appears in the fifth century murals at Ajanta, and proves its antiquity through its importance in ritual and costume.

In Rajasthan and Gujarat, chunari is frequently mentioned in romantic songs and poems in which it serves as a symbol of love and affection. Folk songs from eastern India refer to the chunari of Jaipur as proper gifts for a daughter, sister, or a loved one.[25] Because of such associations, it often is used in the bridal garment of Hindu women. This bridal cloth usually has a red ground color, whereas a type of chunari with predominantly yellow ground is the gift to a new mother from her parents.[26] Paralleling this usage is the custom of Rajasthani women to wear *laharia* at the Teej festival. (Laharia is a resist-patterned cloth that is rolled on the diagonal and tied in a combination of bands.)

The importance of colors within Indian life is well noted and has been expressed by Jayakar:

continued on page 79

53 **Tablecover**
Rajasthan, 18th to early 19th century
Cotton; stamped mordants, dyed
Shades of ocher to yellow, purple to
    pink, green to celadon, black
Warp 92 cm, weft 75 cm
National Museum, New Delhi
    56.48/11

54 Tablecover
Rajasthan, 18th to early 19th century
Cotton; stamped mordants, dyed
Shades of ocher to yellow, purple to
  pink, green to celadon, black
Warp 97 cm, weft 96 cm
National Museum, New Delhi
  56.48/12

The designs of these two small table covers divide the surface in the manner of a patchwork quilt. Large squares are further divided by diagonals or smaller, inset squares. The intervals are filled with a flower cluster, a small diaper pattern, or a similar decorative device.

The subtle range of colors is the textile's charm—it presents a palette brimming with earth tones, brought to life by the small areas left in the white of the ground textile.

All of the design elements have been stamped, but the interplay of the colors gives a keen visual interest that denies the static quality of the blocked forms.

55–56 Patka (sash)
Udaipur (?), 19th century
Cotton; stamped mordants, dyed,
  applied tinsel
Red, yellow, green, black, gold
Warp 356 cm, weft 63.5 cm
Cincinnati Art Museum 1962.478. The
  William T. and Louise Taft Semple
  Collection

55

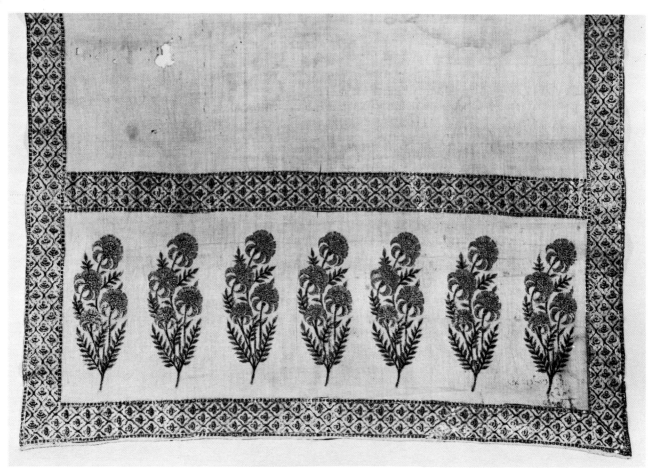

56

57 **Patka** (sash)
Burhanpur (?), 18th century
Cotton; painted mordants, dyed
Red, blue-grey, green, black
Warp 531 cm, weft 66 cm
Victoria and Albert Museum, London
   I.S. 100–1948

58 **Patka** (sash)
Burhanpur (?), 18th century
Cotton; painted mordants, dyed
Red, green, black
Warp 335 cm, weft 63 cm
Victoria and Albert Museum, London
   I.M. 87–1923

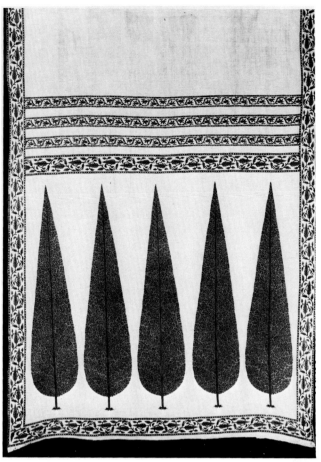

59 **Patka** (sash)
Western India, 18th century
Cotton; stamped mordants, dyed,
   stamped dyes, applied metallic
   fringe
Red, blue, ocher, black
Warp 332 cm, weft 55 cm
National Museum, New Delhi 56–161

60 **Patka** (sash)
Burhanpur (?), 18th century
Cotton; stamped mordants, dyed and
   painted dyes
Green, black
Warp 518 cm, weft 68.6 cm
Textile Museum, Washington, D.C.
   6.111

*Different forms of the decorative
waist sash,* patka, *have been depicted
as an element in Indian costume
since the earliest records.[2] Although
now associated with the tailored coat
of Mughal times, it was first the tie
for dhoti and sari. In its simplest
form, it appears as a long, narrow
cloth that was wrapped one or more
times around the waist and tied with
a knot having a loop in the front. The
hanging ends presented obvious areas
for decoration.*

*The patka was an element in the
costume of all economic levels. It
carried with it an aura appropriate to
ceremonial occasions, and rulers frequently bestowed a patka as a sign of
honor to members of their family,
statesmen, and generals.*

*From its apparently simple begin-
nings, the patka became more elaborate, incorporating silk and metallic
yarns by the time of Jahangir,[3] when
geometric forms and scrolls filled the
long cascading ends. By the 1640s
new design elements came into use,
and the form of the patka displayed
in Figures 55–60 became common. In
these samples narrow side borders
line the cloth and also create a frame
at both ends for the larger design*

area of the pallava. *This area is filled
with a row of individual flowering
plants or regularly placed flower
heads. The area adjoining the pallava
may be patterned, but the center
field, which was worn folded and
creased, is often a plain color. In the
seventeenth century the patka were 2
to 3 meters long and 35 to 50 cm
wide. These proportions increased
with time, and by the nineteenth
century Benares produced patka 5.5 to
9 meters long and about 50 cm wide.[4]*

*The examples shown here were
made in Burhanpur and western India in the eighteenth, and possibly
nineteenth, centuries. On two, Figures 57 and 58, stencils were used;
two were stamped, Figures 56 and 59;
and in Figure 60 it is possible that a
combination of stencil and stamps
was used to create the design in the
pallava and borders. Figure 57 has
red blossoms and delightful fan-
shaped green leaves set on arching
stems that cluster in the form of a
mango. Both the flower and leaf
shapes are repeated in the curving
vine of the border. Repetition of design forms in the end field and its
border was a common convention, although Figure 55 shows a pleasing*

*variation. This particular patka has
been further elaborated by the application of gold tinsel to the outlines of
the design elements. It bears an inscription that, although not completely legible, is written in letters of
a Gujarati type that would have been
used in the Gujarat or Udaipur region. Because the latter area is
known for its tinsel work, this textile
may have been made in that area.
The inscription also indicates that
the patka was made ca. 1899, which
seems late for this quality of work.[5]*

*Figures 59 and 60 suggest the range
of designs appropriate to the patka.
In the latter, abstract cypress trees,
cast in dark green with a veining of
deep red details, form a striking pattern. In the former, the subdued
ocher color and small floral repeat
lend a quiet elegance. In the bordered
end panels, a blue floral head with a
red center set on a single green stem
is the repeated element. The broad
borders incorporate a curling vine
that frames clusters of three similar
floral heads with its leaves. The green
of the flower stems, vine, and leaves
is the result of stamping yellow on
blue. The textile is highly glazed and
has a fringe sewn to the ends.*

◀ 61 Fragment from a curtain
India, before 1666
Cotton; drawn and painted resist and
    mordants, dyed
Red, purple-brown, blue, yellow
Warp 119 cm, weft 83 cm
Textile Museum, Washington, D.C.
    6.112

62–63 Part of a floor spread
India, before 1689
Cotton; drawn and painted resist and
    mordants, dyed
Red, purple, yellow, green
Philadelphia Museum of Art 43-51-
    126. Bequest of Mrs. Harry Markoe

62

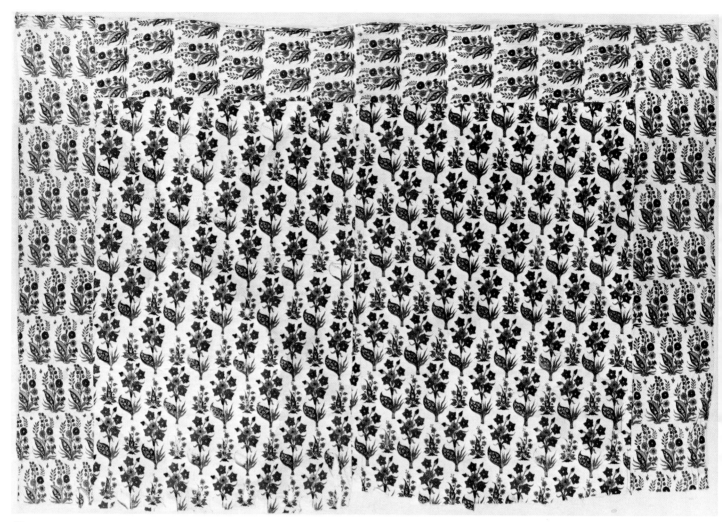

63

A formal flowering plant or cluster of blossoms arranged regularly over a plain surface is a hallmark of Mughal decorative art. Yet Robert Skelton, Keeper at the Victoria and Albert Museum, has convincingly argued that this scheme did not enter the Mughal repertoire until about 1619. Its introduction probably was inspired by the European herbals thought to have been provided as gifts to the court.[6] Ultimately, the significance for Indian textile design was profound, for in the course of the seventeenth century it became the dominant type of textile patterning. The scheme appeared in many types of renderings—woven, embroidered, and mordant painted—on men's and women's costume, on upholstery, and on animal trappings.

Scientific herbals may have provided the initial inspiration for many of the floral patterns, but imagination and decorative sense were important contributors as well, as can be seen in these two extremely fine examples. The flower outlines, probably established with the aid of a stencil, were drawn with a mordant that now yields a purple-brown color. Small designs were worked on the broad leaves with a resist before additional mordants were applied that would eventually give the leaves a red and purple color. The thinner lower leaves were dyed with indigo and top-painted with yellow to yield green. A flower in each cluster in Figure 62 has also been top-painted with yellow dye over a mordanted red.

Figure 63, a large floral patterned rectangle framed on three sides by a textile with a different floral pattern, is all that remains of a floor spread once belonging to a dargah, a Muslim shrine.[7] The textile's use, as well as additional information about the piece, comes from Devanagari inscriptions on the reverse face of the textile, Figure 64. Its original length was 6 yards 12 girah, and its width was 3 yards 5 girah. Along with the 1689 (Hijra era 1101) date, the inscription says that the cost of the spread was 21 rupees 12 annas. A separate inscription records that the spread was still in use in 1701.

Inscriptions on the reverse of Figure 61 provide another rare glimpse into the seventeenth century, Figure 65. These tell us the fragment comes from an abra. This is the face of a padded and quilted curtain, a style of hanging that continued in use in India into this century. In 1666 (Hijra era 1078), which we assume is approximately when the cotton was patterned, the length of the curtain was 4 yards 2 girah, and its width was 3 yards 6 girah. New inscriptions, made in 1695, indicate that the curtain retained the same dimensions, but a price of 18 rupees is added. The last inscription, written in 1701 (Hijra era 1113), suggests that the curtain had been cut because it speaks of "two pieces."

Both of these fragments display the same Persian seal, which indicates that they were once in the same collection. We are delighted at the serendipity that brings these pieces together for a brief exhibition.

Even though the inscriptions suggest that the textiles were used in western or northern India, it does not necessarily follow that the textiles were made in these areas. Fragments (I.M. 57–1933 and 58–1933) similar to Figure 63 were given origins in Golconda and Pulicat by Irwin.[8] The high cost of the textiles suggests they may have been rare in the west, implying an east coast origin. Enough questions remain, however, to leave the provenance of these pieces an open question.

64 *These inscriptions are on the reverse of the floor spread in Figure 63 and indicate it was used in a Muslim shrine as early as 1689. (Courtesy of Philadelphia Museum of Art.)*

65 *Fortunately for historians today, keepers charged with the safety of large wardrobes and stores of furnishings often made notations on the reverse of a piece when holdings entered the* toshkhana, *or storage, and when they were periodically inventoried. This inscription on the reverse of Figure 61 reveals the fragment belonged to a curtain used as early as 1666. (Textile Museum, Washington, D.C. 6.112)*

66 *The sloe-eyed beauty of this miniature, painted in Rajasthan in the mid-eighteenth century, wears a blouse patterned with a design similar to the curtain fragment dating to the mid-seventeenth century in Figure 61. That a design would endure and be used in such widely differing circumstances is of interest. The flower may be a* Crinum patifolium, *an exotic native flower of India. (Courtesy of Museum für Indische Kunst, Berlin.)*

67 Patolu sari
Gujarat, 19th century
Silk; double ikat
Red, blue, yellow, orange, green,
  violet-black
Warp 460 cm, weft 109 cm
Textile Museum, Washington, D.C.
  6.63

This is one of approximately forty traditional styles of patola, an exotic silk textile whose vivid colors and luxuriant texture has made it of great economic and ritual worth in India and Southeast Asia.

The textile is composed of a central field and framing borders, with tumpal (triangles) in the end borders. In the center field various motifs are outlined in white and locked in a regular grid of white lines. Most conspicuous of the motifs is a cross of four heart-shaped leaves, derived from the pipal leaf, which alternate in longitudinal and transverse rows with lozenge shapes and eight-pointed stars. An angular vine with flowers fills the borders, and narrow monochrome stripes create the lateral edges. The dyes are bright red, deep blue, and yellow, and their combinations yield orange, green, and violet-black.

Bühler and Fischer call this kind of patolu Vohra Gaji Bhat, a designation referring to its use by Vohra Muslims in Gujarat.[9] De Bone and Cort[10] have named these patola Waragaji, with a similar explanation. They were worn by the bride or mothers of the bride and groom at weddings and pregnancy celebrations.[11] Both the row of tumpal in the pallava and the narrow stripes of the borders are usually indicative of patola exported to Indonesia.

68 Pichwai (religious hanging)
Burhanpur (?), ca. 1825
Cotton; painted and stamped
  mordant, dyed, applied gold and
  silver tinsel
Red, blue, yellow, green, black
111.5 cm x 92 cm
Jagdish and Kamla Mittal Museum of
  Indian Art, Hyderabad 76.111

This textile is patterned with a trellis of ogival shapes organized in a large central rectangle. Surrounding this field is a border of similar shapes framed by rectangles. Each ogive has an indigo ground and shows milkmaids flanking a blossoming plant. They hold morchal, or fans, carry fly whisks, and wear patterned textiles. In the spandrels of the ogive in the border are flowers and parrots on a maroon ground. A narrow silver border with floral motifs frames the pichwai and encloses all the ogives and rectangles of the border. Gold tinsel was applied to enhance the details in the trellis and the costume. Hangings such as this were used as shrine furniture in a manner similar to that in Figure 69.

69 Pichwai (religious hanging)
Burhanpur (?), ca. 1800–25
Cotton; painted and stamped
   mordants, dyed, surface painting,
   tinsel applied, silk border added
Red, brown, purple, blue, yellow,
   green
122.5 cm x 146 cm; with added
   border 130.5 cm x 154 cm
Jagdish and Kamla Mittal Museum of
   Indian Art, Hyderabad 76.1510

*This type of hanging was used in a
shrine of the Vallabhacharya sect,
which honors the god Krishna. It por-
trays the flute-playing Krishna (Sri-
nathji) as he enchants the milkmaids, gopis. He stands under his
tree, the kadamba, while fruit-laden
mango and banana trees shade his
admirers, who carry fans, or morchal,
and fly whisks. Below is a landscape
showing Krishna with a group on the
left making offerings to a shrine; on
the right are gopis, cowherds, and
cows in attendance at two shrines,
one containing Krishna, the other his
brother Balarama. A river filled with
fish, lotus, flowers, tortoises, croco-
diles, and wading cranes completes
the setting. In the sky above the
trees, the sun appears, flanked by
winged angels and celestial chariots
filled with gods and goddesses. A floral border frames the entire composition.*

continued from page 66

In India the sensitivity to colour has expressed itself in painting, poetry, music, and in the costumes worn both by peasant and emperor. *Raga* was the word used both for mood and dye. Colours were surcharged with nuances of mood and poetic association.

Red was the colour evoked between lovers: a local Hindi couplet enumerates three tones of red, to evoke the three states of love; of these, manjitha, madder, was the fastest, for like the dye, it could never be washed away.

Yellow was the colour of Vasant, of spring, of young mango blossoms, of swarms of bees, of southern winds and the passionate cry of mating birds. Nila, indigo, was the colour of Krishna, who is likened to a rain-filled cloud. But there was another blue, Hari nila, the colour of water in which the sky is reflected. Gerua, saffron, was the colour of the earth and of the yogi, the wandering minstrel, the seer, and the poet who renounces the earth. These colours when worn by peasant or emperor were but a projection of the moods evoked by the changing seasons. The expression of mood through colour and dress was considered of such consequence that special colours were prescribed to be worn by a love-sick person, a repentant person and a person observing a vow.[27]

Also from the western area were patolu textiles, Figure 67, which had designs dyed on both the warp and weft yarns before weaving. Although they are made of silk, and thus theoretically not of central concern in this catalogue, these textiles are one of the finest expressions of the dyer's art. Even if their merit were not great, they would have to be included in this survey because of their effect on certain cotton textiles.[28] The patolu textiles—used as *sari*, odhani, dupatta, or *lungi*—were once made in several regions of western India, but today they are woven only in Patan. They have always been a mark of great wealth and have traditionally been used by certain Hindus, and Jains, and even by one Muslim group in Gujarat, on ceremonial occasions. In certain families brides were given patola as a gift, and some even considered it the bride's wedding garment;[29] or a man might use one as a ritual shoulder cloth in the marriage ceremony. These textiles have a ritual use in the festival for a woman in her seventh month of pregnancy, and people of lesser wealth even sought scraps of patola to use for their protection in certain rites. Whether used as clothing or quilts, the patola carried "irrational qualities" of purity and sacredness, as well as general magical and auspicious powers.[30]

The Deccan

Double ikat worked on cotton, Figures 77 and 78, in designs of a much simpler nature than those of patola is known from Pochampalli, Jalna, and Chirala in Andhra State, where the process is called *pagdu bandu*. The weavers who make them, the *salis*, are by legend descendants of the court weavers of the Vijayanagar Empire.[31] The textiles are called *telia rumals* in the literature, although locally they are termed *chitti rumals*, from the word *chint*.[32] Today they are worn as lungis by fishermen on the east and west coasts of India and by cowherds in the Deccan and Andhra. Jayakar in

70 **Qanat** (tent hanging)
Burhanpur, late 17th or early 18th
  century
Cotton; stamped and painted
  mordants, dyed
Red, yellow-green, black
Warp 107.5 cm, weft 210 cm
Prince of Wales Museum, Bombay
  72.5

her study of these textiles learned that telia rumals had formerly
been woven or embroidered with gold and used as dupatta by the
upper-class women of Hyderabad. It is thought that the work was
introduced originally to Pochampalli from Chirala, and it is probably in this latter area that the *"sacerguntes"* or *"sauruncheras"*
(ikat textiles) of the seventeenth century trade were made.[33] Cloth
merchants in Secunderabad and Hyderabad claim they have been
exporting telia rumals to "Arabia, Burma, and the Middle East for
several generations."[34]

What remains to us today in these telia rumals is very probably
a pale reflection of the original art. Some indication of the original
quality can be seen in Indian fragments dating from the seventeenth century now in Japanese collections.[35] In these, simple squares

71 **Tent wall** (detail)
Burhanpur, mid-18th century
Cotton; stamped and painted
   mordants, dyed
Red, blue, yellow, green, black
274 cm x 914 cm
Trustees of the Powis Estate,
   Welshpool, Wales

72 **Qanat** (tent hanging)
North India, 18th century
Cotton; stamped and painted
  mordants, dyed, painted dyes
Red, green, yellow, black
177 cm x 106 cm
Mme. Krishna Riboud Collection,
  Paris (originally in the collection of
  Mrs. Lizbet Holmes)

*As early as the time of the Ajanta
paintings there exists visual evidence
demonstrating that panels of cloth
were used to define and screen living
areas in India. As portrayed in these
fifth century murals,[12] the cloth walls
were dyed solid colors or had patterns suggesting tie-dye and resist-
patterning techniques.*

*By the time of Akbar, portable cit-
ies were created from cotton textiles;
their walls could be embroidered or
dyed with great floral patterns. The
Ain-i-Akbari gives a picture of the logistics required to establish an encampment when the king moved: "It
required for its carriage 100 elephants, 500 camels, 400 carts, and
100 bearers. It is escorted by 500
troopers, Mansabdars (Grandees),
Ahadis. Besides, there are employed a
thousand Farrashes, natives of Iran,
Turan and Hindustan, 500 pioneers,
100 water carriers, 50 carpenters,
tent-makers and torch bearers, 30
workers in leather, and 150 sweep-
ers."[13] There were two such encamp-
ments, one always being set up at an
advance site.*

*A listing of the functions of differ-
ent tents enumerated in the encampment evokes the atmosphere of the
period: a tent for keeping basins; for
the perfumes; for storing mattresses;
for the tailors; for the wardrobe; for
the lamps, candles, and oil; for keeping fresh Ganges water; for making
sharbat and other drinks; for storing
pan leaves; for storing fruit; for the
imperial plate, kitchen, and bakery;
for spices; for the imperial guard; for
the arsenal; and so on.[14] These and
other tents were set up according to a
predetermined scheme designed by
Akbar himself.*

*The tents, especially those of the
central enclosure, reflected the royal
wealth and the majesty of the imperial presence. Public and private
quarters had an image to sustain,
and they apparently did it with style.
The record speaks of one tent large
enough to house more than 10,000
people; it required 1,000 workmen
and a week to set up. If not decorated, such a tent would cost 10,000
rupees, "whilst the price of one full of
ornaments is unlimited."[15] The em-
bellishments used included embroideries, brocades, velvet, gold ornaments, and mordant-painted and
dyed hangings. The traveler François
Bernier gives us a somewhat more*

73 Qanat (tent hanging)
Golconda, early 18th century
Cotton; drawn and painted resists and
    mordants, dyed
Red, purple-brown, blue, yellow,
    green, black
Warp 208 cm, weft 94 cm
Textile Museum, Washington, D.C.
    6.129

detailed description from Aurangzeb's camp (1664). He tells us the
king's enclosure was surrounded by
qanats, which were screens seven or
eight feet high. ". . . These kanates
are of strong cloth which is lined
with chittes or cloths painted with
portals with a great vase of flowers.
In the center of one side of the square
is the Royal Entrance, which is large
and magnificent and the chittes
[chintz] of which it is made, as also
those which face the exterior of all
this side of the square, are much
more beautiful and rich than the others." Beyond the large official tents
were private quarters also surrounded
"by small kanates of the height of a
man, and lined with painted chittes,
of that fine workmanship of Masulipatam, which represented a hundred
different kinds of flowers. . . ." Bernier also speaks of the interior of
tents lined with "beautiful chittes of
painted flowers made for the purpose,
of that same work of Masulipatam. . . ."[16]
    Bernier attributes these hangings to
Masulipatam, possibly because that
region was reputed to produce the
finest textile paintings. In the seventeenth century, however, fine textile
printing and painting centers—such
as Sironj and Burhanpur—existed
elsewhere, and Irwin has attributed
some of the finest tent hangings that
remain to the latter site. These combine block printing with hand painting of details and a very limited use
of indigo blue. The tent panels of Figures 70 and 71 were probably made
in Burhanpur. Here the flower heads
were first established with the aid of
a stamp, and the green of the leaves
and stems by hand painting yellow
over blue. Figure 71 is only one of a
series of niches contained on a nine
meter tent wall. The wall is part of
the Powis collection formed by Clive
of India and his son and daughter-in-
law, Lady Powis. It belonged originally to Tipu Sahib, Sultan of Mysore
(1782–99) and was acquired by the
second Lord Clive and his wife during his governorship of Madras, 1798–
1803.[17]
    The panel in Figure 72 was proba-
bly made in northern India, but the
precise location is unknown. Outlines
of the major configurations were first
stamped in red to outline the margins
of the red flowers and then in black
to define the leaves. Mordants were

then painted within the flowers. After the red dyeing, stems were drawn by hand and the leaves painted green. The borders show both stamping and brush-applied mordant work. The hanging is of coarse cotton that is lined and thinly padded. It probably served the Jaipur court at one time because it compares with other single panels known to have been in that collection.[18]

With its green background and heavy use of blue, the tent hanging in Figure 73 was probably made in Golconda. It shows a thin vase with a tall floral spray set on a green background. Great fanciful blossoms and fruits weight the stems, while oriental cloud scrolls float in the background. The floral arrangement, flanked by small clusters of flowers that rise from patterned rocks, is framed by a cusped arch. In the spandrels is a finely worked floral tracery set on a deep yellow ground. Above and below is a broad border of crosses and cartouches filled with more floral details. Above the upper border is a frieze of identical flowering plants. Other sections of this wall panel were recently shown in London together with information that the hanging once was in the inventory of the Amber Palace, Rajasthan.[19]

74 This rare glimpse of the manner in which cloth walls might be used shows an Iranian encampment of the nineteenth century. Not unlike the qanats of the exhibition, the designs seem to be of a flowering plant centered on a mound and framed within an architectural niche. This could well represent work done at Masulipatam. The photograph was taken by Antoine Sevruguin, whose other photographs document related hangings used as sun screens. (Archives of Islamic Art of Myron Bement Smith. Courtesy of Freer Gallery of Art, Washington D.C.)

were worked in double ikat and arranged so as to create larger, stepped geometric shapes. This was done in a manner to define blue squares and red squares and areas in the natural color of the cotton. After the textile was woven and these ikat patterns established, the textile was treated as a chintz. That is, designs were drawn in black mordant in sympathy with the ikat forms, wax resists were applied, areas were mordant-painted for red and black, and the textile was subjected to additional dye baths of red and blue. It is this additional designing and processing that probably explains more fully the term chitti, or chintz, rumals. These textiles may also help to explain references to cotton patola.

The conceptualization necessary to create a chintz rumal is not dissimilar to that required to effect the Karuppur textiles (discussed below). These textiles have metallic yarns woven into the textile, which was then worked with wax resists and mordants. It is not impossible that the goldworkers of telia rumals reported by Jayakar and Mittal were ultimately responsible for the gold-worked textiles of Karuppur; these craftsmen may have sought new patronage on the east coast upon the collapse of the Vijayanagar Empire. This avenue of research presents great promise for adding to our knowledge of both the telia rumals and the textiles from Karuppur.

Eastern Regions

Artisans of Orissa State in east India also know the ikat technique, but here still other differences exist. Patterns are tied either only in the weft yarns or only in the warp yarns to make animal and floral designs. These more complex, representational patterns are thought to be recent in origin. Simple squares or geometric patterns are created by joining both warp and weft in a true double ikat.[36] Worked in cotton or silk, this technique is used primarily to create sari. In an area of Cuttack, however, a silk ikat cloth (more properly termed *bandha*, from the Indian word for "to tie") is created that has inscriptions and is used as a temple gift in Puri. The primary creators of bandha in Orissa are the Bhulia. It is possible that these people migrated from Uttar Pradesh in the fourteenth century and before that had made their home in western India.[37]

Very simple ikat patterns were made elsewhere in India. These could be arrowhead patterns arranged in stripes, or simple zigzag configurations. Warp ikat is known in Gujarat (Patan) and Tamil Nadu (Tanjore and Kanchipuram), while weft ikat in addition to that of Orissa is done in the Surat area.[38]

Bengal and the northeast, while producing some chintz, were more famous for textiles that more rightly belong to the category of the weaver's rather than the dyer's art. The region, however, was extremely important for the quality of its cotton textiles because the soil near Dacca grew a particularly fine cotton.[39] For centuries the highly developed skills in spinning and weaving had earned the area a worldwide renown for its fine muslins. These were prized in Indian courts and, although muslins were dyed and

continued on page 114

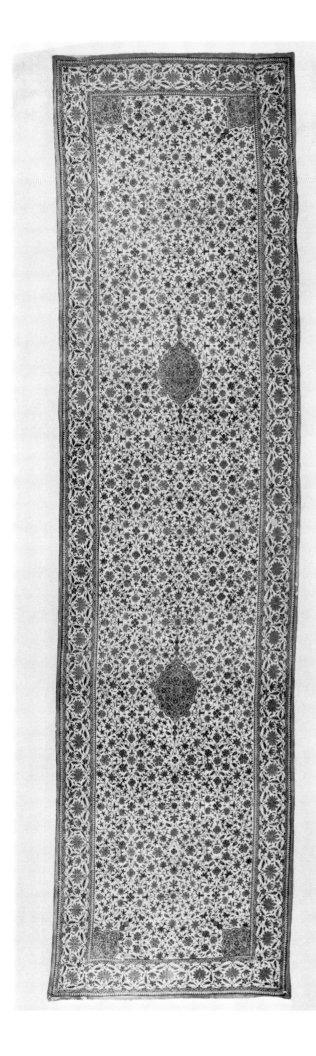

75 **Tablecover**
Burhanpur (?), 18th century
Cotton; stamped and painted resist
    and mordants, dyed
Red, blue, yellow, green, black
Warp 335 cm, weft 87.5 cm
Textile Museum, Washington, D.C.
    6.128

*The format of this textile—with its
two medallions, corner segments, and
broad framing borders—suggests that
a carpet served as a source of inspiration. The narrowness of the textile,
however, seems to preclude its use as
a floor spread.*

*The surface is filled with flowers
delicately arranged on their stems;
together the flowers and stems form
large circles over the face of the
cloth. Some flowers are blue, others
are red and purple outlined in red.
The green of the leaves was produced
by painting yellow over indigo. The
combination of painting and stamping, together with extremely fine
workmanship, suggests an origin in
Burhanpur.*

76 Chandova (canopy)
Burhanpur, ca. 1825
Cotton; drawn resists, stamped and
   painted mordants, dyed
Red, blue, yellow, green, black
245 cm x 143 cm; with added border
   274 cm x 170.5 cm
Jagdish and Kamla Mittal Museum of
   Indian Art, Hyderabad 76.1512

*This delightful canopy can best be
described as a scene of celestial celebration. Winged musicians and dancers, worked in a welter of fine details,
fill the surface. In the center the figures are arranged in three concentric
tiers; elsewhere they dance in single
file about a nucleus featuring still another winged figure. Heavenly musicians, as well as parrots and a round
floral form, fill the spaces between
the medallions. The smaller medallions have sky-blue centers on a ma-
roon-red ground bounded by white
floral borders. In the tiers of the large
central medallion, the ground alter-
nates between maroon and deep
green. This green is also the color of
the background of the textile.*

*The celestial females wear earthly
skirts,* choli *(blouses), and* odhani
*(shawls). Their male counterparts
wear dhoti with patka. These costumes have been meticulously patterned with motifs that would have
been familiar at the time.*

*The contours of the winged figures
were created with the aid of stamps,
and their details were added with
brush-applied mordants. The outlines
of the medallions were freely drawn,
lending a pleasing irregularity to the
formal shape. Two layers of light
brown handloomed cotton line the
canopy.*

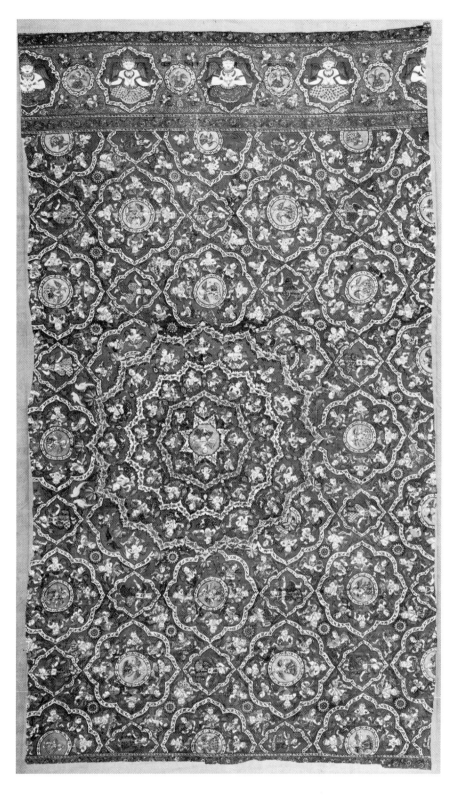

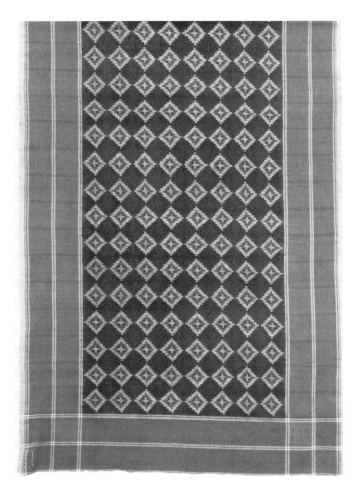

77 **Dupatta** (woman's shawl)
Pochampalli, 19th century
Cotton; double and warp ikat, dyed,
   supplementary weft
Red, black
Warp 234 cm, weft 120 cm
National Museum, New Delhi
   56.105/12

78 **Dupatta** (woman's shawl)
Pochampalli, 19th century
Cotton; double and warp ikat, dyed
   Red, black
Warp 260 cm, weft 119 cm
National Museum, New Delhi
   59.178/2

*These are light, almost diaphanous
cottons worked by double ikat. The
deeply saturated colors of dark red
and black, and the ecru of the cotton
ground, give form to simple geometric
patterns of stepped squares and patterned stripes. These designs fill the
center field, which is then framed by
wide borders defined by three pairs of
thin white stripes. The stripes cross
in the corners to form four squares;
one of these is always patterned by a
grid of fine white lines. This faint,
crosshatched design was created by
double-ikat patterning in Figure 77,
but by a warp ikat crossed with a
white supplementary weft in Figure
78. This crosshatching, although a
seemingly minor detail, has required
substantially more work. It appears
on many cotton double ikats from
this region.*

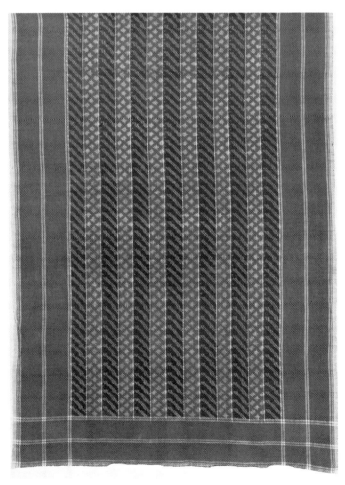

*   Textiles such as these are referred
to as* telia rumals. *Literally translated, this term means "oiled
squares," but in common usage it
connotes the square textiles exported
to the Middle East or used by local
laborers.[20] "Oiled" refers to the oily
feel that remained in the textile after
the cotton yarns had been soaked
and kneaded in oil during an initial
stage in the dye process. Locally, they
were called* chitti rumal, *a term discussed in the text. How these textiles
were used is not known, but their
size suggests a head covering; thus
they are defined as dupatta, but this
is open to question.*

81   85   92

The Brooklyn Museum Hanging

By NINA GWATKIN

The Brooklyn Museum wall hanging is an outstanding example of the fine cotton painting produced on the Coromandel Coast in the first half of the seventeenth century.[21] Three panels from this most unusual mordant-painted and dyed curtain are on display, Figures 81, 85, and 92. In its original state the hanging measured approximately 8 by 23 feet and depicted a series of seven tall, architectural alcoves containing a range of people from elaborately dressed and bejeweled Hindu courtiers, to foreign visitors, to tribal hunters dressed in leaves. The size of the hanging and the variety of figures represented suggest that it was commissioned to decorate a grand room in a cosmopolitan center.

Of the approximately twenty cotton paintings attributed to the first half of the seventeenth century, the

Brooklyn curtain may be the earliest. It is clearly a product of what Irwin has defined as the Madras-Pulicat school of cotton painting,[22] but such elements as the costume and the rendering of the figures suggest that the piece should be dated somewhat earlier than other surviving specimens of this school. Drawing and costume details are more indicative of a date in the first quarter of the seventeenth century than in the second quarter. The bulk of European costume evidence, for example, suggests a style current around 1600–10. While there could have been a time lag before such fashions appeared in India, some of the indigenous costumes depicted seem to be of that period as well. Architectural aspects of the piece also fit within this earlier time frame.

The curtain was in such fragile

condition when acquired by the Brooklyn Museum that it was cut into seven sections and mounted on canvas to ease the strain on the old fabric. Unfortunately, no record of the original sequence of the panels seems to have been made.

Architectural setting, costume, and portrayal of the figures all illustrate the richness of this hanging and warrant closer examination.

Format

The format of the Brooklyn hanging shows the architectural type of framework common to all pieces of this school. The principal figures are contained within seven Islamic-style alcoves, each of which is topped with a leaf-shaped finial as in Figure 81. Three of the arches are outlined in red with a resist decoration of alternating flowers and endless knot designs; the other four are delineated by a chevron pattern in white, blue, and red. The upper edge of each arch is bordered by a garland of leaves.

Across the top of the hanging, as if behind the alcoves, are several tiers of sketchily drawn, onion-shaped domes and chhatries that may derive from the contemporary Islamic architectural style of such Deccan kingdoms as Golconda and Bijapur. In Figure 79, however, the domes alternate with sikhara-topped pavilions that are clearly from the Hindu canon. In the original curtain, each alcove with its surmounting domes seems to have been separated from its neighbor by a tall floral "pillar" that was also topped by a dome. Similar floral strips form part of the border of the whole piece. The upper edge of the whole is finished with an additional border filled with crenelations, another borrowing from Islamic architecture that also appears around the edges of some Persian carpets and some of the Golconda painted textiles.[23]

Although it is impossible to determine the order in which the panels were once arranged, it seems probable that the alcoves were meant to depict a series of courtly audience scenes. Elaborate hanging flower garlands, some with perching birds, decorate the topmost sections of the alcoves. Below, each alcove (except Figure 92) is subdivided into four, sometimes five, separate compartments. The compartments are set apart from each other by rather cursorily drawn architectural elements: brick platforms, moldings, wall niches, onion domes, and variously shaped small arches; in fact, almost every figure has its own flower-filled arch. Within the compartments richly dressed figures sit on ornate couches, and beneath the couches stand vessels for food and drink. All these features suggest the curtain's aristocratic milieu.

Costume

The most striking aspect of the principal figures is their international character. Only two (possibly three) panels are dominated by local Indian figures, Figures 79, 92, and 97; the other four textile segments show figures in what is obviously meant to be foreign apparel.[24] The figures are dressed in what appears to be Persian or Turkoman style, Figure 80; Southeast Asian costume, Figures 85 and 89; and European garments of the early seventeenth century, Figure 81. The details of these costumes are not always accurate, but the artist has used various costume profiles, as well as differences in the textiles being worn, to indicate the diverse nature of the groups. Obviously the artist had available a great repertoire of both foreign and domestic textiles to imitate. Varieties range from what appear to be European brocades and velvets, to indigenous striped and patterned textiles, to what might be Javanese batiks.

Aside from adding to the interest of the panels, the costumes provide useful evidence for dating. The European and Indo-Persian costumes are the most helpful in this respect since there is more comparative material available for them. It is, however, dangerous to rely too heavily on details of dress to date these panels because the Indian artist was probably working with patterns or stencils that he did not always completely understand. This confusion occasionally yielded quaint ambiguities: in Figure 81, several men have what appear to be cloak collars but wear no cloaks, or stockings end in bare feet (for example, the seated man, Figure 82). Even indigenous costume was prey to misunderstanding (see the necklines of the seated men in Figure 97, for example); sometimes patterns were simply reversed, showing costume elements in the wrong position, right hands attached to left arms, and so forth.

Shortcuts were also taken in delineating different garments. Variations on the sashed jerkin worn by both men and women appear as elements of many of the diverse costumes shown in five of the seven panels, Figures 79, 80, 81, 85, and 89; this rendering seems to be an artistic convention for depicting a torso covering when the exact style was in doubt. The overall look could be modified by changing the sleeve length and adding an undershirt, a ruff, or a different collar line.

Given the discrepancies that crept into the renderings of European costume, the Indian artist did manage to depict correctly the general silhouette of a European costume common at the turn of the seventeenth century. Such a silhouette would not have been seen in India much earlier than the 1580s, and by the 1620s it had begun to change to the more relaxed and flowing silhouette of the mid-1600s, an appearance familiar from the portraits of such contemporary artists as Rubens and Van Dyck: wide, plumed hats topping long hair or wigs; flat lace collars worn over long doublet coats; and longer breeches meeting wide boots. That this great a costume change was not lost on the Indian artist can be seen in later painted and dyed wall hangings, Figure 103.[25]

There is, of course, the question of how quickly these changes in European fashion would have been seen in India, but volumes published by the Flemish engraver and publisher Bry and his sons in the first decade of the seventeenth century show Dutchmen in Asia wearing costumes[26] similar to those shown in Figure 81 of the Brooklyn curtain, Figure 123. The Indiae Orientalis of Bry also contains engravings based on the Dutch traveler Linschoten's sketches of the Portuguese done in the 1580s when he was living in the Portuguese enclave of Goa on the Indian southwest coast.[27] Some of these men are shown in knee breeches, with hats and shoes similar to those of the Brooklyn figures; a number of the women also wear comparable dress. The evidence from Bry suggests that the European costumes depicted in the Brooklyn hanging could have been seen in India not too long after they appeared in Europe, and that stencils for this piece could have been made in the early 1600s.

Stencils were reused, of course, within cotton paintings and from one painting to the next, so it is possible that earlier elements could appear in later textiles. Most of the Indo-Persian dress shown in Figure 79, however, corroborates the European evidence and seems to correspond to that worn by the Mughals at the end of Akbar's reign (1590–1605). Later cotton paintings, some of which can be dated fairly accurately from stocktaking dates on their backs, show forms more congruent with those worn in the second quarter of the seventeenth century at the Mughal and Persian courts, Figures 101 and 103.

Function and Antecedents

The cotton paintings appear to have served more than one purpose; all are decorative, of course, but some also seem to have a narrative or instructional function. Unfortunately, there are no known examples extant of what preceded the early seventeenth century cotton paintings, but almost certainly there were contemporary Hindu narrative cloths derived, perhaps, from temple and palace wall paintings. Since the Brooklyn curtain stands somewhat apart from the main body of cotton paintings, it may show a transition from the Hindu narrative tradition in both wall and textile painting to the more purely decorative form of the majority of the surviving textiles: from a style in which the story is the unifying principle to one in which the design elements provide cohesion.

Irwin points out that pieces such as the Brooklyn hanging were probably specially commissioned.[28] He adds that they were not usually designed to tell a single connected story; rather, the intention was to create something "purely fanciful and decorative."[29] While this curtain is certainly fanciful and decorative, it is also possible that it was designed for more than just an ornamental purpose. At the very least, the audience scenes and the international cross-section they depict indicate that the patron for whom the curtain was made must have been a powerful ruler of an important city, someone who could attract such a cosmopolitan group to his court.

A contemporary description of Vijayanagar reveals that the walls and ceilings of at least some of the palace buildings were hung with rich cloths "adorned with figures in the manner of embroidery."[30] Although this account does not reveal the subject matter of such cloths, it does describe some palace wall paintings that might have provided a prototype for the Brooklyn curtain: "On this same side is designed in painting all the ways of life of the men who have been here even down to the Portuguese, from which the king's wives can understand the manner in which each one lives in his own country."[31] Not only would such paintings have acclaimed the worldly stature of the king, they could also have served to edify the women of his harem, who would have been absent from the scenes depicted because of the custom of strict purdah that aristocratic Indian women observed.

Such wall paintings as prototypes for the curtain would also help to explain its architectural framework. The few surviving fragments of wall painting from Vijayanagar show figures in similar alcoves and compartments with dividing pillars;[32] there are no domes in that purely Hindu work, but along the top of one of the alcoves gopura-topped buildings interspersed with palm trees are shown in a manner that foreshadows their depiction in both the Brooklyn hanging and a similar type of hanging shown in Figure 104.

The combination of Islamic arches and domes with Hindu gopura and sikhara in these two textiles appears rather peculiar, but it may have had its antecedents in such Islamic-influenced buildings at Vijayanagar as the Lotus Mahal and the so-called Elephant Stables.[33] This fusion of architectural styles was continued in other buildings such as the raja's palaces at the later capitals of Penukonda and Chandragiri.[34] The palace facade at Chandragiri, for example, consists of three stories of arcades made up of typical Islamic arches; the whole, however, is topped with seven Hindu sikhara, several of which have rather domelike summits. The influence of such a hybrid architectural style seems evident in these two cotton paintings and suggests that perhaps the raja's palace at Chandragiri served as an inspiration for the layout of the Brooklyn piece.[35] During the reign of Venkata II (1584–1614), Chandragiri would certainly have been able to provide the international ambiance to inspire such a hanging.[36] Since the textile was presumably made in Pulicat, and this port was under the control of Chandragiri, the hypothesis does seem feasible.

All the existing cotton paintings of the Madras-Pulicat school reflect Vijayanagar influence in their architectural format and decorative conventions,[37] but the relationship appears most clear in the Brooklyn curtain. Details of costume and of drawing firmly link this piece to the Vijayanagar mural tradition as it can be seen in the surviving wall paintings at Lepakshi, Anegundi, and Vijayanagar itself.[38] Striking parallels exist in the rendering of the figures: profile legs and feet, frontal upper body, and profile head. The treatment of faces is also similar; the majority of the faces are depicted in profile in both the murals and the Brooklyn hanging. In the frontal view a person is often cross-eyed, and three-quarter renderings are rarely successful; for example, see the seated man in Figure 83. Several women in Figures 92 and 97 even retain the projecting further eye that is so noticeable in murals at Lepakshi.

Some of the figures are seated in conventional Indian poses indicating that they are granting audiences; a hand is often raised in what appears to be the Hindu mudra, or gesture, of exposition or admonishment, Figure 99. Other figures show hands raised in greeting or the arms folded across the chest in respectful attention. Still others hold or offer various objects such as cups, surahi, food, fans, musical instruments, weapons, or jewels.[39]

It seems clear that this usage of both gesture and pose to link the figures is another inheritance from the wall painting tradition in which Hindu myths and stories were often vividly portrayed. As already proposed, the Brooklyn curtain may show a transition from this earlier narrative style derived from wall painting to the more purely decorative style that historians attribute to the later cotton paintings.

79 Wall hanging

Madras region (Pulicat?), ca. 1610–20
Cotton; drawn and painted resist and
  mordants, dyed
Red, violet, brown, blue, yellow,
  green, violet-black
275 cm x 96 cm
The Brooklyn Museum 14.719.1

*While this panel is similar in format
to the others, several variations distinguish it. The most striking differ-
ence is the two sikhara-topped pavilions that nestle among the more
usual onion-shaped domes. The
whole is divided into five parallel
rows, rather than the usual four, and
there is a frieze of deer and comb
ducks along the bottom.*

*Even though aspects of the archi-
tecture may be Hindu inspired, the
figures are dressed in Indo-Persian
style; variations on this mode could
be seen both at the Mughal court in
the north and among the Muslim
courts of the Deccan. Here there may
be an attempt to show representatives from both groups; for example,
two different kinds of turban appear.
Figures in the top row wear closely
fitting styles similar to those worn in
the Deccan at the turn of the century;[40] in profile the turban gives the
head an elongated oval shape. Others
wear a much fuller form of turban,
usually with an upstanding end piece
or feathers. A comparable type of turban can be seen in many Mughal
paintings done during the later years
of Akbar's reign (1590–1605);[41] in
general, this mode gives a more
rounded form to the head. Other differences in style can be seen in the
dress of the two men seated in the
top row, who seem to be wearing the
full-length jama that was worn in the
Deccan at this period; most of the
other figures favor the short one that
was in style at the court of Akbar.
The long straight swords of the first
row also appear to be Deccan, while
the other swords are shown with the
shorter curved outline of the Mughal
weapon.*

*As Irwin points out, there was defi-
nitely direct Persian influence in the
Deccan at this period,[42] but it seems
more likely that the stylistic influences in this section of the panel owe
more to local Indo-Persian fashion
than to Persian. Irwin cites the
rounded turbans with the projecting
end pieces shown here as evidence
supporting a post-1630 date for the
Brooklyn curtain; he seems to consider the turbans a Safavid type that
was unlikely to have appeared in India before the 1630s.[43] The turbans
shown in Figure 79, however, are
quite round and compact in contrast
to the loosely wrapped ones Irwin
specifies;[44] they seem to resemble
more closely turbans worn at the
Mughal court in 1590–1605.*—NWG

80 Wall hanging

Madras region (Pulicat?), ca. 1610–20
Cotton; drawn and painted resist and
  mordants, dyed
Red, violet, brown, blue, yellow,
  green, violet-black
275 cm x 96 cm
The Brooklyn Museum 14.719.4

*The style of the costumes portrayed
in Figure 80 may be Persian, or Turkoman as Irwin suggests.[45] Most of
the figures wear the conventional
sashed jerkins with close-fitting trousers, but their hats add a distinctive
note. Of interest, too, is the short
costume of the three musicians in
row three. Two of these men seem to
be drummers; the third holds what
appears to be a lyre attached to the
body in some manner. Other figures
hold swords, drinking cups, and
jewels.*

*The identity of the women in row
one poses a problem. Their dress appears to be predominantly European,
but no European woman would have
worn such a short skirt at this period,
even with leg coverings. Perhaps they
are native women in a combination
of local and European dress.—*NWG

81 Wall hanging

Madras region (Pulicat?), ca. 1610–20
Cotton; drawn and painted resist and
  mordants, dyed
Red, violet, brown, blue, yellow,
  green, violet-black
275 cm x 96 cm
The Brooklyn Museum 14.719.2

*The most intriguing feature of this
panel is the European-style dress of
the figures. Aside from adding to the
charm and eclectic nature of the
hanging, these costumes are useful in
helping to date the Brooklyn curtain.
This is one of the panels in which
jewels are a focus of interest; other
figures hold drinking cups, surahi,
pan, or fans. Even though in European
dress, the figures sit in conventional
Indian poses and use some of the traditional Indian hand gestures; their
surroundings are similar to those in
the other panels.*

*The style of dress seen here resem-
bles that worn in Europe from about
1590 to 1620, but it is more difficult
to determine the exact nationality
being portrayed. Portuguese, as Irwin
proposes, is an obvious possibility;[46]
however, Italian travelers were
known on the Coromandel Coast as
early as the 1500s, and Dutch and
English merchants were active there
from the beginning of the 1600s. This
difficulty is compounded by the
spread throughout Europe of an international style of fashion beginning in
the mid-sixteenth century. Further-*

more, although the dress shown is definitely European in cut, its bright colors and varieties of textile patterns owe more to Indian decorative taste than to European fashion.

The most conspicuous aspect of the men's profile is their baggy knee breeches, or "Venetians"; these were worn in Europe from about 1570 to 1620, but were most popular in the 1580s and 1590s.[47] The breeches were worn over colored stockings secured by garters; the garter ties vary from simple bows to ones with tasseled ends. Several of the men are shown barelegged and barefooted, but most are wearing stockings and either slippers or flat-heeled tie shoes. The shoes and garters appear to be in turn-of-the-century styles; from 1600 European shoes began to develop heels, and their simple bow ties grew into large rosettes.[48] Big rosettes also began to appear on garters after about 1610.

Another eye-catching feature of the costume is the copotain, or tall crowned hat, that was popular throughout Europe from the 1580s into the early 1600s. After 1585 the copotain was often worn tilted to the back or side, as many of the gentlemen in the hanging are doing.[49] The hatless men may be servants or of a lower rank, for gentlemen of this period removed their hats—even when indoors—only out of respect for persons of higher rank. Elaborate hatbands were also the fashion, with feathers and jewels as typical ornaments. The hat decorated with feathers and an animal skin worn by the seated male in Figure 83 is possibly an adaptation of this style to local materials.

As already discussed, the jerkin and its sash seem to be an artistic convention. To portray Europeans, the artist has added a neck ruff—a salient feature of European dress from the 1560s to the 1640s—and a long-sleeved doublet with wrist ruffs. The ruff shown here is quite moderate compared with the huge cartwheel affairs that appeared at the height of this fashion;[50] worn with matching wrist ruffs, it suggests a style more common in the late sixteenth century than in the early seventeenth. There is some confusion in the neck and shoulder area of the costume: most of the jerkins appear to have "wings," pads or rolls of cloth projecting from the shoulder and sleeve seams, that would normally be of the same color as the body of the garment. On several of the figures, however, this piece is shown as white and appears to be attached to the ruff (seated man in Figure 83). The artist may have tried to portray a ruff worn over a falling collar, another fashion of the turn of the century.[51]

82 Detail of Figure 81.

83 Detail of Figure 81.

84 Detail of Figure 81.

The rapiers and daggers that many of the men wear were fashionable weapons of this period. In the panel most of the rapiers are depicted upside down and are arbitrarily hung about the belt, not just on the left as was the custom. In Elizabethan England the dagger was carried in the waist belt on the right side; here, the daggers are shown on either side of the waist, as suits the artist's convenience. After 1605 daggers began to go out of fashion as a costume element.[52]

The women in this panel could be European, but they are more likely Indian, either the wives or mistresses of the men shown. Portuguese women were present in Goa as early as the 1580s,[53] but the earliest mention of European women on the eastern coast dates to the 1620s.[54] Both the English and the Dutch remarked on the Portuguese custom of taking local women as mistresses and wives; for a time at least the Dutch followed suit, seeing these mixed marriages as a way of maintaining their power in India. In the 1620s, however, this attitude changed; men married to Indians were not allowed to return to Holland, and Dutch women were sent out to the East in order to make marriages with their countrymen.[55]

It is also possible that the women portrayed were drawn from European paintings or engravings rather than from life; such representations were available on the subcontinent at least as early as the mid-sixteenth century and were studied with great interest by local artists and connoisseurs alike. For example, the Jesuit mission present at the court of the Vijayanagar ruler Venkata II at the beginning of the seventeenth century included two lay brothers, one English and one Italian, who were painters. They did portraits for him as well as religious subjects such as the Virgin Mary and Child.[56] The nursing woman in Figure 84 brings to mind the many European-inspired renderings of the Virgin and Child by both Mughal and Deccan court artists.[57]

Whether the women are European or Indian, their dress owes its inspiration to European prototypes. They wear the same ruffs and upper garments as the men, but theirs are worn over ankle-length skirts and flat-heeled shoes. A close look at their hair reveals that it is not curly, as Irwin suggests,[58] but dressed in a knot on top of the head and elaborately ornamented with what appear to be pearls. Similar top knots with jewels may be seen in contemporary Deccan paintings of Indian women,[59] but this mode of wearing the jewels on the crown of the head seems to be of European inspiration.[60]—NWG

85 Wall hanging

Madras region (Pulicat?), ca. 1610–20
Cotton; drawn and painted resist and
　mordants, dyed
Red, violet, brown, blue, yellow,
　green, violet-black
275 cm x 96 cm
The Brooklyn Museum 14.719.3

This panel, too, adheres to the general format of the others. The ladies of the upper row resemble those in Figure 81, but the male figures wear what appears to be Siamese costume. There is not the wealth of costume evidence for Southeast Asia that there is for Europe, but some late seventeenth century descriptions of Siamese costume seem quite similar to what can be seen here.[61] *French visitors to the court of the king of Siam described high, pointed hats, open-necked shirts, and painted cloths worn wrapped about the thighs and pulled up between the legs to leave an end hanging down in front; they also noted the style seen here of wearing one wrapper over the other. As in other costume renderings in the curtain, there are probably inaccurate details: the shirt all the men wear, for example, is obviously an open-necked version of the conventionalized torso covering seen throughout the panels, but the overall profile of the Siamese costume has been captured.*

Some of the men hold jewels or fans while others hold sheathed daggers similar to those shown in Figure 89.—NWG

86   Detail of Figure 85.
87   Detail of Figure 85.

88 Detail of Figure 85.

89 Wall hanging

Madras region (Pulicat?), ca. 1610–20
Cotton; drawn and painted resist and
   mordants, dyed
Red, violet, brown, blue, yellow,
   green, violet-black
275 cm x 96 cm
The Brooklyn Museum 14.719.5

*More men of Southeast Asian origin
appear in this panel. A definite attempt has been made to show an ethnic type different from those rendered
in the other panels: the men have
short, brushlike hair styles, tiny
wisps of chin whiskers, and almond-
shaped eyes, Figure 90. Although the
physical features are not definitive,
aspects of their costume such as the
head ties, the textiles, and the kris-
like knives suggest that the men are
Javanese or Malay.*

*The overall look resembles that of
Java; however, specific costume details are difficult to identify. The
men's tunics are the stock ones seen
in some of the other panels, but here
they have a different hem profile and
are worn with the neck open and no
undershirt. The short "skirts" of the
men are probably meant to be loincloths; as in some of the other panels,
they are rendered more like baggy
pants when the men are shown
seated. All the standing men have
bare legs and feet.*

*The knife carried by so many of the
men might be the Javanese kris, but
its shape and the way it is worn are
more akin to Indian custom than Indonesian. According to one expert,
the rendering of the knife more
closely resembles the Indian khanjar
than the kris;[62] the differences are revealed in both the carved hilt and
the shape of the blade.[63] The way of
wearing the knife is also more Indian; in Java the kris is usually
tucked into the sash at the man's
back.*

*The head ties are another problem.
Although it is not uncommon in Indonesia to see head ties that leave
the top of the head bare, these fish-
fin-shaped end pieces are not recog-
nizably Javanese; however, people of
the archipelago often styled their
headgear in fanciful ways, and perhaps that is what is expressed here. It
would seem that the Indian artist
was unfamiliar with this headgear
because it is always shown from the
same view, no matter how the wear-
er's head is turned.*

*The textile designs shown in this
panel are especially interesting. Some
are similar to those used elsewhere in
the curtain, but others are more distinctive. The wrapper on the man to
the left in Figure 90, for example,
brings to mind Indian block-print
work, while the pattern of the tunic
on the man in Figure 91 is reminis-*

90 Detail of Figure 89.

91 Detail of Figure 89.

cent of Indian tie-dye work. The rendering of the tunic on the central
man in Figure 90, on the other hand,
might be interpreted as Javanese patterns of the **parang rusak** variety;[64]
the tunic of the sixth figure in the
bottom row of Figure 89 reminds one
of Javanese **kawung** designs.[65] Traditionally, however, these Indonesian
patterns would have appeared on
wrappers rather than on shirts.

This is another of the panels in
which drinks and jewels seem to be
the primary focus of attention. The
men are shown in surroundings similar to those of the other panels.—NWG

92 Wall hanging

Madras region (Pulicat?), ca. 1610–20
Cotton; drawn and painted resist and
   mordants, dyed
Red, violet, brown, blue, yellow,
   green, violet-black
275 cm x 96 cm
The Brooklyn Museum 14.719.6

The framework of this panel is similar to that of the others, but its alcove encloses a tropical jungle full of animals and tribal hunters rather than a courtly audience scene. Even the carefully arranged hanging garlands are absent from the point of this arch; in their place what seems to be the chief of the group talks with some of his men. Below, the rows are divided from each other by lush vegetation instead of architectural elements, and individual spaces for the figures are outlined by trailing leaves, not the flower-lined, domed arches of the other panels. Rather than on brick platforms and ornate couches, the hunters stand and sit on rocky hillocks from which sprout grasses, flowers, and large plants; among the plants hide many small animals and birds.

The costumes worn here and in Figure 97 show the most direct Vijayanagar influence. In murals at Lepakshi, too, leaf-skirted hunters, both male and female, are shown, and the simplicity of their garments contrasts with the elaborateness of their jewelry.[66] The jewelry of the men on the textile is comparatively simple: bracelets and chestbands of beads, unusual pendant earrings, and, on the seated man, anklets. The women wear large earrings and many bracelets as well as ornate necklaces.

While the men wear only leaf skirts and headbands, the women appear to be wearing transparent garments beneath their leaf skirts as well as long-sleeved choli, Figure 95. Both sexes have long hair tied back at the neck, but the women's hair continues in a single thick braid down to the knees; in addition to the headband, the women each wear a garland of flowers at the nape of the neck. Some of the women also seem to have flower-like tattoos on their cheeks. Several of the women here and in Figure 97 are drawn with the protruding further eye, Figures 95 and 98, another link with the Vijayanagar style as seen at Lepakshi.

The seated man with the striped animal skin on his head is perhaps the leader of the group, but the woman seated below seems to be directing some of the activities, too. In fact, the women appear to be the hunters of the band; the men carry arrows and snares, as well as the day's bag, but it is the women who are actually shooting arrows.

93 Detail of Figure 92.

94 Detail of Figure 92.

95 Detail of Figure 92.

96 Detail of Figure 92.

The identity of these hunters continues to be a puzzle. Stewart Culin even suggests that they are from outside India,[67] but there were many tribal groups in the Deccan; as Irwin points out, leaf-skirted hunters, both male and female, have been a convention in south Indian art since the twelfth century.[68] It is, of course, possible that the artist did not intend to depict a specific tribal group, but rather some kind of myth or hunting story. The leaf-skirted hunters at Lepakshi, for example, represent the god Shiva and his entourage and are part of an episode from the Hindu epic the Mahabharata.[69] Such an explanation based on an unidentified myth would account for the elaborate jewelry of these jungle folk and might explain why one of the hunters is greeting the mother tiger so reverently, and why she in turn is addressing her cubs, Figure 94. Such a theory, however, must also await further documentation.—NWG

97 Wall hanging

Madras region (Pulicat?), ca. 1610–20
Cotton; drawn and painted resist and
    mordants, dyed
Red, violet, brown, blue, yellow,
    green, violet-black
275 cm x 96 cm
The Brooklyn Museum 14.719.7

*In this panel the full effect of the Vi-
jayanagar influence can be seen; from
the hanging garlands to the confront-
ing elephants, echoes of this style of
Hindu court life abound. Such scenes
as the king surrounded by members
of the seraglio or interviewing his
courtiers would have been common.
Elephants were among the most
prized of royal possessions, and almost all the early European travelers
to India commented upon the importance and abundance of jewels in Vijayanagar life.*[70] *Here most of the figures (including the elephants) are
elaborately bedecked with jewelry,
and jewels seem to be the principal
interest of the figures themselves.*

    *The women show the most obvious
parallels to Vijayanagar mural painting as we now know it; both their
stance and the sharply pointed profile
of their sari are reminiscent of the
women in the Lepakshi murals. The
first and fourth women in row one
even retain the projecting further eye
so common at Lepakshi, Figure 95. In*

98 Detail of Figure 97.
99 Detail of Figure 97.

both mural and textile renderings the women wear long-sleeved choli with the end of the sari carried across the chest and over the shoulders; the sari end is crossed to either side, as suits the artist's convenience. In contrast to figures at Lepakshi, these ladies wear their hair in a long, single braid down the back, but the hair is still elaborately dressed with jewels and flower garlands as in the wall murals. Both sets of women display jewelry at the ears, neck, arms, and ankles, and in three or four chains around the hips. Several of the women in the Brooklyn hanging may be dancers or musicians, since they are holding what appear to be wooden castanets. Two others offer pan to the seated man, and one waves a fly whisk, Figure 98.

The men, too, are dressed in Vijaya-nagar style, but their dress varies from the simple costume of the water carrier in row four to the rich apparel of the seated figure in row one. The courtiers wear loincloths with narrower cloths tied over them, a style that can also be seen at Lepakshi. Most of the men are barechested except for their jewels; however, several wear a shirt with a low, square-cut neckline, and a hanging medallion is partly covered by the top of the shirt. The shirt seems to combine elements of the open-necked Hindu shirt with the ties that would appear on the Muslim jama. This ambiguous style is also present in Figure 104, but it does not appear to have an antecedent in the mural paintings. The men's headgear is also quite different from any shown in the murals. The man in row one wears what appears to be an embroidered velvet cap, while the rest of the men wear various styles of turbans, none of which seems to have a prototype in the murals.—NWG

100 Coverlet

Golconda region (Petaboli?), ca. 1640–50
Cotton; drawn and painted resist and mordants, dyed
Red, violet, brown, blue, yellow, green, violet-black
71.75 cm x 81.9 cm
Cincinnati Art Museum 1962.465. The William T. and Louise Taft Semple Collection

In this attractive coverlet a wide border filled with hillocks, flowering plants, and birds surrounds a white center field. The two guard stripes of the border have a violet ground filled with a running floral motif.

As in the other coverlets, the field is decorated with a series of unrelated vignettes. In the upper left corner, a tiger attacks two deer while just beside them a Persian man obliviously drinks from a surahi. In the upper right corner, a man in Persian dress plays a tambourine. Next to him another man, who is perhaps a singer, wears what appears to be Indian dress; because of a draftsman's error, both of his arms are depicted as being on the right side of his body. In the lower left corner, two Persian men appear to admire one another. Below the central figure, a hunter in a loincloth walks toward a herd of deer. He carries a club and leads a reluctant dog on a leash. Surrounding the larger figures are trees, plants, and flowers, as well as assorted birds and butterflies.

With the exception of the hunter and the "singer," the figures in this textile are in Persian dress of a style quite similar to that seen in the other coverlets, Figures 101 and 102. Irwin has pointed out that several of the figures repeat in the coverlets;[71] this practice has been followed here as well. The closest parallel can be seen between this textile and a coverlet at the Metropolitan Museum of Art (no. 28.159.3). Although not exact replicas, as in several of the coverlets, some of the figures are analogous in dress or stance, and several of the textile patterns on their clothing are repeated in different colors. For example, the costume of the central figure in the Cincinnati coverlet is similar to that of two seated figures in the Metropolitan Museum piece (lower left and upper center), and forms comparable to the standing figure wearing a cone hat (bottom left) appear in the Metropolitan Museum piece (upper right) and in a piece in the National Museum, New Delhi (lower right).[72]

These and other more general similarities that can be seen in this textile as well as in the rest of the coverlets indicate that the Cincinnati piece must also have been produced in the Golconda region around the mid-seventeenth century.—NWG

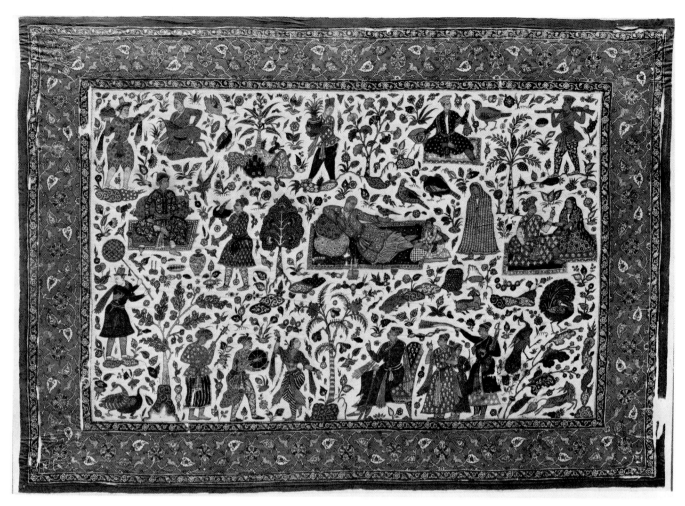

101 Coverlet
Golconda region (Petaboli?), ca.
  1640–50
Cotton; drawn and painted resist and
  mordants, dyed
Red, violet, brown, blue, yellow,
  green, violet-black
92.1 cm x 64.1 cm
The Metropolitan Museum of Art,
  New York 28.159.2. Rogers Fund
  1928

This fine coverlet is one of several
that survive from the seventeenth
century. It has a white field surrounded by a broad red border filled
with palmettes and scrolling leaf motifs; the border is bounded by two
guard stripes with a running floral
design on a darker brownish ground.

Twenty human figures are sprin-
kled about the field of the textile
with no apparent attempt at a narrative rendering; rather, the figures
seem to provide a sampler of such
everyday pastimes as feeding a bird,
watching a musical entertainment, or
having a foot massage. Even the
placement of the figures appears to
have been decided on largely decorative grounds. While some figures
stand firmly on the bottom guard
stripe, others seem to float in space;
one sits on a European-style chair,
and some rest on carpets; still others

perch on their own private clouds.
Fanciful plants and flowers, as well
as goats, rabbits, peacocks, ducks,
parrots, and other birds, enliven the
setting.

The reverse side bears an impres-
sion in black of a circular seal with a
Persian inscription. Joseph Breck
translated this as "the servant [of
God] Rustam the undisputed master
who spread the table of Jemshid (i.e.,
who emulated this legendary Persian
king in entertaining)."[73] The inscription suggests that the vignettes of the
coverlet may show ways of offering
hospitality to guests, or perhaps the
coverlet itself was a gift of welcome.
Also on the reverse of the textile are
two decipherable dates that correspond to A.D. 1689 and 1701 and two
Devanagari inscriptions that, according to Breck, are probably the names
of clerks.[74]

The format of coverlets such as this
with the center field surrounded by
borders and guard stripes is reminiscent of Persian carpets: some even
have a central medallion, Figure 102.
History records strong Persian influence on both trade and social life in
the Golconda region at this period.
There was even a settlement of Persian carpet weavers at Ellore (about
70 miles north of the Golconda port
of Masulipatam) who could have sup-

plied the inspiration for these formats. By the time English traders
noted the presence of these weavers
in 1679, they had been there for over
100 years, ample time for them to
have influenced local textile-painting
designs.[75]

There seems to be less European influence in the coverlets than in many
of the larger cotton paintings, but the
device to render the animal pelts by
circular dotted designs may, in fact,
derive from European engravings. A
similar treatment of animal skins can
be seen in Figure 102. Further European influence can be noted in the
chair at bottom center and in the hat
worn by the figure at the bottom far
left.

With the exception of the Indian
dancing girl, the figures appear to be
dressed in a pastiche of Indo-Persian
costume. The majority of the male
figures wear Persian headgear that
Irwin dates to the 1630s or 1640s,[76]
but both the man playing the tambourine for the dancer and the one
holding two birds wear turbans in
the style of the Mughal court during
the reign of Shah Jahan (1627–58).
Figures attending the man seated on
the chair appear to wear styles of
jama and turban popular in the Muslim courts of the Deccan in the first
quarter of the seventeenth century.

Further Deccan influence can be seen in the composition of several of the coverlet scenes. As Irwin has already pointed out, the reclining youth in the center calls to mind "The Siesta" miniature painting in the Staatliche Museen, Berlin.[77] The group attending the man seated in the chair is reminiscent of another Deccan painting: a portrait of the Ahmadnagar ruler Burhan II, that shows him seated in a similar chair with three attendants.[78]

Inscriptions and costume details, as well as comparison with other coverlets, indicate that this textile was probably made about the middle of the seventeenth century. The storage inventory dates on the reverse provide a date for its latest possible production (about 1685); however, a similar piece at the Metropolitan Museum of Art (no. 28.159.3), said to have been stored in the same treasury, bears the inventory dates A.D. 1650 and 1651.[79] These earlier dates seem to indicate fabrication of both pieces in the late 1640s. A much earlier date does not seem feasible since most of the headgear shown in the coverlet would not have been seen in India before the 1630s.—NWG

102 Coverlet

Golconda region (Petaboli?), ca. 1640–50

Cotton; drawn and painted resist and mordants, dyed

Red, violet, brown, blue, yellow, green, violet-black

89.5 cm x 62 cm

Victoria and Albert Museum, London I.S. 34–1969

With its central medallion, floral border, and guard stripes, the Victoria and Albert coverlet is closer in design to its Persian carpet prototypes than most of the other coverlets. The dark center field is surrounded by a light border filled with palmettes and scrolling flower and leaf motifs. A slightly different repeat has been used to finish the bottom left border: note the different kinds of flowers, the two rabbits, and the two birds. The border is framed with two guard stripes with a floral motif on a dark ground.

In the center field unconnected scenes are set off by exotic flowering trees and plants. Cloudlets and fancifully decorated animals drift about the ground. The genre scenes are similar to those portrayed in the other coverlets: men dallying with women, listening to musicians, feeding birds, meditating, or hunting; both women

and men are depicted drinking. The horse and elephants shown are larger than the typical animals that grace these textiles. There is little evidence of European influence in this piece, but the circular dotted designs on some of the animals may be an attempt to imitate the appearance of European engravings.

The costumes are a medley of both Persian and Indian dress and appear to be congruent both in style and period with those of the other coverlets. There seem to be no exact parallels between these figures and those of the other coverlets, but the Indian man embracing a woman is reminiscent of a similar couple on one of the coverlets at the Metropolitan Museum of Art (no. 28.159.3). In both cases the man's arm has been drawn out of socket to allow him to embrace his companion.

There are no storage inventory dates for this piece, but there are enough similarities in format, subject matter, style, and costume details between it and the other coverlets to confirm that it, too, must have been made in the Golconda region around the middle of the seventeenth century.—NWG

103 Wall hanging

Madras region (Pulicat?), ca. 1640–50
Cotton; drawn and painted resist and
    mordants, dyed
Red, violet, brown, blue, yellow,
    green (?), black
198 cm x 114 cm; with borders
    295 cm x 152 cm
Victoria and Albert Museum, London
    687–1898

The architectural format of this remarkable textile is a significant characteristic in establishing it as one of
the few surviving pieces from the
Madras-Pulicat school of cotton
painting. Two large panels are framed
by a series of small architectural
niches containing figures, vases, or
floral garlands. In the upper panel
four figures wearing Indo-Persian
styles are depicted. The lower scene
shows two couples in European-style
dress gathered around a table. Sepa-
rating the two compartments is a
blue band containing vases, chests
with swords, and surahi. At the top
of the main section of the hanging
are a series of domes and pavilions, a
feature common to the other pieces of
this school, Figures 81, 85, and 92. A
blue border containing Indo-Persian
figures engaged in various pastimes
runs along the bottom; the figures
stand in a floral ground filled with
whimsical animals and birds.

The central area is composed of
two textiles seamed horizontally
along the lower edge of the upper
panel. A band formed of blue floral
fragments, which seem to be of a
later date, has been added above the
domes. The surrounding eighteenth
century borders were also added at a
later date.

Irwin has expertly analyzed this
piece,[80] but several of his points may
be open to question. He suggests, for
instance, that the format was probably inspired by a type of Jesuit engraving of the Virgin and Child that
was in circulation in the East in the
1620s.[81] This comparison is interesting, but it seems unnecessary to turn
away from Indian artistic traditions
to seek a prototype for the layout of
this piece. In south Indian wall
painting there was already a long-
established practice of dividing the
space to be dealt with into smaller
compartments. Frequently a large
scene is shown surrounded by
smaller panels and niches, and quite
often the framing of these sections is
done with such architectural elements as pillars, arches, pavilions, or
roofs. Examples of this style can be
seen in fifteenth century wall paintings of the Virupaksha Temple of Vijayanagar,[82] or in seventeenth century
wall paintings illustrated in a recent
edition of Marg.[83] Such wall paintings
were widespread in the seventeenth
century Deccan and were much more

accessible as a source of inspiration
for the cotton paintings than the rarer
European engravings.

There is, of course, obvious European influence in these textiles, but it
is to be seen more in subject matter,
costume details, and decorative effects than in format. In the lower
main scene, for example, the two
men, who are probably Dutch, wear
their native costume. Their female
companions wear a combination of
European and local styles; it is unclear whether the women are European or Indian, or a mixture like
their costumes. The four-legged creature with tiger stripes, leopard spots,
dewclaws, and fringed tail is presumably a European dog; Irwin notes that
dogs were regularly shipped to India
in the early seventeenth century
where they were highly coveted presents suitable for Indian rulers and
nobility. He also identifies the sweets
dish as seventeenth century Italian
Latticinio work and the goblet on the
table as contemporary rib-molded
European glass.[84] The crosshatching
on the man's hat and the dog's stom-
ach may be an attempt to imitate
that seen in European engravings.

The European style of costume is
helpful in dating this piece. The
men's doublets and breeches are similar to those worn in the Brooklyn
hanging, Figure 81, but the wider hat
brim, lace cuffs, and flatter falling
collars with the accompanying longer
hair styles all indicate a period several decades later than that of the
Brooklyn piece, at least in the second
quarter of the seventeenth century.[85]
The upper garments of the woman on
the left appear to be European, but
she wears them over a skirt wrapped
like a sari, complete with a patka, or
sash. It is difficult to ascertain what
the second woman wears under her
wrapper, but the rounded décolletage
with the scalloped edging looks more
European than Indian. These European styles would not have been seen
in India much before the late 1620s;
they could have been seen for several
decades after that because styles per-
sisted in the distant Eastern settle-
ments, and stencils for painting such
textiles were frequently reused.

Other figures in the scene wear assorted forms of Indo-Persian dress. In
the upper frame the two main figures
wear large turbans with stiff, upstanding ends. Irwin indicates that
this style first appeared in Persian
paintings of the 1620s and became
common in the reign of Shah Abbas
II (1642–67). The shape seen here
probably would not have reached India before the 1630s.[86] Many of the
small niche figures wear variations of
either this Persian turban or a style
of turban that was popular at the
Mughal court during the reign of

Shah Jahan (1627–58).

The principal figure on the left
wears a jama tied to his left; this
usage could indicate that he is
Hindu, but since he wears a Persian-
style turban, it is more likely that the
draftsman reversed the stencil. The
feather-like article around the man's
neck may be the collar of an outer
coat such as his companion wears,
but the details, including what appear to be European-style buttons applied to his sleeve, are unclear. The
smaller figures accompanying the two
men wear skullcaps, with long locks
of hair hanging in front of their ears;
their jama are of conventional Indo-
Persian style. Again, these fashions
do not give a cut-off date for the cotton painting, but they do indicate
that it would not have been produced
much before the 1630s.

The decorative patterns shown on
the costumes may be purely fanciful,
or the artist may have attempted to
depict actual fabrics of the time. The
white-ground floral textiles shown in
the two sleeveless jerkins and the
man's knee breeches, for example,
appear to be schematic renderings of
the fine sarasa, or chintz, for which
the Pulicat area was famous. The
skirt of the woman on the left displays a pattern similar to ones that
can be seen in some of the earliest
Jain miniature paintings.

There are many striking parallels,
both in format and decor, between
this hanging and a similar one at the
Metropolitan Museum of Art (no.
20.79); it is tempting to think that
the two once formed parts of the
same large hanging. Certainly they
must be of the same date and origin.
As Irwin has already indicated, both
pieces have the same horizontal join
at the middle, and both show signs of
crude cutting along the edges where
the eighteenth century borders have
been added. The fact that some of
the eighteenth century fragments
used to frame them are identical indicates the two cotton paintings may
have passed through the hands of a
common owner as well.[87]—NWG

continued from page 85

printed,[40] the finest were patterned on the loom or by embroidery.

Seemingly inexplicable dye practices are associated with certain items of clothing made from this muslin and from muslin woven elsewhere. The practice involved the deliberate use of fugitive dyes. Singh cites eighteenth century documents from Jaipur that list muslin ordered to be printed in fugitive colors and other records that note motifs rendered in fugitive colors.[41] We also know that laharia, worked on muslin, was and is worked with fugitive dyes. There is no apparent technical reason for this, and it must be founded on ritual or custom. (Inquiry in parts of Gujarat and Rajasthan in 1981 brought no satisfactory answers.)

The Coromandel Coast

The third major area, in addition to western India and the Bengal-Orissa area, that produced patterned cotton textiles was the Coromandel Coast, known simply as the Coast. This extends on India's eastern shores from the Kistna River in the north to Point Calimere in the south. Because the majority of records come from European trade contacts with Masulipatam and the vicinity of present-day Madras (and Pulicat to the north), less effort has been made to consider the importance of the region of Negapatam-Tanjore-Madura as a truly significant region creating mordant-painted and dyed textiles. Few writers actually try to assign textiles a provenance in this region;[42] possibly they are disillusioned by the examples illustrated by Hadaway that were done in Kumbakonam for the Aceh market.[43]

Yet when Northern Europeans arrived in the East, textiles were traded from this southern area to Malacca by the Portuguese and other traders, and it was because of the Portuguese presence in the south that the English and Dutch did not trade here. When the situation permitted, the Dutch, the most successful seventeenth century traders, attacked the Portuguese who held Negapatam and seized that city and fort in 1658 for their own needs, which at that time were primarily political. As their political and economic fortunes waned in 1690 at their headquarters at Pulicat, the Dutch moved their headquarters to Negapatam. Early historians of the move establish this as the moment of decline for the Dutch trade in India.[44] Other research has shown quite convincingly that "... Dutch trade in the subsequent decades ... does not substantiate the view that the shift had any appreciable effect on the nature of this [textile] trade. ... What was lost in the northern markets was soon made good by more intensive exploration of the southern markets."[45] After 1740 there is a decline in the Dutch exports, but not before.[46] Therefore, during the years of peak consumption of chintz in Europe, and when the Indian textiles carried to Japan (in the Dutch-held monopoly) had finally found a stable market, the Coast headquarters for this trade was Negapatam.

In her work on *palampore*, or bedcovers, that contain family crests, Hartkamp-Jonxis dates examples of this class to the first half of the eighteenth century, most of them in the first quarter, and believes at least some of these come from Negapatam.[47] One could cite other historical reasons why the extreme south must be considered a significant area for mordant-painted and dyed textiles that were important in the trade to Europe and the Far East. At the present time, however, the evidence is lacking to indicate the specific depth and range of this production.

There is little doubt that, at least for the Mughals who ruled in north India, Masulipatam was the major source of finely painted and dyed textiles on the Coast. Akbar's (1542–1605) own tent hangings were painted there,[48] and standards of comparative skill were reckoned by the products of Masulipatam. (Other foreign sources herald the works of Pulicat, claiming they were particularly desired in the markets of Southeast Asia.)

In addition to large tent hangings, Figure 73, other types of figured hangings were made along the Coast, but very few of these remain today. The approximately twenty pieces of this type known from the seventeenth century present tantalizing problems of art history, which have been admirably addressed by Irwin.[49] He has identified two schools represented within these pieces, assigning some to a Golconda category and others to Madras-Pulicat. The former were actually made in Petaboli, which was near Masulipatam, Golconda's seaport. Because of plentiful evidence of the affinity that this court had for Persian tastes, and because of the sizable population of Persians in residence, those textiles with conspicuously Persian details, Figures 100–102, are thought to have been made in this more northern region. A fine red dye is another characteristic of these because, as mentioned earlier, calcium in the soil of an island in the Kistna delta promoted a particularly effective dye agent in the chay plants grown there.

In a more southerly direction, the second school was bounded by Pulicat in the north and St. Thomé, now a suburb of Madras, in the south. Irwin describes this school as containing no Persian influence; rather, it was "imbued with what might be called the fantasy of the Hindu imagination."[50] "Close parallels," he continues, "can be recognized with the style of Hindu mural paintings which survive at Lepakshi and Anegundi, both of which sites were formerly part of the Hindu Vijayanagar kingdom. When this kingdom was destroyed in 1565 by a confederacy of Islamic forces, most artists and craftsmen ... fled south and sought ... patronage ... in the small Polygar states of the Coromandel Coast. A secondary influence [on this school] is that of European (especially Jesuit) art ... explained by the presence at St. Thomé of a Jesuit mission ... since 1547."[51] Irwin believes that Jesuit engravings—which depicted the Virgin and Child in a center panel, with saints in adoration on a lower register, the whole surrounded by smaller panels illustrating the mysteries of the Holy Rosary—inspired the format in some of the dyed hangings that have a conspicuous European subject matter, such as Figure 103.[52] This proposed secondary influence, although interesting, is not convincing.

There is a possibility, however, that two of the known dyed wall hangings, Figures 104 and 108, may not have been made in either of the regions defined by Irwin. Their subject matter and details of architecture, costume, and jewelry suggest that the artist intended to render a more southern scene. For reasons of purposeful vagueness, this southern locale could be termed the Cauvery River area, which would include at least Srirangam, Tanjore, Kumbakonam, and Madura. In the period in which the two textiles were created, the region was under Nayak rule, which lasted from the mid-sixteenth century to approximately 1736; before this, in the fourteenth century, the region owed allegiance to Vijayanagar. Influences from the more northerly region had been felt for centuries, and artists fleeing from the empire's collapse would have found their work in harmony with existing tastes. The stylistic affinity these two textiles have with the Vijayanagar work of Lepakshi and Anegundi is therefore understandable, but their details are more southern.

Other details, discussed in connection with the individual wall hangings, place their subject matter even more securely in the south. It is not clear, however, whether the southern locus for the artistic renderings proves that they were actually dyed in the far south. Musters or samples could have been drawn in the Cauvery area and placed on order in the Madras or Pulicat area. If the dating now proposed for these two textiles is correct, the contact between the two sites would have been politically feasible because the Dutch controlled both Negapatam and Pulicat, having finally ousted the Portuguese from their coastal enclave at Negapatam in mid-century. It would have been in the interest of the Dutch to have cooperated with the local elite in having such hangings finished in Pulicat.

The evidence presented above, however, suggests that the hangings could actually have been made in the far south. Furthermore, some of the earliest European records state that the finest chay root was available on the north and northeast coasts of nearby Ceylon, and one reason we do not hear of this in European shipping records is that much of the trade between south India and Ceylon was carried by local coasting vessels for which no records exist.

In addition to secular wall hangings, such as the ones shown here, the southern Coast was famous for its religious hangings. These were commissioned for temples, used as coverings for great *raths* (temple cars), or carried in religious processions. Textiles for processions could be great didactic displays in a tubular form. The subject matter dealt with the life and exploits of one or more of the Hindu gods. Varadarajan points out the close interaction between the south Indian temple and its patron. She proposes that the patron's desire for figural representation cast in a narrative context, as in the temple hangings, encouraged the use of the brush, not the more stilted woodblock used in western India, for applying mordants.[53]

Far less well known because of their comparative small number is a group of textiles from Karuppur, Figures 117 and 118. Their excellence derives from the wedded skills of the weaver and the dyer that were focused in service of the court at nearby Tanjore.[54]

The existing Karuppur pieces, consisting mostly of dhoti and sari, seem to have been made in the late eighteenth or early nineteenth century in the declining years of the royal house of Tanjore.

Pieces were worn by royalty and given as gifts of special note. Information accompanying a turban, Figure 117, in the Prince of Wales Museum, Bombay, says that such turbans were presented by the Raja of Tanjore as a dress of honor to each *peshwa*. At the time Hadaway investigated these textiles in 1915, only a few small pieces were being woven.[55]

In these singular textiles, gold- or silver-wrapped yarns were worked in the manner of a tapestry on the cotton warp in pre-determined patterns as the textile was being woven. Lines that further delineated these gold areas as actual design forms or as a background were subsequently drawn in a wax resist. The textile was mordant-worked and dyed red and black. When finished, the resist-worked areas remained a pleasing ecru on a maroon ground. An initial dye immersion intensified the red around the gold areas, lending an aesthetic depth to the final design.[56] The dyeing also colored the core of the sparsely wound metallic yarn, causing it to blend completely with the color of the dyed cotton. The gold yarn of the weave, which is normally brightened and enhanced by its fiber core, thus remains a subtle nuance in the rich maroon of the textile. In most of these textiles the resist was applied with a pen, or kalam, on both sides of the textile, but a few have been worked on one side only. Certain examples indicate that blocks may also have been used to apply the mordant.

The predominant design of the Karuppur textiles tends to be geometric forms organized within framing borders and a large central field. That this was not the limit of the Karuppur repertoire can be seen from fragments now in the Madras School of Arts. One has a delicate tracery of vines, deer, and birds, and another has stolid elephants arranged in a grid pattern. Also, a small tracery of figures appears in the narrow border of the turban in Figure 117. Both the patterns and the format of the Karuppur textiles resemble features found in classic Southeast Asian textiles. This resemblance strongly indicates that textiles for the Tanjore court were merely a refinement of existing south Indian traditions of textile design that had profoundly influenced the east through the textile trade as early as the sixteenth and seventeenth centuries.

The patterns of the Karuppur textiles at the end of the eighteenth and nineteenth centuries also seem to have been made in a modest mordant-painted and dyed version lacking wax-resist patterning and gold yarns. At least a fragment once used as a wrapper for a book, in the Saraswati Mahal Library in Tanjore, carries designs similar to those on the Bombay Karuppur turban in Figure 117.

The Tanjore book wrappers, or what remains of them in their present neglected circumstance, constitute additional evidence of the hand-painted mordant textiles being made in this area at the time carved blocks began to displace this work in the early nineteenth century. The wrappers, usually square with a dimension up to approximately 90 centimeters, were made of one layer of cloth that was often lined with a patchwork of two to three textile pieces. Most of the textiles were mordant-painted and dyed cot-

continued on page 131

105 *The interior courtyard of Tiru-mala's palace is surrounded with an arcade of tall lofty columns approximately 18 meters high. (Drawing from Chisholm 1876.)*

106 Detail of Figure 104.

104 *This hanging is believed to be a mordant-painted and dyed cotton, although the actual textile has not been available for contemporary scholars to examine. In the early part of this century, a Japanese journal reported that the piece originally came from China. The textile probably entered a Japanese collection, but efforts to locate the cloth have failed. Because of the style of the hanging, there is little doubt that it was made in south India in the mid-seventeenth century. The details of the costume and architecture are discussed in conjunction with Figure 108. Some of its details are addressed by Irwin.*[88] *(Courtesy of Victoria and Albert Museum, London.)*

107 *This ivory carving from the Srirangam temple museum shows Nayak Tirumala and one of his wives or possibly consorts. The neck ring with the simple disk that she wears compares with that shown on the women in the textiles of Figures 104 and 108. This comparison and others suggest that the subject matter depicted on the textiles belongs to the Madura vicinity where this nayak ruled from 1622 to 1662. (Courtesy of Smeets Photographer, Weert, the Netherlands.)*

108 **Hanging**
South India, second half of 17th
century
Cotton; drawn resist and painted
mordants, dyed
Red, violet, brown, black
155 cm x 202 cm
Mme. Krishna Riboud, Paris

*When an area of art history is starved
for examples, even a fragment may
have significance for the entire disci-
pline. To come upon an example as
richly endowed as the Riboud textile,
Figures 108–116, however, is of extraordinary import.*[89] *The content of
the textile hanging provides a rare
glimpse of secular life in a Hindu
court of south India in the second
half of the seventeenth century and
opens questions of where and when
other hangings were created.*[90]

*As it exists today, the hanging has
three horizontal registers that share a
subject matter of high celebration.
The intent is obviously narrative. On
the upper left, women musicians en-
tertain a man. In the center, the man
dresses more formally, dons platform
shoes, and proceeds, in the next alcove depicted on the right, to engage
in an amorous encounter. He is probably the same person who is again
rendered in the lower left alcove,
where he and his consorts seem to
await a great procession.*

*In the upper and lower registers,
vignettes are set within an architectural frame of cusped arches, which
spring from tall pillars. Behind and
above the arches are storied roof lines
and a welter of architectural detail
meticulously elaborated. Lacing between these major registers is a file of
exuberant "troops" who apparently*

*complement a procession depicted in
the lower right.*[91]

*Fragments that accompanied this
textile before it was restored, Figures
113–116, suggest that the original
hanging was even more imposing.
The procession in the lower register
evidently included an elephant carrying a figure of a rank worthy of two
umbrellas and, undoubtedly, an appropriate horde of attendants. This
would have extended the right hand
margin of the hanging by several feet
at least. Fragments appropriate to the
top of the hanging, Figures 114–115,
suggest the original skyline.*

*The cloth is unrestrained in its
feeling of festival: the figures have
mass and volume; they overlap one
another, crowd, lounge, dance, and
careen, carrying with them the
sounds of Indian celebration. All the
action is achieved, however, by a
fairly stock set of conventions. Feet
are rendered in side view; with a few
exceptions, the torso is drawn fron-
tally, with the head in profile. The
exceptions are done with bravado
and artistic command. For example,
the shoulder of the woman in amorous dalliance in the upper right alcove turns forward in the picture
plane; a woman in the third alcove
on the left daringly confronts the
viewer en face; and, in a similar location in the lower register, a woman's
face is given a three-quarter rendering. There is also a sense that arms
and legs are applied with the aid of a
limited number of stencils—variation
being supplied by an assortment of
skin colors, by the object held in a
raised hand, but even more by the array of different textile patterns that*

109   Detail of Figure 108.

clothe the figures portrayed.

The eyes are rendered as great ovals, with the large pupils set well forward; the nose is sharply ridged, and in some cases it curves downward. The appearance of mass is created in the bare arms and legs by shading of the dye at the edges. An intriguing convention, for which an explanation will be proposed, concerns the bare shoulder and upper arm of many of the men. An elon-gated teardrop shape spills from the shoulder onto the muscle of the upper arm. This is clearly visible on the man seated in the lower left alcove as well as on some of the troops.

The pleating of the sari worn by standing women flares forward at the feet, and in most instances the extreme end is wrapped horizontally across the torso either to the left or right side, Figure 110. This seems to be a south Indian style of wrapping a sari. Another south Indian style of sari wrapping appears on the dancer in the lower register, fourth alcove. All the women wear the blouse, choli, that here has three-quarter-length sleeves. In many instances the sleeve is embroidered (?) with a narrow design that extends from the shoulder seam a short distance down the outer arm. The women's hair is parted in the middle and tied in a large bun at the nape of the neck

110 Detail of Figure 108.

where it is covered with flowers. All the women are heavily bedecked with gems—ornaments in the hair, large earrings, nose rings, necklaces, bracelets at the wrist and elbow, heavy girdle ornaments, and ankle bracelets over bare feet.

There are several men's costumes. The troops, or attendants, wear dhoti and have their hair confined in a snood or cap at the back of the head. Seated at ease in the major alcove on the left is a man draped in a long dhoti. Where he stands in the central alcove of the upper register, he wears a white muslin (?) dhoti, or vetti, draped over with a large scarf in a floral pattern. On his feet are elaborate platform shoes. These important figures wear striped, tightly wrapped turbans. The equestrian shares this type of turban, but he seems to wear the Muslim-style jama over striped pajamas with a separate cloth wrapped about his hips. His shoes are soft slippers. On his back is a shield, and at the waist hangs a sword holder. These principal male figures are bejeweled at the ear, wrist, upper arm, neck, and ankle and carry feathered fans (in the case of the horseman, a sword).

That the equestrian wears Muslim-style costume is no reason to assign him that identity. Muslim dress had been assumed by the upper classes

111 Detail of Figure 108.

throughout much of India by the time of this textile.[92]

The patterns on the textiles are rendered with such loving attention to detail that one might surmise the artist designed textiles for clothing as well as for these more imposing wall hangings. Certain sari appear to be delicately patterned muslins; others are dyed floral patterns, such as the one in the upper right corner with the large lotus buds. Many of the dhoti worn by the crowd look as though they imitate kalam-drawn designs of large circles, small flowers, or colorful checks. Less certain is the type of textile-patterning technique implied on the dhoti and scarf of the man featured in the main alcoves. In each instance this central figure appears, the pattern is different, ranging from

twisting vines to metrically arranged flower heads. Given the imposing context, it seems logical to assume that these particular fabrics are intended to be silk, but precisely how they might have been patterned poses a problem. The hypothesis of a clamp-resist procedure should be considered because the designs here compare well with the evidence presented in connection with this technique as it was practiced in western India, and it is thought that clamp-resist techniques were used in south India.[93] As added support for this hypothesis, it is significant that the major caste of silk weavers in Madura, the pattu-nul-karans, originally came from Surat in western India[94] and could possibly have brought this technique with them.

The architectural style of the hanging undoubtedly belongs to south India. This can be seen from the bulbous-eyed lion, simha-mukham, that crowns the principal arches in the upper register and from the yali, or rampant lions, that form the brackets for each of these three arches.[95] In the fragments left of the skyline, Figures 114 and 115, appear schematic renderings of yalam moldings, characteristic of Dravidian, or south Indian, architecture. The name yalam is given to the detail because yali decorations appear at the ends.[96] A general location in south India seems unquestionable.

A small but distinctive detail suggests additional, important information for understanding this hanging. A part of the woman's costume is a

112 Detail of Figure 108.

necklace drawn with great precision; it is a simple disk suspended from a plain neck ring, Figures 109 and 121. The disk, which may carry a cursive "v" inscription, is flanked on the left or right by a small rectangle that is probably the clasp of the neck ring. In a scene of general opulence, this necklace, worn by each of the women in the hanging, is conspicuous in its very simplicity.

Exactly the same necklace is worn by certain female figures carved in stone in the mid-seventeenth century colonnade built by the Nayak Tirumala in Madura.[97] It may also be found on two ivory statues of this same nayak and his queen (or consort) now in the Srirangam Museum, Figure 107. Also in that museum are similarly ornamented women in am-

orous engagement carved on the panels of an ivory casket that may be dated within this same general time period.[98] Because of the paucity of published photographs portraying the details of south Indian art, it is difficult to establish that Madura is the only place in which this particular necklace existed in the seventeenth century,[99] but there is little doubt of its importance in the arts of that city. The presence of this necklace in the Riboud hanging suggests that it, too, may have been made in the Madura region. Assigning the hanging to a source in Madura would of course posit an origin other than the two major "schools" of cotton painting now recognized (that is, Madras-Pulicat and Masulipatam).

There are other details in the tex-

tile that suggest it should not be classified with either of the previously identified schools. The figures are viewed in an architectural frame of tall pillars and cusped arches. These are portrayed as actual architecture, in which the arch springs from either a tall column or (in the upper register) from columns ornamented with rampant lion brackets. These yali brackets appear larger in the top center alcove and are lacking completely in the lower registers; clearly the variation indicates different areas within a building. The architecture and composition of the hanging make one "read" the textile horizontally. The type and use of architecture here contrast markedly with the style and function of architecture in another group of hangings from this period.

113 Fragment originally associated with Figure 108.

114 Fragment originally associated with Figure 108.

115 Fragment originally associated with Figure 108.

116 Fragment originally associated with Figure 108.

These are the magnificent examples in the Victoria and Albert Museum, Figure 103, the Calico Museum (no. 647), and The Metropolitan Museum (no. 20.79). In these three examples "pillars" or walls are merely decorative framing elements that terminate in onion domes. The architecture is not functional, nor does it participate in an interpretation of the scene. These textiles, which are assigned to the Madras-Pulicat region,[100] are more closely related in a generational sense to the Brooklyn Museum textiles, Figures 79–99, if we consider those panels in their original form as a single, broad hanging. If the Brooklyn hanging were reconstituted, it would be seen that the lateral mar-

gins of each segment are schematic columns or walls ending in an onion dome. Further, each section of the Brooklyn hanging, if it may be "read" at all, follows a vertical sequence, whereas, as mentioned before, the Riboud piece can only be interpreted horizontally.

The Riboud textile does, however, align very clearly in virtually all details with the now lost hanging of Figure 104. In that hanging, too, the scene reads horizontally. The architecture is rationally constructed and seems to consist of similar cusped arches set on tall pillars. In contrast with the lion brackets of the Riboud textile, however, here the ornamental brackets are smaller renderings of horses with riders. The manner in which the women wrap their sari is the same as in the Riboud piece, and each of these women wears the simple disk necklace described above in the Riboud textile and known to have existed at Madura. In this rendering, however, the disk is considerably smaller in diameter.

Although it is probable that these two hangings, Figures 104 and 108, should be seen as a group separate from the other hangings, and that this group may have had an origin in the south, possibly Madura, they were made in different periods. In the lost hanging the illusion of the tilted body, created by the curved legs, the sharp downturned nose, and the flared sari line have their source in the earlier art of Vijayanagar. These very traits, however, were being repeated in the mid-seventeenth century sculpture in the great colonnaded hall built by the Nayak Tirumala, and they surely were part of the currency of style available to the contemporary artist.[101]

While costume is often of help in dating, it is not distinctive enough to help in the case of the lost hanging. The central man in Figure 104 is probably a European wearing some Indian costume elements. It was common for Europeans to dress "according to the custom of the country."[102] Therefore, his long sash and dhoti (?) may be accurately rendered. His doublet, the cuffs at its sleeves, and its falling collar would still have been elements of costume worn in the first half of the seventeenth century, especially by a European overseas. The costume of the men in the flanking alcoves seems to be a combination of Mughal and Hindu elements. The hybrid nature discourages dating with conviction.

It is interesting to speculate that the lofty pillared setting of the lost hanging, Figure 104, might represent the palace built at Madura, Figure 105, by Nayak Tirumala around 1646. The architecture of the palace,

which is thought to have utilized the expertise of workers who had experience in the construction of European architecture in Goa,[103] was renowned for a large colonnaded court with extremely tall pillars and cusped arches.[104] Nayak Tirumala, who was responsible for this palace, also substantially rebuilt the nearby Shiva temple, and some reflection of this may exist in the textile hanging, which, in this otherwise secular context, depicts Shiva's son Ganesha in an ornament above one pillar.

On the basis of the small disk neck ring—which, as noted earlier, corresponds to similar features in stone and ivory dating to the reign of Nayak Tirumala (ca. 1622–1662)—as well as of the possible rendering of the pillared colonnade built by this nayak, a date of the mid-seventeenth century seems appropriate for the lost hanging.

Dating the Riboud textile is equally problematic and remains in the realm of speculation. Many of the small details of this textile are reinterpreted in the murals at nearby Srirangam.[105] In these murals a necklace very similar to that on the textiles and on statues at Madura appears, the woman's choli often carries the embroidered decoration down the outer seam of the sleeve, and the men carry a marking on the bare upper arm at slight variance with that seen in the Riboud hanging. The murals were done under the "inspiration of the Nayak of Madura,"[106] so their affinity with other art forms located within that center of cultural influence is not surprising. The Srirangam murals, however, which date from the end of the seventeenth century to 1720, lack the sophistication in style and detail that is so much a part of the Riboud textile. The eloquence bequeathed by the arts of Vijayanagar had been lost by the time of the murals, which suggests the textile hanging would have been done earlier.

In the search for additional evidence to aid in dating, the details of the procession in the lower right of the Riboud hanging are critical. They tend to confirm a date in the last quarter of the seventeenth century. Among the objects carried on tall standards appear the conch shell (sangu) and the disk (chakram), emblems of Vishnu. From an early, simple rendering of the sea mollusc Murex tritonis, the shell gained embellishment in the iconography of southern India. By the eighteenth century it is shown with flame elements on the sides and top and with the scarf (vastram) encircling the top and tied to the sides, with the two ends hanging down below the flames. A similar evolution occurred in the simple disk.[107] As the conch and disk

appear in the Riboud hanging, however, the scarf does not encircle the top of either emblem. This seems to indicate a date slightly earlier than the eighteenth century—more evidence supporting a date for the hanging in the last quarter of the seventeenth century.

The emblems also reveal that the principal of the procession was a follower of Vishnu—a member of the sect that, after vying with the devotees of Shiva for much of the seventeenth century, ultimately became dominant in the southern region.[108] It is also possible, indeed probable, that the tear-drop mark, mentioned earlier, on the upper arm of many of the men in the Riboud hanging is the tiruchurnam, or center stripe of the Vishnu emblem, the tirunamam. It was not uncommon for followers of Vishnu to use this single mark on the upper part of the torso.[109] It also seems that many of the men who surround the equestrian carry marks of Vishnu on their foreheads.

The third emblem carried on a standard in the procession seems to be a makara. This mythical, long-snouted creature of the sea has a venerable history in the classical art of India. Whether the intent in the hanging was to render the makara or another sea creature is open to question. The fidelity to type in the rest of the hanging, however, argues that the rendering of the classic makara was the intent of the artist. This identification may, in the end, be critical to identifying the scene depicted in the hanging.

Such specific evidence as the Riboud textile contains will ultimately lead to a more precise explanation of its content. The history of the southern area of Madura, Srirangam, Chidambaram, and Tanjore is complex and poorly documented, however, and this makes the search for the precise incident depicted in the hanging a task that is mutually dependent on serendipity and hard work. There seems little doubt that the hanging relates to this southern region and that it was made perhaps in the last quarter of the seventeenth century. In its conceptualization, the Riboud piece relates more closely to the lost hanging of Figure 104, which probably depicts a scene in Madura in the middle of the seventeenth century, than it does to the existing textiles of the Madras-Pulicat school. These two hangings may have been drawn in the south and taken to Pulicat to be worked, but all the current evidence suggests they were also dyed in the more southern region around Madura. Whatever the historical verdict, these hangings are both important pictorial documents that add to our vision of south Indian courtly life.

Karuppur, a village near Tanjore, 19th
  century
Cotton; gold wrapped yarn; drawn
  resist, painted (?) mordants, dyed
Red, dark maroon, black, gold
Warp 907 cm, weft 107 cm
Textile Museum, Washington, D.C.
  6.78

deep brick red. To lend depth to the
geometric forms, selected outlines
were rendered in a still darker red.
The dyeing affected all the cloth not
reserved by the wax. This included
the yarns that formed the core for the
loosely wrapped gold, causing these
elements to blend gracefully into the
texture of the cloth. What remains is
a subtle hint of gold imbedded in the
deep red texture.

These textiles were made in Karuppur for the ruling family of Tanjore;
they apparently had no significant
distribution elsewhere. It is generally
believed that the surviving pieces
were made for the last Raja of Tanjore and the women of his court in
the nineteenth century.[110] The skills
required, however, are based on those
known to have been practiced in the
area long before.

Technically, the textiles of this
group found in museums reveal several features that suggest a history of
declining skill. Some superb examples, such as those presented here,
have had the resist applied to both
sides and then both faces of the textile have been worked. In others
(Prince of Wales 15.73), stamps have
been used to apply the design to only
one face of the cloth.

The designs and their arrangement
are fairly limited, but this may be a
result of court preferences rather than
the range of skills and design vocabulary of the artist. Sari, such as this
example, have broad borders and a
broad pallava filled with geometric
patterns; often these are set in a trellis or grid.[111] The center field contains
a single pattern of circles, as we find
here, quatrefoils, teardrops, or
squares.

The turban cloth was woven with
gold metallic yarns as a continuous
weft on one end, as well as tapestry
interlocked in leaf-like forms. This
gold patterning extends for only part
of the length; the remainder is patterned with resist and mordants but
in a different design, one considerably smaller in scale. Working the
entire turban with gold would have
made it unwieldy to wrap and wear.
Even so, it is interesting that care
was taken to pattern minutely fabric
that would not be visible when the
turban was worn. Such a turban was
a gift of honor from the Raja of Tanjore to his peshwa.

117 **Turban**
Karuppur, a village near Tanjore, 19th
  century
Cotton; gold wrapped yarn; drawn
  resist, painted mordants, dyed
Red, dark maroon, black, gold
Warp 3614 cm, weft 37 cm
Prince of Wales Museum, Bombay
  15.10

These two textiles are superb examples of a splendid group once made in
a small village in south India; their
beauty is difficult to capture in a
photograph. Each textile contains
several shades of deep red and black
touched with hints of gold and the
warm ecru of the natural cotton that
usually outlines the design configurations. Nuances of color and texture
change as the cloth is moved.

An abbreviated description of the
weaving and dyeing of these textiles
can help to understand their unusual
properties. As the original textile was
woven, gold-wrapped yarns were
worked into the ground, in the manner of tapestries, in the areas that
would become the centers of configurations, in the background area, or in
both. The rest of the textile was
woven in a plain weave. Before
dyeing the designs were reserved with
a wax resist, the mordant for black
was drawn, the mordant for red was
applied, and the cloth was dyed a

119a–119i *These figures illustrate book wrappers once used in the Saraswati Mahal Library in Tanjore. They provide a sampling of the patterning done with mordants and dyes on modest textiles in the early nineteenth century. Astonishingly, most were hand drawn even though the small repeated motifs could have been done easily with stamps. Stamps were, however, used in parts of Figures 119h and 119i. In the former, the zigzag elements in two bands imitate patterning in silk ikat. Most of the designs have not involved the use of resist, an obviously expensive additional step. Figure 119f is the exception, and here the color range includes red, blue, and yellow. The other textiles are shades of red or red and black. (Mattiebelle Gittinger, Washington, D.C.)*

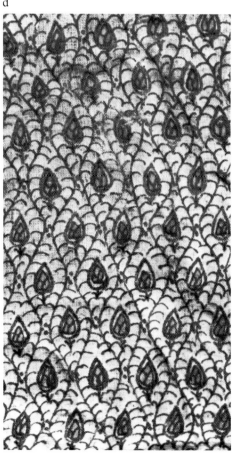

a

b

c

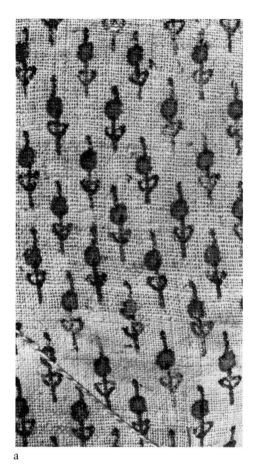

d

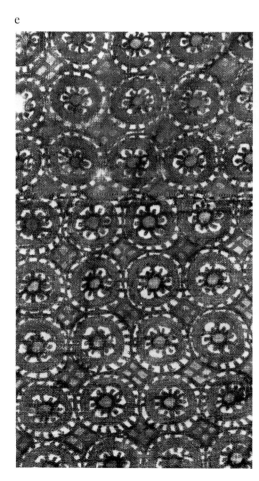

e

f

g

h

i

continued from page 117

tons, a few were mordant-stamped, and some were ikat-patterned silk. Of the book wrapper fragments illustrated here, Figures 119a–119i, Figure 119h is a stamped cotton fragment that imitates a silk ikat pattern. Notably absent in these fragments, except in Figure 119f, is the use of wax-resist patterning and indigo dye. We know at the time of the Beaulieu manuscript that blue dyeing was done by special dyers. The lack of it here, in more modest textiles from Tanjore, suggests that the two steps of wax-resist patterning and indigo dyeing continued to be an added expense that was not un-intentionally incurred.[57]

We do not know precisely where the book wrappers were made. Hadaway assumed in his work that they had been created in Karuppur along with the gold- and resist-worked courtly wear.[58] He also adds in his survey that cottons from Negapatam were painted with a pen and mentions other nearby places where cloths were painted in very rich detail and were covered in shades of red, black, yellow, and blue. Together with other information from this far southern region, the evidence suggests several potential sources for the book covers in addition to Karuppur. We do not know enough about these local styles, however, to give more specific provenance to the fragments.

The use of the brush and kalam continued as block printing appeared in the work of the Coast in the nineteenth century. Block

120 Fragment
India (exact provenance unknown),
  17th century
Cotton; painted mordants, dyed,
  painted dyes, tinsel added
Red, purple, blue, yellow, green, black
Warp 45 cm, weft 48 cm
Textile Museum, Washington, D.C.
  6.41

*Although undeniably interesting, this
fragment presents perplexing problems of interpretation and prove-*
nance. *It carries a water scene, complete with aquatic plants and long-
legged wading birds, in which a man
seems to founder while another is
being swallowed by a water monster.
Above them, at the shoreline, are two
strange animals and two bowls. Additional forms at the very top of the
fragment suggest that this is only a
small part of what was once a much
larger composition.*

Compared with other mordant-
dyed cottons, *this is relatively coarse,
both in the open weave of the cotton
and in the quality of the dyework.
Nevertheless, the design elements are
complex and the surface details have
been embellished with gold tinsel,
qualities that suggest the original
cloth was of considerable value.*

*It has been suggested that this
composition may derive from paintings done in Goa by Indians who had
seen Swiss woodcuts that depicted*

121　Detail of Figure 108.

sea monsters devouring Portuguese ships.[112] *This does not seem completely satisfying given the richness of Indian mythology.*

printing eventually reached the Masulipatam area at that time and is associated with the work exported to the Persian market.[59] Kalahasti (in the southern corner of Andhra Pradesh), one of two places in which the kalam and brush are still in use to fashion temple cloths, came to importance early in this nineteenth century period.[60] The technique used in Kalahasti involves free application of the mordants, but no wax-resist work.

Many factors contributed to the decline of the dyer's art, and of the whole of the handloom industry, in India through the nineteenth and twentieth centuries. Today—and to some degree since 1956, when the All India Handloom Board started Weaver's Service Centres—there is an effort to improve work, and "official" recognition that these are arts to be preserved is in evidence.

NOTES TO TEXT

1. *Letters Received* I:29. By the time of the Roques manuscript in 1678, the chintz here is described as coarse, suitable only for village use (Schwartz 1969:10).
2. Mundy 1914–19 II:56.
3. Schwartz 1969:10.
4. *English Factories* 1637–41; Naqvi 1968:157.
5. Cited in Moreland 1923:211.
6. Moreland 1975:216.
7. Ibid.:217.
8. *English Factories* 1646–50:163.
9. Irwin and Hall 1971:111.
10. Chaudhuri 1978:251.
11. Ibid.:253.
12. Ibid.:252.
13. Brennig 1975:274.
14. *English Factories* 1634–36:14.
15. Havart 1639:14.
16. Shah, R. 1977–78.
17. Carré 1947:595.
18. Varadarajan 1981.
19. *Census of India* 1961 Vol. V, Part VIIA.
20. Chaudhuri 1978:475ff. The author lists the characteristic trade textiles of each area. Some form of these would have been available to local markets.
21. Victoria and Albert Museum I.M. 89–1936.
22. Chandra 1973: illustrations following 176; Shah 1976:Fig. 33.
23. See Shah 1976:Figs. 51, 53.
24. Singh 1979:xxxvii.
25. Ibid.:xxxviii.
26. Ibid.:xxxvii.
27. Jayakar 1980:78.
28. Although there is no standard set of colors in patola, those most common are white, yellow, orange, red, blue, green, and violet-black. These were obtained from dye baths for red, yellow or orange, and blue (Bühler and Fischer 1979 I:234) and from the neutral white of the reserved fibers. The source of the natural dyes seems to have varied. Mentioned for red are resin from the boradi tree (*Mimusops Elingi*), or pipal tree (*Ficus religiosa*), as well as kirmaj or majith (Ibid.:237). Cochineal from a dried insect (*Dactylopius coccus*) and pistachio (*Pistacia vera*) were also used for red; for brown, an acacia (*Acacia arabica* and *A. catechu*) was used; for yellow, tumeric (*Curcuma domestica*) or powder from the kamila tree (*Rottlera tinctoria*) (Ibid. II: fn. 118, 119, 295). Black was obtained with iron or by overdyeing red and blue. Naphthol and other manmade agents enter into the dyeing today; De Bone 1976 gives details of this contemporary work.
29. Bühler and Fischer 1979 I:267.
30. Ibid.:304 and Tavernier 1925 II:3.
31. Jayakar 1955:55.
32. Ibid.:56.

33. Irwin and Schwartz 1966:40.
34. Mittal 1962:28.
35. Yoshioka 1980:16–17.
36. Nabholz-Kartaschoff in Fischer 1980:300ff.
37. Mehta 1957:68.
38. Bühler 1972 and Bühler and Fischer 1979 discuss ikat and its distribution in detail.
39. Chaudhuri 1978:241.
40. Singh 1979:xiv.
41. Ibid.
42. Hartkamp-Jonxis (1980) has been an important exception. Varadarajan (1981) points out the general importance of Tanjore for kalamkari work. Irwin and Brett (1970) use a general term "southern region" to designate sources other than Masulipatam on the Coast, but it is not clear if this refers just to Madras or elsewhere.
43. Hadaway 1917.
44. Raychaudhuri 1962:74.
45. Arasaratnam 1967:329.
46. Ibid.:341.
47. Hartkamp-Jonxis 1980:8.
48. Bernier, cited in Irwin and Hall 1971:23.
49. Irwin 1959a and Irwin and Brett 1970:13ff.
50. Irwin and Brett 1970:14.
51. Ibid.
52. Irwin 1959a:23.
53. Varadarajan 1981.
54. Hadaway 1917:9.
55. Ibid.
56. Irwin and Hall 1971:139.
57. From a letter from North Sumatra at the turn of this century we know that textiles made in this general area of the Indian Coast virtually doubled in basic price if they were worked with wax on both sides (Hourgronje 1899).
58. Hadaway 1917:10.
59. Varadarajan 1981.
60. Ibid. and *Census of India* 1961 Part VII-A(1):39.

NOTES TO ILLUSTRATIONS

1. Singh 1979:xxxiii.
2. Chandra 1973:14.
3. Sonday and Kajitani 1970:52; Kahlenberg 1972:154.
4. Singh 1979:xxix.
5. Chandramani Singh kindly read the inscription on this patka.
6. Skelton 1972:147ff.
7. Chandramani Singh read the inscriptions on these two textiles and supplied information about the meaning of abra.
8. Irwin and Brett 1970:66.
9. Bühler and Fischer 1979 I:104.
10. De Bone 1976:62 and Cynthia Cort: personal communication.
11. Bühler and Fischer 1979 I:272.
12. Yazdani 1930:Pl. XVIIa.
13. Abu'l-Fazl 1975:49.
14. Ibid.
15. Ibid.:56.
16. Bernier, cited in Irwin and Hall 1971:23.
17. Murphy in Skelton 1982:84.
18. Ibid.
19. Ibid.
20. Jayakar 1955:56, 57.
21. Stewart Culin, a former curator of the Brooklyn Museum, bought the piece in Delhi from a curio dealer named Imre Schweiger about 65 years ago. According to Culin, Schweiger himself seemed to have only a very general idea of the age and origin of the curtain, but Culin acquired from another dealer similar pieces that came from an old palace courtyard in Jaipur and felt that his curtain had probably come from there, too (Culin 1918:142).
22. In 1959 Irwin was the first to attempt a systematic classification and analysis of these cotton paintings. He placed the Brooklyn piece in what he called the "Golconda school" and dated it to 1630–40 (Irwin 1959a:38). In more recent writings he has characterized two separate but distinct schools: the Golconda school (centered at Petaboli, or Nizampatam), with conspicuously Islamic and Persian subject matter and with border patterns borrowed or adapted from Persian carpet designs, Figure 101; and the Madras-Pulicat school (located in the region bordered by Pulicat on the north and St. Thomé, now a part of Madras city, on the south), with designs set within decorative architectural alcoves and showing conspicuous Hindu elements revealing stylistic influence from Vijayanagar art and with borders, when broad, filled with a continuous panorama of human figures, fauna, and flora, Figure 103. Irwin now places the Brooklyn hanging in this second category (Irwin and Brett 1970:13).
23. Irwin 1959a:Pl. XII, Fig. 16; Pl. XV, Fig. 19.

24. It is difficult to determine whether the wearers of the Indo-Persian dress in Figure 79 are meant to be Persian, Mughal, or members of one of the Persian-influenced Deccan courts, such as those of Bijapur or Golconda. What makes this panel even more problematic is that it is the only one to have the Hindu-derived sikhara along its top.

25. See also Irwin 1959a:Pls. X and XI.

26. See also Bry 1606 Part VIII: Pls. IX and X.

27. Bry 1606 Part II:Pls. XXXII–XXXVI.

28. Irwin 1959a:21.

29. Irwin and Brett 1970:65.

30. Sewell 1900:264.

31. Ibid.:286.

32. *Splendours* 1981:109–10.

33. Devakunjari 1970:Pls. IV and V.

34. Sherwani 1974 Vol. II:Pl. LVI, Figs. a and b.

35. The format of Figure 104 seems to be derived from a similar but different source.

36. After the military defeat of the Vijayanagar Empire in 1565, its ruler, accompanied by some 1,500 elephants laden with gold, diamonds, and precious stones, managed to flee to a secondary capital at Penukonda (Heras 1927 Vol. I:222). From there and from other capitals such as Chandragiri and Vellore, the Empire managed to survive in a diminished fashion into the middle of the seventeenth century. Under Venkata II, however, the Vijayanagar Empire even made somewhat of a comeback. A great scholar himself, Venkata fostered scholarship in others and was responsible for a general patronage of all cultural activities, including encourgement of painters both native and foreign. He strengthened his realm, both internally and externally, and made his court once more a cosmopolitan center. At Chandragiri, Venkata received missions from the Mughal Emperor Akbar and from the Qutb Shahi ruler of Golconda; he also treated with Portuguese, Dutch, and other embassies to his court (Sherwani 1973 Vol. I:133).

37. For example, all the known pieces of the school continue the Vijayanagar convention of filling in open space above heads with flowers and hanging garlands; animals and plants become fillers at foot level.

38. Surviving examples of Vijayanagar mural painting range in date from fifteenth century murals in the Virupaksha Temple at Vijayanagar, through early sixteenth century paintings at Lepakshi, to early seventeenth century fragments at Anegundi. The remains are so sparsely published and the dates so widespread that, at least until further work is done, it is practically impossible to develop a dating sequence for this Vijayanagar group of wall paintings.

39. It is relevant to note that in at least four of the panels, Figures 81, 85, 89, and 97, figures are holding round and egg-shaped objects that appear to be jewels. Pulicat was the Vijayanagar port on the Coromandel Coast, and the early European travelers Varthema and Barbosa both comment on the importance of the jewel trade there, a trade in which the raja took a close interest. Varthema adds further that the colored cotton goods produced as a specialty at Pulicat were exported to pay for the rubies of Burma and the elephants of Ceylon (cited in Lach 1965 Vol. I, Bk. I:411).

40. See Barrett 1958:Pls. 5 and 6; Barrett and Gray 1978:122.

41. See Atil 1978:nos. 61, 65, and 68; or Beach 1981:Cat. nos. 26 and 27.

42. Irwin 1959a:21–22.

43. Ibid.:36 and 39.

44. Ibid.:Pls. IV and XII, for example.

45. Ibid.:39.

46. Ibid.:38.

47. Cunnington 1972a:121.

48. Cunnington 1972b:54–55.

49. Cunnington 1972a:135.

50. Ibid.:112.

51. Ibid.:110–11; and Reynolds 1951:Pl. 50.

52. Cunnington 1972a:146.

53. Linschoten 1970:205–6.

54. Raychaudhuri 1962:204.

55. Ibid.:203–4.

56. Heras 1927:487–91.

57. See Beach 1978:Pl. 8; or Beach 1981: Cat. nos. 16a recto and 35 and Fig. 44.

58. Irwin 1959a:40.

59. See Barrett 1958:Pl. 7.

60. Davenport 1948:603.

61. La Loubère 1693:25–26; or Tachard 1755:190–92.

62. Garrett Solyom to M. Gittinger, July 3, 1981: personal communication.

63. See Stone 1934:Fig. 444.

64. See Gittinger 1979:Fig. 86.

65. Ibid.:Fig. 82.

66. Gopala Rao 1969:Pl. V.

67. Culin 1918:138.

68. Irwin 1959a:40.

69. Gopala Rao 1969:83.

70. Lach 1965 Vol. I, Bk. I:374.

71. Irwin 1959a:43.

72. Ibid.:Pl. XV, Fig. 19.

73. Breck 1928:10.

74. Ibid.

75. Irwin and Schwartz 1966:41; Irwin and Brett 1970:13–14.

76. Irwin 1959a:36 and 43.

77. Ibid.:46; Barrett 1958:Pl. 6.

78. Barrett 1958:Pl. 5.

79. Breck 1928:6.

80. Irwin 1959a:35–37; Irwin and Brett 1970:64–65.

81. Irwin 1959a:23 and Pl. XIX; Irwin and Brett 1970:65.

82. *Splendours* 1981:109–12.

83. Nagaswamy 1980:116–19.

84. Irwin 1959a:36.

85. Reynolds 1951:12–13; Thienen 1951:11.

86. Irwin and Brett 1970:65.

87. Ibid.

88. Gangoly 1919:325 and Irwin 1959a.

89. Mme. Krishna Riboud, Paris, acquired this textile in 1964 from a dealer, Lucien Lepine, in Paris. Previously the textile had been in the possession of a Mr. Kevorkian (brother of the well-known art dealer Hagop Kevorkian of New York), who had purchased it originally from an Indian merchant, possibly in Cairo. It was restored to its present dimension at the Victoria and Albert Museum, London.

90. This essay has benefited considerably from the assistance of my colleague Nina Gwatkin.

91. Veronica Murphy interprets this scene differently. She believes that the central register depicts the principal shown in the top register, possibly on a hunting expedition (Murphy in Skelton 1982:83).

92. Sherwani 1974:521.

93. Bühler and Fischer 1977:26, 27, 105, 106.

94. Nelson 1868:87.

95. The yali is a lion with the trunk of an elephant. The animal bracket in the center alcove seems to have this form.

96. Jouveau-Dubreuil 1978:12, 13.

97. Zimmer 1964 II:Pl. 449 and Thiagarajan 1966:67.

98. Chattopadhyay 1980:132.

99. I. Job Thomas, June 28, 1982: personal communication. Dr. Thomas suggests a similar necklace exists in the murals at Chidambaram. Certain textile patterns worn by women in the Chidambaram murals are the same as those which appear in the Riboud hanging.

100. Irwin 1959a and Irwin and Hall 1971.

101. See Zimmer 1964 II:Pl. 449.

102. Bühler and Fischer 1977:41.

103. Zimmer 1964 I:285.

104. See drawings in Chisholm 1876 and Zimmer 1964 I:Fig. B12b.

105. Nagaswamy 1980:119.

106. Ibid.:123.

107. Jouveau-Dubreuil 1978:60–61.

108. Heras 1927:554. This author points out that Telugu chiefs sent from Vijayanagar to the south were nearly always followers of Vishnu and that these chiefs were responsible for founding the Nayakship at Madura (Ibid.:542).

109. I. Job Thomas, June 28, 1982: personal communication.

110. Hadaway 1917:9.

111. See Hadaway 1917; Irwin and Hall 1970:Pls. 80–85.

112. Born 1946:172.

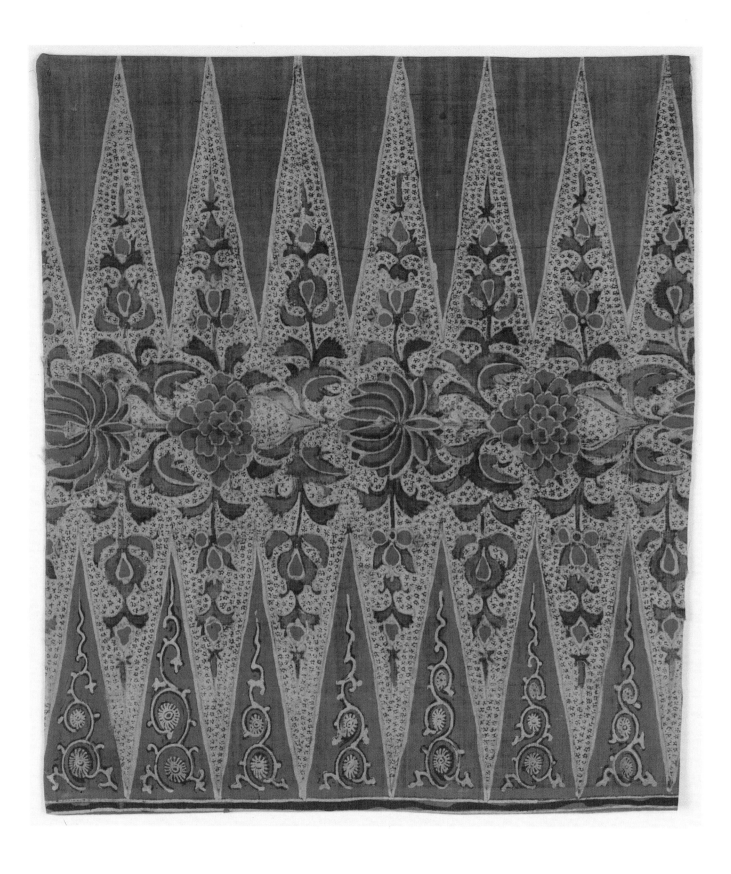

Master Dyers to the East

As the first Dutch ships arrived in Bantam, northwest Java, in 1596, "There came such multitudes of Javanese and other nations as Turks, Chinese, Bengali Arabs, Persians, Gujarati, and others that one could hardly move . . . ," according to one Dutch report.[1]

Bantam was one of the great emporiums for a trade that had gone on long before the Dutch came upon the scene. The ports of Southeast Asia such as Bantam and Malacca—the latter called "the richest seaport . . . in the whole world" in 1518[2]—acted as an interface between the east and west of Asia. Here the Indian trader's cloth, opium, and minerals met the Chinese merchant's raw silk, silk textiles, tea, and porcelain and the island world's wealth of spices, aromatic woods, and gums.

The major areas of India taking part in this trade were Bengal, the Coromandel Coast, and Gujarat.[3] Through the years the merchants had been able to cater to the demands of individual islands, courts, and countries to such an extent that specific product preferences were well established throughout much of the East. What exasperation and incredulity emerges from this European merchant's letter from a Malay port in the early seventeenth century:

> A great oversight hath been comitted in the bespeaking [ordering] of the foresaid Maley's cloth . . . for they have all of them a little narrow white edge, and the upright [acceptable] Maley cloth must be without it . . . wherein the Maleys are so curious [particular] that they will not once put forth their hands to look upon them; and, if I had not now found it by experience, I had never believed it, that so small a fault should cause so great an abatement in the price.[4]

As a result of this market specialization, the Indians had developed a great many kinds of cloth. One of the earliest English traders in western India despaired of being able to enumerate the many traded to Sumatra, Java, and the Moluccas, calling them "infinite, they being of so many sorts and of such different prices."[5] The historian W.H. Moreland counted forty-three textile types handled by the earliest Dutch traders on the Coromandel Coast and thirty that were carried on a single ship sailing from western India to Java in 1619.[6]

Thus, Indian textiles had become the dominant currency of exchange in the spice trade and were critical for the acquisition of nutmeg, cloves, mace, pepper, and other valued commodities in the East. When Western Europeans entered this trade in the six-

122 **Fukusa** (used to display tea ceremony objects)
India, 17th or 18th century
Cotton; drawn resist, painted mordants, dyed; silk lined
Red, blue, black
31 cm x 36 cm
Konjaku-Nishimura Collection, Kyoto

In the Japanese tea ceremony, an object may be set on a small square of cloth in recognition of its precious nature. This fragment of an Indian textile was used in this manner. It is lined with a striped silk textile called kapitan—*an obvious reference to a time of trade with the Portuguese.[1] The fragment shows facing rows of* tumpal, *or triangular forms, which is a design scheme more commonly associated with Indian exports to Southeast Asia. The Japanese market, however, never restricted its preference in Indian textile imports to the same degree as other importing areas of Asia.*

123 *This engraving from the early seventeenth century shows the 1602 meeting of the King of Kandy and the Dutch Admiral van Spilbergen. The tumpal, row of long triangles, that line the flared end of the king's costume was a design element particularly favored on Indian textiles traded to Southeast Asia, suggesting this textile had an Indian origin. The admiral wears a turn-of-the-century costume similar to that portrayed in the Brooklyn hanging, Figure 81. (Bry 1606, part VII: Pl. X. Courtesy of The Folger Shakespeare Library, Washington, D.C.)*

teenth and seventeenth centuries, they had to procure these textiles in India as a prerequisite to other trade. The following is a brief glance at this trade of the seventeenth century.

The initial expectation of the European companies to export European manufactures, in particular excess woolen textiles, was dashed when the novelty value of these goods was exposed to tropical reality. The Indians did not need the commodities the Europeans could supply. Unless their governments back in Europe were to allow a continued drain on national reserves of precious metals, the trading companies had to acquire additional capital in the East. Europeans thus entered the existing intra-Asian trade (commonly called the "country trade") in an effort to make a profit; with this they would buy Indian textiles to barter for commodities that would be of value in Europe.

Although the Portuguese had been in Asian waters for a hundred years before them, it was the Dutch and English East India companies that emerged as the most important European contestants in the commerce with Asia in the seventeenth century. The Dutch United East India Company (or the V.O.C., Vereenigde Oostindische Compagnie), founded in 1602, had more substantial funding and quickly established trading enclaves, called factories, on Java, in the Celebes, and in India at Surat, Masulipatam, and Petaboli. The English founded their East India Company in 1602 as well. Although economically more modest, it was well served by a background of trade experience in the eastern seas and early wrested a position in the textile trade of western India that would allow for its further growth.

continued on page 145

124 Kain (hip wrapper)
Gujarat (for the Indonesian market),
    18th century
Cotton; stamped mordants, dyed
Red, black
Warp 335 cm, weft 85.7 cm
Anonymous loan

The high economic and ritual value placed on the patola in Indonesia led to imitation of the textile in less expensive forms such as this example, in which the designs were created by stamping rather than by ikat.

This particular example was acquired on Sumba, where such textiles are valued and saved as sacred family heirlooms that enter into use only on ceremonial occasions. Similar imitations were found in North Sulawesi and Bali.[2] Cotton textiles with other patterns imitating patola have been found in Sumatra, Sulawesi, Bali, Lomblen, and in Western New Guinea. They continue to be reproduced in contemporary form in Java today.

This textile carries the stamp of the Dutch East India Trading Company (V.O.C.) on the reverse. Some of the black of the stamping has penetrated to the face in the lower right corner. Bühler has suggested that this particular kind of imitation patolu may have been made in Ahmedabad.[3]

125 **Tapis** (hip wrapper)
India (for the Indonesian market) 17th
    or 18th century
Cotton; drawn resist, painted
    mordants, dyed
Shades of red, blue
Warp 345 cm, weft 104 cm
Konjaku-Nishimura Collection, Kyoto

The textile pattern is a complex but regular interchange of blue floral heads and sinuous scrolls set on a red ground. The pattern, probably established with a stencil, abounds with white resist details. Its ornately formal quality recalls patterns of Italian velvets, a not improbable source of inspiration because these velvets were traded to India before the seventeenth century.

126 **Tapis** (hip wrapper)
India (for the Indonesian market),
   18th century
Cotton; drawn resist, painted
   mordants, dyed
Red, blue, yellow, green, black
Warp 262 cm, weft 107 cm
Konjaku-Nishimura Collection, Kyoto

The clearly discernible repeat of a trailing floral vine in the center field of this textile makes it easy to compare parallel forms, and there is little doubt that a stencil was used to create the pattern. One can follow the hurried branchwork from flower to flower. This casual, relaxed rendering in the center field contrasts sharply with the meticulously drawn row of tumpal in the end borders. The care-
fully rendered tumpal are a common device in textiles exported to Southeast Asia but are also seen in some textiles traded to Japan. The green in the center field is the result of top-dyeing yellow over indigo.

127 Idja Pateunom (hip wrapper)
Negapatam (collected in Aceh,
  Sumatra), 19th century
Cotton; drawn and stamped
  wax resist, dyed
Orange-brown, two blues
Warp 268 cm, weft 112 cm
Tropen Museum, Amsterdam H1172

*The background color of this textile
is a warm brown-orange, while the
details appear in a dark indigo and
the ecru of the reserved cotton
ground.*

*The following procedure seems to
have been used to create the surface
decoration. After an initial preparation, the cloth was treated with a
mordant. A resist was subsequently
stamped on one surface and the textile dyed its rich brown-orange color.
The initial resists were removed and
new wax was applied, probably by
hand, in a rapid, casual manner to all
areas except those to be colored blue,
such as the center of the dots in the
body, the center of the palmettes,
and so forth. The textile was then
dyed in indigo. During this process—
by accident or design—the wax surface was severely cracked, allowing
the indigo to vein the brown surface.
A startlingly contemporary feeling results from the imprecision of each of
the patterning steps, giving the textile
an appearance of accomplished work
to the modern eye. Such imprecision
may not have been as highly valued
when the piece was created.*

*Additional information concerning
this particular type of textile, as well
as other textiles traded from India to
the extreme northern part of Sumatra, is left to us from the turn of the
century. This may be found in two
letters from Snouck Hourgronje, the
famous scholar of Aceh history and*
*Islamic religion, to the textile expert
G. P. Rouffaer. The letters were in response to queries from Rouffaer regarding the practice of batik in North
Sumatra.[4] Hourgronje was able to
confirm Rouffaer's suspicion that the
textiles in question (samples were apparently sent with Rouffaer's initial
enquiry) were actually made in India.
Soon after this exchange Hourgronje
gave a group of these textiles—including this example, donated by a
Dutch officer stationed in Aceh—to
the Kolonial Museum in Haarlem
(which later was absorbed by the
Tropen Museum).*

*Hourgronje's letter equates the
name Pateunom with [Nega]patam,
an interpretation apparently suggested by local textile traders who
said such* idja *(the local word for the
Indonesian* kain, *a wrapper worn
about the hips) were made in the region near Negapatam. These traders
claimed that their forebears had
come from that Indian region and
continued to import the Negapatam
textiles, as had their ancestors.*

Kling *was the general term for
these and other merchants engaged in
the textile trade in Southeast Asian
markets at the time of the arrival of
the Portuguese in the sixteenth century. It is thought that the name derives from Kalinga, an ancient name
for the Gingelly Coast of India. In an
attempt to control commerce, the
Portuguese seized major entrepot centers. Their capture of Malacca in 1511
at first severely curtailed and eventually destroyed the trading patterns of
the kling that served Malaya, Java,
and other eastern islands.[5]*

*It seems that the kling were able to
maintain some trade in North Sumatra after the Portuguese onslaught, at
least according to the later evidence*
*of Hourgronje. According to earlier
records, however, the important traders in North Sumatra through the
third quarter of the seventeenth century were Gujarati merchants carrying textiles from the west coast of India. As the power of the Dutch
increased in the last half of the seventeenth century, this trade and access to Gujarati textiles dwindled,
causing a shift to textile sources on
the Coromandel Coast.[6] Although we
do not know, we would assume that
Gujarati textiles acceptable to the
Aceh market were sent to the Coast
for replication to satisfy the demands
of the North Sumatran market.*

*At the end of the nineteenth cen-
tury, Hourgronje described some of
the major Negapatam textiles. He
wrote that there were three lengths
averaging 183, 229, and 274 cm, and
that the width of the pieces ranged
between 101 and 104 cm. One textile, called* idja patanilam, *had a central yellow area and a border. It was
made exclusively for the Aceh market. Other types, such as this example, sold not only on the Aceh market
but were appropriate in Rangoon as
well. The type was characterized by
the design known as "mousefood" in
the center and, according to the
Acehnese, one called "sandal" in the
border (the palmette). The third textile, called* katjekarom, *was distin-
guished by a design named "onion
blossom" in the main field, which
was bordered by three rows of sandal
designs. There were numerous combinations and variations of these three
basic textiles. Some of these imported
cotton textiles were held in as high a
regard as silks, according to Hourgronje's informants.*

128 **Tapis** (hip wrapper)
India (for the Indonesian market),
  17th or 18th century
Cotton; drawn and painted resist and
  mordants, dyed
Reds, blue
Warp 325 cm, weft 100 cm
  (approximate measure)
Konjaku-Nishimura Collection, Kyoto

*A large-scale floral lattice covers the
surface of this textile. The components are boldly drawn and worked
in a muted red and blue. In the intervals small filling elements vein the
surface and frame a simple three-
branched flower. The work seems to
have utilized a stencil, but the subsequent hand application of the mordants gives the textile a lively variability.*

continued from page 138

Both companies established factories at critical trade locations in India and Southeast Asia in the first quarter of the seventeenth century. The bills of lading, communiqués, and letters issuing from the intra-Asian trade they sought to control provide the primary records for reconstructing patterns of trade within Asia, particularly in the seventeenth and eighteenth centuries. This is not to deny that other traders—Portuguese, Arab, Indian, Thai, Chinese, and Japanese—were active, but simply to state that these are the records available.

Textiles of the Trade

The English captain John Saris, passing through the Moluccas in the early seventeenth century, wrote in his journal that "... we traded with the Naturals for Cloues [cloves], which for the most part was by bartering and exchanging Cotton cloth of Cambaya and Coromandell for Cloues." The sorts requested, and prices that they yielded (ca. 1614) as he cites them, were:

Candakeens of Barochie—six Cattees of Cloues [cloves]
Candakeens Papang, or flat—three Cattees
Selas, or small Bastas—seuen and eight
Patta chere Malayo—sixteen
Dragam chere Malayo—sixteen
Fine Cassas—twelve
Coarse of that kind—eight
Betellias, or Tancoulos red—fortie foure and fourtie eight
Sarassas chere Malayo—fortie eight and fiftie
Sarampouri—thirtie
Chelles, Tapseils, and Matafons—twentie and foure and twentie
White Cassas or Tancoulos—fortie, and foure and fortie
Dongeryus, the finest—twelve. Coarse of that kind—eight and ten
Pouti Castella—ten
Ballachios, the finest—thirtie
Patta chere Malayo, of two fathomes—eight and ten
Great Potas, or long foure fathome—sixteen Cattee of cloues
Parcallas white—twelve
Salalos Ytam—twelve and fourteene
Turias and tappe turias—one and two
Patola of two fathomes—fiftie and sixtie. Those of foure one fathome accordingly.[7]

With a few exceptions, Saris' list enumerates the principal textiles traded to the islands of Southeast Asia in the early part of the seventeenth century. Their purchasing power in catties of cloves (a catty, from the Malay *kati*, is a measure varying around 1⅓ pounds) provides a comparative measure of the worth of the various cloths within the group. As this range suggests, by far the majority of textiles traded east were simple cottons that can be most broadly classified as calicoes and muslins.[8] The muslins were a more open weave than the calicoes and used more finely spun yarns, but both groups contained varying goods and were sold bleached, unbleached, or dyed.

The names aligned within these two categories may distinguish a size, a quality, a place of manufacture, or the ultimate function.

129 Hanging
Western India (?) (for the Indonesian market), late 17th century
Cotton; stamped resists and mordants, dyed
Red, blue
Warp 460 cm, weft 82 cm
Yōzō Nomura, Tokyo

This textile was originally traded to the Toradja people of Sulawesi in Indonesia. Like other exotic textiles from abroad, it undoubtedly entered a Toradja family treasury and over time acquired a sacred status. Such textiles were critical elements in rites accompanying birth, death, illness, and other periods of social stress. On certain of these great occasions some of the textiles were flown from high poles; this may explain why the long narrow shape was retained in this piece. It was obviously designed to be cut into smaller segments.

In one portion a bird with its head turned over its back is repeated as the design element; in two additional panels, one not illustrated, a branched floral configuration is repeated. The work was hastily done, but repetition of form in one portion, and interplay of positive and negative elements within similar shapes in the other portions, create interesting designs.

Further complicating this nomenclature is a tendency for meanings to shift over time. The calico *bastas* or *baftas* is an example; as it appears on Saris' list in 1614, the term would have designated a calico woven in Gujarat with a length of about 15 yards and a width of 25 inches or less. Later in the century, the term bafta was used for textiles from many other areas and increasingly became a more generic term in textile trade. The word, derived from the Persian *bafta*, "woven," was used for many different grades of cloth—from gifts suitable for kings to humble trade cloths.[9] Other calicoes on the list are dongeryus, ballachios, and sarampouri or salempore.[10]

In contrast to calicoes, which were woven throughout India, most muslins came from Bengal or the Deccan. The latter area exported to both coasts; on the east coast these muslins were called *betilles*, the betellias in Captain Saris' list, a term deriving from the Portuguese *beatila*, "veiling." These could be dyed red, striped, embroidered, or could include metallic yarns.[11] From Bengal came the muslin *cassas* and *mulmuls*. The former, from the Persian *khass*, "choice or select," were in great demand in the Asian trade. As a traveler in 1629 wrote, "the finest and richest cassas are produced in this country [Bengal], from 50 to 60 yards long and 7 to 8 handsbreadths wide, with borders of gold and silver or coloured silks. . . ."[12]

These textiles in their standard lengths could be tailored—or according to Moreland's terminology, "transformed"[13]—into specific products that carried new names. Thus Saris' candakeens (or

130 *The Toradja of Sulawesi ultimately gave their rare imported textiles a sacred status. Examples such as this, dating probably from the seventeenth century or early eighteenth century, have gained irrational powers and are important elements in family treasuries. (Hetty Nooy-Palm. Courtesy of Koninklijk Instituut voor de Tropen, Amsterdam.)*

candekins or cannikens) were pieces cut from a bafta, usually dyed blue or black, and sold on the Asian market; *tricandees* were cut from dutties and dyed red for sale in Java; and *ardeas*, which were also sold here, were cut from *buzzees*, a long stiff calico woven in north India.[14]

Other textiles were "patterned in the loom." Most numerous and widely distributed were the Guinea cloths, whose stripes and checks were created with yarns dyed before weaving.[15] Saris' chelles, selas (zelas), and matafons are types of Guinea cloth.[16]

Ordinary calico in western India and longcloth (Guinea cloth), salempores, betilles, morees, and occasionally percales on the east coast could have been patterned by stamping or painting of resists and mordants, and dyeing. Called chintz and pintados in the trade lists, these were made into specific articles such as the turias, patta, and sarasa of Saris' list. In tappe turias, tappe corresponds to the present day *tapis*, the general term for the tubular or untailored skirt of the Southeast Asian archipelago. Turia refers to a type of patterned textile that evidently disappeared from the eastern trade lists. In 1603 it is described as an inferior painted cloth, usually patterned in stripes, florals, or circles in red or green. A piece measured 5½ yards by 33 inches and a bundle of twenty could be bought for 3 or 4 reals on India's west coast and sold in the Moluccas for 16 reals, with red turias claiming a slightly higher price. A confirming description elsewhere says turia (or toorya) were dyed cloths similar to sarasa but coarser.[17]

Patta were made in several styles, and here the "chere Malayo" means patta in the Malay style. (This seems to refer to a size rather

131 *Imported Indian cottons such as this example are called* maa' *among the Toradja of Sulawesi. Certain examples possess powers to bless man and his animals and have been highly valued by the Toradja for centuries. This example is red and dark blue and carries the name* lotong boko, *black back. The amount of resist patterning in both this example and Figure 130 seems extraordinary. (Hetty Nooy-Palm. Courtesy of Koninklijk Instituut voor de Tropen, Amsterdam.)*

than a particular pattern, 3 yards 28 inches by 1 yard 5 inches). Examples from Pulicat on India's east coast had ends dyed red or blue and the center area striped in the weft direction. *Patta malam* came from Masulipatam and were similarly patterned but of lesser quality.[18]

Sarasa were a trade textile prized in Southeast Asia and Japan, commanding 100 reals for a unit of twenty pieces in the Moluccas.[19] The term itself may derive from the Gujarati *saras*, meaning "excellent, beautiful,"[20] and seems, at least in this early trade period, to have designated textiles patterned both by weaving and dyeing.[21]. The sarassas chere Malayo of Saris' list simply means sarasa in the Malay style. These, like patta in the Malay style, were 3 yards 28 inches by 1 yard 5 inches, a dimension still used in Indonesia today for the traditional *kain panjang.* An early Dutch record describes them as being "painted" with foliage and birds and as coming from Pulicat on India's Coromandel Coast.[22] The word was adopted in both Southeast Asia and Japan, to become

132 Tapis (hip wrapper)
South Coromandel Coast (Tanjore?),
  (for the Indonesian market), 17th or
  early 18th century
Cotton; drawn resist, painted
  mordant, dyed
Red, blue, black
Warp 325 cm, weft 98 cm
Konjaku-Nishimura Collection, Kyoto

An intricate mosaic of geometric forms fills the four framing borders and the central field of this textile. Small, fern-like resist patterns and cleverly concealed birds are tucked in the borders, but the primary design elements are squares joined to form stepped configurations and interlaced knot figures. The filling details of the squares, which create these larger shapes, have been painstakingly worked with an interplay of simple geometric shape and twisting organic form. There is a comparable juxtaposition of the colors red and black with the light blue and the white filigree worked in the resist patterns. Consummate craftsmanship and total mastery of linear design come together in this extraordinary textile. An important detail contributing to the success of this design structure is the white resist outline that encloses and echoes every geometric shape. This, together with one of the two styles of birds used in the border, suggests an affinity with the Karuppur textiles.

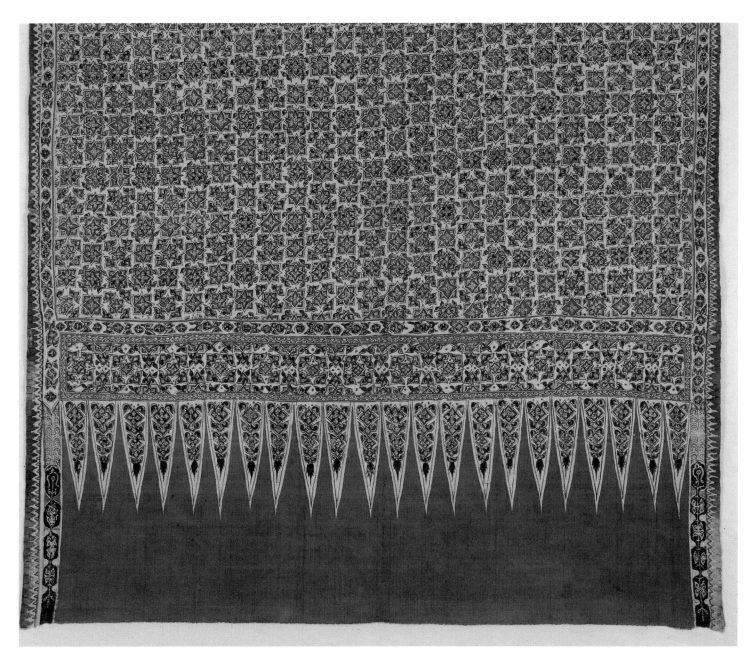

133 **Tapis** (hip wrapper)
India (for the Indonesian market),
    18th century
Cotton; applied resist and mordants,
    dyed
Red, blue, black
Warp 325 cm, weft 100 cm
    (approximate measure)
Konjaku-Nishimura Collection, Kyoto

*The textiles traded to insular South-
east Asia tend to have an affinity in
format. They display side borders and
ends marked by a row of tumpal. It
is not clear if this design scheme
originated in the Indonesian archipelago or if the taste was acquired from
early trade textiles. Within this format the details may vary widely.
Here small geometric configurations
fill the textile surface.*

the *serassah* of Malaya and the *sarasa* of Japan; in Japan the term designates mordant-worked and dyed textiles.[23]

These sarasa, a few of which are represented in Figures 124–133, must have had a significant influence on the design awareness of the Indonesians and very likely stimulated in Java the existing art of batik, which at that time may have been practiced only on a modest scale. Many batik from the north coast of Java (the major trade region) show more than just reflections of designs common to Indian sarasa; they suggest that some distinctive patterns, for instance the Cheribon cloud patterns, owe a profound debt to designs such as those in Figure 158.

An important term in the eastern trade that does not appear in Saris' list is *tjindai* or *chinde*, which is related to the Indian word chint, meaning "spotted" or "many colored."[24] Originally these tjindai were mordant-painted and dyed cotton fabrics, but at some time the term tjindai or *tzinde* becomes associated with silk; when we first encounter it in the trade lists of 1603 and 1605 it is given as *tschyndes* and tzinde and is described as being colorful silk cloth or silk with red stripes.[25] In Indonesia the word now seems to be associated primarily with weft or double ikat on silk, especially when done in floral patterns. Originally, however, this term may have referred not to ikat silk but to dyed cottons.[26]

The Prized Patola

The term tjindai or chinde is readily substituted in certain areas for patola, the Indian trade textile we know most about. Because of its inherent beauty, value, and importance in Southeast Asia, patola have been the subject of considerable study.[27] As we know the textile today, it is a multicolored silk patterned by double ikat, Figure 67. In this process sections of both the warp and weft yarns are reserved from the dye in carefully arranged patterns. When these yarns are woven, the reserved areas coincide to create the design. It is an extremely complex procedure that is practiced now by only a few weavers in Patan, in Gujarat. Other western Indian sites such as Surat, Baroda, Cambay, Ahmedabad, and Broach[28] may also have produced this textile prized in India as in Southeast Asia.

It is not certain that all references to patola in the early trade lists refer to the textile we recognize today. At the beginning of the sixteenth century, the Portuguese traveler Duarte Barbosa recorded that every year ships came to Burma bringing an abundance of printed Cambay (and Pulicat) cloths, both cotton and silk, that were called patola. He wrote that "these are colored with great skill and are here worth much money."[29] Cambay was then the preeminent seaport of Gujarat, and Pulicat on the Coromandel Coast was famous for its mordant-painted and dyed cottons, not ikat. From its use in the literature of the sixteenth century, one Indian scholar has concluded that the term patola was used for both patterned silks and cottons, although later it was applied exclusively to the Gujarati double-ikat silks.[30] Therefore, when this term is used in *early* trade lists we cannot be sure what variety of multicolored textile is intended. At least in the literature that comes down to us, it is not until Jean Baptiste Tavernier's description in around 1650 that we unquestioningly recognize the patola of today.[31]

Tavernier also tells us that patola were traded to the Philippines, Borneo, Java, Sumatra, and other neighboring regions. We know from other sources this included the Malay peninsula and possibly Thailand, Cochin-China, and China.

Nowhere was the effect of these cloths and their imitations more profound than in Indonesia. The prestige of the textiles was so great that their designs or basic format were adapted in locally made textiles. These adaptations were executed in batik, plangi, and weft ikat on Sumatra and Java and in warp ikat on such islands as Sumba, Flores, and Roti.[32] In only one area, the village of Tenganan Pageringsingan on Bali, were similar designs actually worked by the double-ikat process—but in cotton, not silk. A possible historical relationship between the processes of Bali and Gujarat has not been proven but is probable.

The designs most frequently copied in local textiles—the eight-pointed stars, blossom motifs, and tigers and elephants—reflect the popularity of specific types of patola in the archipelago. Very large elephant motifs are associated more singularly with Bali and Lomblen.[33]

Even more telling of the nature of the patola than the imitation of motifs is the sacred aura attached to the textiles themselves. In Java they are esteemed as garb for weddings and the rites marking other transitions in life, and at one time certain motifs were reserved for private use by the royalty in Central Java.[34] In the royal palaces sacred patola heirlooms continue to adorn ceremonial beds and are components of sacred dance costumes. By tradition, sacred objects—kris, and *wayang* figures—are protected by patola wrapping. On Bali patola are hung in the temples, and in times of illness small fragments of the textile are burnt for the patient to inhale or to put his feet into the smoke.[35] On Sumba possession of certain patola remained the exclusive prerogative of the highest class, who had the designs copied into their own textiles, which were used together with imported pieces at royal funerals and important occasions.[36] In Sulawesi, in the Minahassa areas, men's ceremonial sashes were patola; elsewhere in North Sulawesi they were used at weddings and funerals as wall hangings and, apparently, to cover coffins of deceased noblemen.[37] One could cite many other examples of past and present customs regarding patola in the islands of Indonesia to confirm the exalted position this particular Indian cloth held there.

Almost as valued as the patola in Indonesia's outer islands were the Indian block-printed cotton imitations, Figure 124. The instance of the Sa'dan Toradja of Sulawesi provides an intriguing, albeit extreme, example. Over time, awareness of the foreign origin of these Indian textiles was lost, and sacred origins were attributed to them.[38] Together with a few other exotic, Indian-made textiles, Figures 129–131, these cloths were given individual identities and were attributed special powers. Some had "the power to bless man, his animals and his crops . . . to ward off illness from

134 **Quilt lining** (detail)
Ahmedabad, Gujarat (for the Chinese
    market ?), 18th century
Silk; clamp resist, dyed
Red, blue, blue-green, yellow
Warp 243.8 cm, weft 122 cm (single
    panel)
The Metropolitan Museum of Art,
    New York 1975-208. Rogers Fund
    1975

Only recently has it become known
that clamp-resist processes were practiced in India; this knowledge is the
result of a search and research effort
with all the mystery and intricacy of
a hunt for buried treasure. The pur-
suers in this case were Alfred Bühler
and Eberhard Fischer. It is their envi-
able research that gives a provenance
of western India to this silk and provides our knowledge of this aspect of
the Indian dyer's art.[7] The quest began in 1964, when Bühler identified
some carved wooden blocks in an
Ahmedabad antique shop as the type
used in clamp-resist patterning. In
this process, designs are carved in
mirror image on a pair of large
blocks. After a cloth is folded and
laid between the pair, these blocks
are firmly clamped together so that
the edges of the design coincide per-
fectly. Holes that had been cut

through the blocks served as chan-
nels for the pouring of the dye. The
wooden edges of the design dammed
up, or acted as a resist, preventing
the dye from spreading. Different
color dyes could be poured in appropriate holes, allowing a range of
colors such as that displayed in this
quilt lining. Dyes penetrated through
all layers of the cloth, creating a repeat pattern.

The blocks identified by Bühler
had come from a house demolished
in the older part of Ahmedabad, but
its exact location was unknown. It
was not until 1970 that more of the
blocks were found, built into several
houses. They were considered merely
carved decorations by their owners.
Through questioning and research, it
was concluded that the blocks were
certainly used in the sixteenth century, and very probably only to pat-

domestic animals . . . or have the power to increase the stock of buffalo or pigs."[39] Every important family treasured a store of these textiles, which were brought into use at times of social crisis.

Further to the east, in the Bird's Head region of New Guinea, the Indian printed imitations of patola, and a few textiles made in eastern Indonesia, became the focal point of the social pattern of the Mejprat people. Not only were the textiles saved as precious heirlooms to be used in rites such as funerals and initiations, and as marriage gifts, but they became the critical objects in an elaborate barter system. Pieces were lent as credit to exchange partners at extraordinary interest rates of 100 percent or more. Prestige dictated a continual borrowing and lending of pieces of these cloths in an all-consuming occupation that created an elite class of people within the society. So valued were these textiles that any crime could be vitiated by payment in them. This system and its use of textiles has been studied in depth by Elmberg (1968) and Kamma (1970).

From the remaining evidence it is not clear if the importance of patola and its imitations in the Indonesian islands was matched in other areas of the East. Because some patterns or arrangements of textiles in Cambodia and Thailand recall patola features, it seems probable that this Indian textile was known and valued there.[40] Certainly the textiles would have been used to some degree in the Malay peninsula, and it is known that Indian textiles were traded to the southern Philippines as early as the mid-sixteenth century[41] and that in the mid-seventeenth century Gujarati merchants were sending ships to Manila.[42] The evidence that some of this cargo must have been the precious west Indian ikat remains in the designs of certain textiles made in Mindanao that replicate patola designs.

The patola and their imitations would have represented only a small proportion of the possibly 400,000 Indian textiles imported into the Spice Islands in one year of that early seventeenth century period.[43] By far the majority—as Saris' list suggests—were simple, plain, striped or checkered cottons that Moreland characterized as "just a humdrum, useful, business directed, so far as Asia was concerned, to supplying cheap cloths to poor people. . . ."[44] This is a harsh economic judgment concerning a trade that stimulated new local textiles, entered into peoples' sacred customs and myths, and changed the historical fortunes of many islands.

The Trade to Thailand

Indian textiles in their specialized market forms were established even on the mainland of Southeast Asia before the Europeans appeared. When the Portuguese arrived at the beginning of the sixteenth century, they learned of cloths "in the fashion of Siam."[45] We can only assume these were similar to those of a later date, Figures 136–139. This trade was carried by Arab and Indian merchants to Tenasserim on the contemporary Burmese coast, where it was transported overland to the Thai capital of Ayuthia.[46] The volume of the early trade with Thailand may not have been large, but it was sufficient to establish market preferences that were

tern silk. Other evidence supports an assumption that they were carved and used by local people. In addition to evidence for Ahmedabad, there is a suggestion that the technique was known in south India.

The quilt lining is attributed to Ahmedabad because its designs are virtually identical to those on some of the Ahmedabad blocks and because of the absence of this type of design in other regions of the world where clamp resist is known to have been practiced.

When the lining was removed from the quilt face, the conservator determined that the original stitching was Chinese.[8] This evidence supports the previous assumption that the lining was added to the embroidered face in China.

135 *Thai pictorial arts abound with representations of Indian imported textiles. They are worn as clothing or, as in this example, serve as a setting for an important figure. Here Queen Mahamaya, at the moment of her miraculous dream in which she conceives the Bodhisattva, reclines on one of the Indian cloths. The textile is recognizable by its ornate row of tumpal in the end border, broad framing borders, and lattice-patterned center field. Depictions such as this may explain the enormous size of some "Thai" textiles in museum collections. This scene, painted at the end of the eighteenth century, appears in the Buddhaisawan Chapel, Bangkok. (Courtesy of Chira Chongkol, Director, National Museum, Bangkok.)*

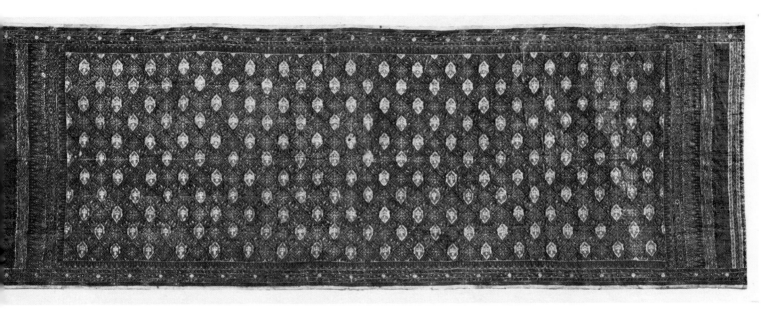

136 **Phanung** (wrapper)
India (for the Thai market), 18th
  century
Cotton; drawn and stamped resist and
  mordants, dyed
Shades of red, blue, tan, black
Warp 33.8 cm, weft 117 cm
Indianapolis Museum of Art
  47.184. Jacob Metzger Fund

*This textile exemplifies the lattice-
work patterning so preferred by the
Thais. It is a consistent device in
their art, so it is not surprising to see
it used on textiles designed for that
market. In this example, a filigree of
resist details worked on maroon and
rose grounds forms decorative
squares that are joined to create a
net across the textile. In the intervals
appears the torso of a heavenly being.
Decorative borders, again worked
with extensive resist elements, frame
the sides and ends. Included in the
borders is the ornate tumpal, or triangular form, characteristic of Thai
textiles.*

*This piece, highly calendared and
lined, was purchased in Bangkok in
1938 by the art historian Carl Schus-
ter.*

137 Detail of Figure 136.

138 Detail of Figure 139.

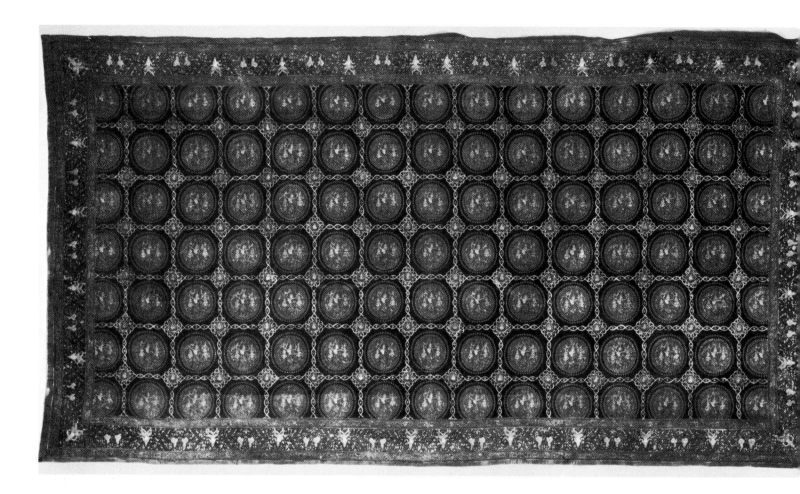

139 Pha Kiao[9]
India (for the Thai market), 18th
century
Cotton; drawn and stamped resists
and mordants, dyed
Shades of red, purple, brown, pink,
blue, ocher, green, black
Warp 215 cm, weft 114 cm
Victoria and Albert Museum, London
T. 53-1909

*A border with guard stripes and a
large center field were used to form
this textile composition. In the border, amid leaves and vines, pairs of
heavenly beings in a cartouch alternate with standing figures set with
arms akimbo. The center field is divided into a broad grid with a
twisted rope-and-knot device. The
knot frames a torso of a figure with
hands in a gesture of adoration. In
the intervals of the grid are great medallions containing a dancing figure
flanked by two adoring heavenly
beings. Outlines of the figures have
been stamped in red or black, the
medallions are deep red, and the
background color is a purple-brown.
Details in the border are light blue
and green. Although the mordant-
worked areas appear stamped, the resist wax was freely drawn, lending a
pleasing variability to the surface
pattern. The center field pattern is
not exclusive to textiles of this format; it also appears on textiles with
broad end borders.[10]*

*The cotton textile is lined with
three colors of plain silk. In this lining the center field is a rich red bordered by a narrow green frame. There
is a narrow purple rim where it joins
the cotton.*

140 *Some textiles patterned in India for the Thai market have subsequently been lined with silk and meticulously edged with silk piping. Such care suggests the textiles were to be seen on both faces much as the textiles encompassing the group of monks and the curtains in the doorway in this scene. The grid pattern that covers these textiles is reminiscent of the design detail on Indian-made textiles such as in Figure 136. This scene, painted in the nineteenth century, appears in the Lacquer Pavilion in the Palace of Suan Pakkad, Bangkok. (Courtesy of Chira Chongkol, Director, National Museum, Bangkok.)*

quickly noted by the Dutch, who complained in 1616 that not even Malay-style textiles from Coromandel would sell in Thailand.[47] In the following years there was no broadening of this taste, as this 1622 description of Siam witnesses: "This place vents other kinds of cloth than Java or Malaya do, and the people are very curious [particular] of their cloth, especially painted, whereof those of Sct. Thomae [near Madras] and Palliacat [Pulicat] have the most trade. . . ."[48] In 1663 we learn again of the strong preference for Coromandel textiles over those of Surat.[49]

These textiles traded to Thailand were used as hangings, area dividers, floor spreads, and clothing. A description of the costume of Thailand in 1693 states, "They go with their Feet naked, and their head bare; and for Decency only they begirt their Reins and Thighs down to their Knees with a piece of painted Cloth about two Ells and a half long, which the Portuguese do call *Pagne* . . . ; sometimes instead of a painted cloth the *Pagne* is a silken Stuff, either plain or embroider'd with a border of Gold and Silver."[50] Later in the same work the writer says, "Those *Pagnes* that are of an extraordinary beauty and gaudiness, as those of Silk with Embroidery, or without Embroidery and those of painted Linnen very fine, are permitted to those only to whom the Prince presents them. The Women of Quality do greatly esteem the black *Pagnes* and their Scarf is frequently of plain white Muslin."[51] "Linnen" here has become a generic term Europeans often applied to a plain-

141 and 142 *These pages from a Thai divination manuscript of the early nineteenth century clearly depict Indian patterned cottons worn as costume. The textile rendering in the first illustration may be compared with that in Figure 119f. In the second illustration, the rendering is more schematic but derives directly from the bold patterns of stepped squares commonly found in the Indian textiles traded to Southeast Asia and Japan. (Courtesy of British Library, London; Or.12167, folios 28,42.)*

weave cotton with which they were less familiar than the linens of home.[52]

The details of these Thai preferences assumed great importance for the trading companies for reasons other than the immediate market these preferences secured in Thailand. A triangle of trade was involved. In their quest for sources of increased capital, the Europeans learned that the Japanese would pay for imported goods with silver and copper. These metals could then be traded else-where for sizable profits.[53] The range of items acceptable to the Japanese, however, was limited. Only skins, sappanwood for dyes, and silks consistently found a market there, and Thailand could supply the first two. Japanese, Thai, English, Muslim, and Dutch merchants all vied for this trade, but it was the Dutch V.O.C. in the 1620s that "laid the foundation for a very profitable, though limited, trade that continued for the remainder of the cen-tury. . . ."[54] In this early period the chief import of the company to Thailand was Coromandel Coast cloth,[55] a trade which company representatives tried to monopolize. They were never successful in their efforts, and periodically in the course of the seventeenth century they had their profits cut as other nationalities flooded the Thai market with the Indian textiles. At certain times, such as between 1680 and 1689, the Dutch abandoned the textile trade here altogether because competition had made it unprofitable.[56]

A continual and steady flow of Indian textiles into Thailand is an accurate picture of trade in this early period. So great was the commerce that in 1690 the king decided to try producing fine cloth in Thailand to stem the flow of wealth from the royal treasury. He enlisted the aid of the V.O.C. to acquire cotton seeds and dyes from India as well as Indian dyers, painters, and weavers to train local workers.[57] (The results of this enterprise and the development of a local Thai textile industry are not recorded in the correspon-dence.) The imported Indian textiles came from both coasts of India, but those from the west never had the same esteem as those from Coromandel.[58]

In 1617 the following types of cloth were some of those rec-ommended for trade to Siam.[59] From the west coast: cheap calicoes such as blue *byrams*, white baftas, and types of candekins and turban cloth called zelas (Saris' "candakeens" and "selas"); also from this region, chintz from Ahmedabad and Burhanpore and ta-peh sarasa (skirts) and chawdor *pintathos* (painted shawls). From the Coromandel Coast: painted Guinea cloth, *jeckandames* (a painted wrapper of two cloth widths), and *tallepines* and woven and painted *tanipie*, which are terms not understood; in addition, red and white betilles and salempores—the staple muslin and cal-ico of Golconda and the Coast.

From this and later lists, there is evidence of continuing demand for "painted" wares and chintz in the Thai markets (including the mention of *palampore*, a bedcovering more commonly associated with trade to Europe than to Asia).[60] In the use of the two terms "chintz" and "painted" there may be an implied distinction on the part of the seventeenth century writer between stamped and painted mordant dye work. Both types remain in collections today,

143 Su'a Senakut (warrior's jacket ?)[11]
Coromandel Coast (for the Thai
  market), 18th century
Cotton; drawn resists, painted
  mordants, dyed
Red, blue, black
Center back length 69 cm; sleeve
  width between the cuffs 155 cm
Henry Ginsburg, London

*The textile used to create this jacket
was designed and dyed with a clear
understanding of its eventual function. The intention was to recreate a
protective armor in spirit, if not in
fact. On the flat cloth were drawn
and worked two large demonic faces
with fangs that gripped a painted belt
in front and back, and monster maws
on the shoulders to disgorge the
sleeves. A basket or wicker plaiting
was imitated in the lower sections in
red, and the sides have an overlapping scale pattern, probably to represent still another layer of armor. The
border of the sleeves and hemline
were created as part of the original
textile, but the collar was added, apparently by using a piece cut from
the center front opening of the jacket.*

*The jacket is joined at the under-
arm and sides. In the original flat
textile these areas were a solid blue,
possibly to allow for some adjust-
ment in size that would not interrupt
the designs when the textile was cut
for a specific person. There is also a
join at the breastline, across the
front, that was made before the textile was dyed. The entire garment is
lined with a plain, undyed cotton.*

*The textile seems to have been pat-
terned first with resists, then painted*

*with mordants for red and black, and
dyed these colors. In the final step
blue was added with a brush.*

*The precise use of this jacket
within the Thai context is not
known. From a late seventeenth century visitor's report we learn that it
was ". . . a general Custom at Siam
that the Prince, and all his Retinue in
the War or Hunting, be cloath'd in
Red. Upon this account the Shirts
which are given to the Soldiers, are of
Muslin dy'd Red; and on the days of
Ceremony, as was that of the Entry
of the King's Ambassadors, these Red
Shirts were given to the Siamese
which they put under their Arms."[12]
There is little doubt that these jackets were made from imported Indian
textiles, but whether this piece resembles the general form of such
jackets is not known. Perhaps specific
officers received this more elaborate
style. Certainly Thai art of the eighteenth century has representations of
armor of similar design worn by war-
riors and guardian figures.[13] It is also
possible that jackets such as this
served as costume pieces in theatrical
presentations. They are one of the
more exotic forms of market specialization the Indians mastered.*

although it is virtually impossible to trace these examples to their precise location in India.

By the mid-twentieth century knowledge of the trade to the Indian east coast seems to have been forgotten in Thailand. Steinmann, inquiring about the old "phanung," or wrappers, worn at the court in Bangkok, was informed by H.R.H. Prince Dhani Nivat and by Reginald Le May that these "were made to order in Surat" and, because the Indian artists copied imported Siamese patterns, were called *pha lai yang*, "garment designed after patterns."[61] This raises questions in itself—how "old" were the phanung indicated, and what were the patterns taken to be copied?

The majority of these textiles are structured in one of two formats, Figures 136 and 139. In the first there are broad lateral and even deeper end borders that frame a single large, central field. Each of these areas is filled with a tracery of white filigree (done with a wax resist) describing floral, geometric, or animal forms. Particularly striking in this type are the one or more rows of tumpal (a motif of long triangles) in the end borders outlined with a welter of organic white lines that terminate in a single straight line. In the second type, a single ornate border of equal depth frames the textile on all four sides, encompassing a broad and patterned central field. According to Henry Ginsburg, specialist for Thai and Cambodian languages at the British Library, this framed type is called *pha kiao* and was used on elephants where all four borders could be seen.[62] It is possible that textiles with this format were also used as space dividers, in association with figures of the Buddha, and as curtains, Figures 135 and 140.[63]

Textiles in the first format served functions other than clothing according to wall paintings from the eighteenth century. In one such painting, Queen Mahamaya reclines on a textile of this type at the moment of her miraculous dream.[64]

Characteristic of these textiles, whether the mordants were stamped or painted, is the extraordinary amount of resist patterning that outlines and details every element, enlivening the surface with a tracery of white lines.

Lesser sorts of cloth that did not have such fine details were surely exported to Thailand. These more modest textiles may have resembled the groups of sample pieces preserved at the Victoria and Albert Museum, which were made by dyers "at Peethapoor and Wasna" in Gujarat for the Thai trade before 1879 (I.S. 1707). The samples have very small geometric repeats in the center field and grossly stamped tumpals in the end border. The white tracery of the more precious examples is lacking. Because the evidence in the samples is late, it does not allow us to conclude that the more elaborate textiles were made on the Coromandel Coast. There is evidence to suggest this, but not to form a final opinion about where in India the more elaborate Thai textiles were made.

A difficulty in interpreting the trade lists to Thailand in the seventeenth century is that Ayuthia served ships sailing to and from China, Japan, Formosa, and Manila. At least some of the textiles loaded for Thailand would have been transshipped to these other destinations.

144 *This is a detail from a Japanese Namban screen of the Momoyama period, 1573–1615. The person depicted has been variously identified as a Japanese or as a Portuguese warrior rendered through Japanese eyes.[14] The European ruff and long gun encourage such speculation. The patterning of the textiles of the man's trousers and wrapper, however, clearly suggests imported cottons of India. Designs on the trousers may be compared with Figure 146. The resist pattern in the wrapper recalls work done in western India. The Portuguese who would have traded such textiles, together with the priests who accompanied them, may be seen on the ship in the distance. (Courtesy of Seattle Art Museum, Seattle 63.151. The Thomas D. Stimson Memorial Collection.)*

The Trade to Japan

The importance of Indian textiles in the trade to these other regions of Asia was never as significant as in the trade to Southeast Asia. Indeed, there was virtually no demand for these cottons in China[65] or Japan in the early part of the seventeenth century. Pepper in China, and steel, lead, silk, hides, and dyewoods in Japan were the primary elements of exchange. As the Japanese would tell the English, "you commend your cloth unto us, but you yourselves wear least thereof, the better sort of you wearing silken garments, the meaner fustians."[66] Indian textiles initially sold more because of their novelty and their painting, "the Japanese being a people desiring change."[67] In the first quarter of the century the English would complain that one line of textiles might sell well, but when it was repeated, could meet with complete rejection. It was also noted in this period that cloth sales were better during Japan's internal wars because the textiles were used to sheath weapons.

The Dutch had a real incentive to persist in their efforts to change this inclination, because after 1625 they enjoyed a virtual monopoly on the trade between Japan and India. Their success was such that by 1680 the Japanese were consuming 10 percent of all cotton goods shipped from the Dutch Batavia factory.[68] By 1692 the physician to the Dutch factory in Japan would write that "all sorts of stuffs and cloth yield a considerable and sure profit. . . ."[69] He mentions half-silk India chintz, silk and cotton striped goods from Bengal and the Coromandel Coast, and several staple types of cotton.[70]

These and other cursory listings that mention such textiles as sarasa give little preparation for the extraordinary range that entered the country in this period—at least as shown by the examples remaining in private and public collections in Japan today.[71]

As a group, these dyed textiles seem to have little stylistic or aesthetic affinity with one another. Some are coarsely woven cottons that have been stamped with mordant and dyed in roughly executed floral repeats. Others are finely wrought textiles with an extraordinary wealth of detail in the painting of the mordants and resists and in the dye procedures. Some that arrived in Japan at the beginning of the seventeenth century even show applied tinsel.[72] Designs range from stiff floral repeats to sinuous vines, from geometric patterns to fans and patterns with animals and snakes.

Some of the Indian textiles imported to Japan form an aesthetic classification called *oni* sarasa, meaning "demon" sarasa. Originally applied to a form of classical Japanese verse, the word came to be used for categories in other arts, such as a style of utensil used in the traditional tea ceremony. When applied to an Indian textile, it refers to an exceptional size, to handspun, relatively coarse yarn, and to forthright patterning. It is certainly not pejorative, as seen in this sixteenth-century explanation of the quality of oni: "The true meaning of oni is to be unmoving, showing fierce mein, yet in practice possessing the quality of a flower."[73]

Oni sarasa is merely one category of imported textiles. Another, *meibutsu-gire*, has over 350 major types.[74] This term—meaning

145 and 146 Furoshiki (a textile used as a wrapper)
India (probably Gujarat), 17th or early 18th century
Cotton; stamped resist and mordant, dyed
Red-brown, blue
104 cm x 106.7 cm
Danziger Collection, New York 81.07

In the course of the seventeenth century, the resistance that had initially greeted Dutch efforts to trade Indian textiles in Japan reversed itself, and the textile imports were eagerly sought. In time, fragments of these textiles, along with other varieties of imported textiles, came to be referred to as meibutsu-gire, meaning "famous" or "named-cloth-fragment,"[15] connoting that which is rare and precious, fit for ritual use in the tea ceremony. Some pieces were sewn into bags to hold utensils for the ceremony, and others were fashioned into simple rectangles to wrap boxes crafted to store specific utensils. The example in Figure 146 usually encloses a simple wooden box fashioned to cradle a freshwater jar, as shown in Figure 145. There is a com-

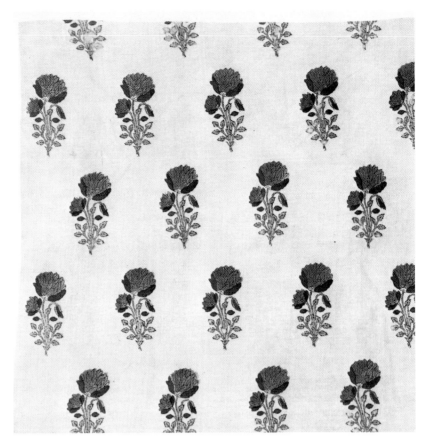

plete harmony in the sympathetic association of imported Chinese porcelain made especially for the Japanese tea ceremony, the broad-grained wood box, and the handspun cotton with its muted dyes.[16]

The design of a recurved vine with a floral head appears on textiles depicted in west Indian manuscripts from the fourteenth century onward. It also can be seen on a Fostat fragment of indeterminate date, illustrated in Bühler and Fischer.[17] This textile from Japan probably was crafted in the late seventeenth or early eighteenth century, when textile imports from India increased. Judging from its worn condition, it may have been stitched onto a furoshiki soon after reaching Japan. (Photographs courtesy of Schecter Me Sun Lee, New York.)

147   **Furoshiki** (a textile used as a wrapping)
India (probably Gujarat), 17th or 18th century
Cotton; stamped mordants, dyed
Red-brown, purple, black
50.8 cm x 49.5 cm
Danziger Collection, New York 79.10

This meibutsu-gire, or "named-cloth-fragment," has been sewn into a square wrapper that enfolds the tea scoop used in the Japanese tea ceremony. Each element in the ceremony—from the physical setting to the smallest detail—contributed to a desired mood; thus, concern for every aspect was profound. This was true for the accessories as well as the major utensils. Precious imported textiles from China and India were used as wrappers and to create small protective bags for the utensils central to the ceremony.[18] In time, people made scrapbooks of some of these fragments for personal study and devised categories named after renowned owners of prototypes such as a warrior, a temple, and the like.[19] (Photograph by Schecter Me Sun Lee, New York.)

148   *These wood-block prints are pages from a small book,* Sarasa benran, *published in Japan in 1781, that was a contemporary "how to" publication.*[20] *The designs, adaptations from imported Indian textiles, are offered to the reader complete with notation of the appropriate colors. The book's introduction claims it to be a "handy survey" of new designs for textiles, including patterns for decorating cotton fabrics by hand "with a description of the dyes and how to stain them to make them look old. These patterns are for* fukiye *[blown pictures]. In this process the coloring is blown through a stencil onto the cloth. The process was introduced by the Dutch." This book was published in Edo. A similar book with the same introduction was published in 1784 and 1808 in Kyoto. The Kyoto edition carried a wood-block print of an "orientalized" Dutchman seated in pensive deliberation at his desk. The pages reproduced here are approximately 27 cm x 17 cm. (Courtesy of Victoria and Albert Museum, London E.6924–1916.)*

148a

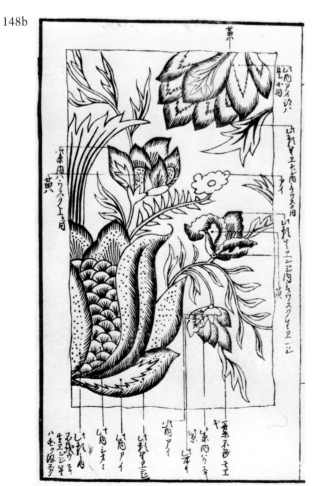

148b

148c

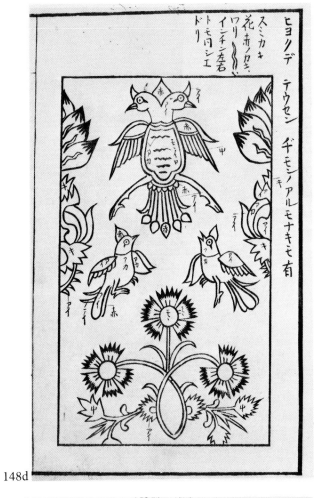

148d

148e

148f

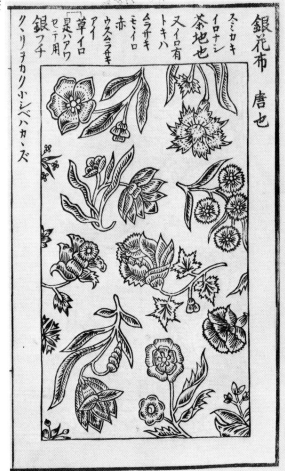

148g

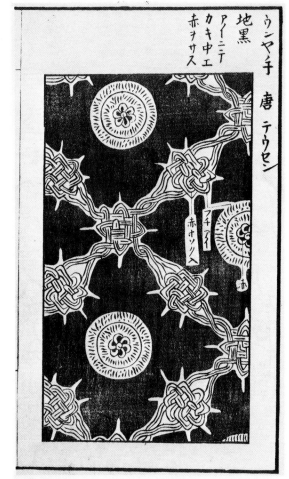

roughly "famous" or "named-cloth-fragment"—is applied to imported textiles used in connection with the ritualized Japanese tea ceremony.[75] The disparate fragments used as wrappers, Figures 146 and 147, sewn into bags, or used as a display napkin, Figure 122, could be of a strikingly different character. Each was prized, however, for the harmony it might lend when joined with a particularly appropriate setting of tea bowl, flowers, water bucket, and the like.

Other categories of meibutsu-gire include *To-santome*, which derives from *To*, meaning (Chinese) "foreign," and St. Thomé, the seventeenth century enclave on the east coast of India from which textiles were exported by the Portuguese. Another is called *moru*, which is thought to derive from Mughal (not the textile termed moree).[76]

Throughout the centuries an extraordinary number of these trade textiles have been honored and saved as family and national treasures in Japan. They constitute one of the most valuable resources for reconstructing the details of this art.

As political and individual events both in Asia and the West changed the nature of the trade in the East, Indian textiles lost their preeminent position. The legacy bequeathed to regional designs, organizational concepts, and textile technology itself, however, was profound and lasting. Although each region of South Asia, Southeast Asia, and East Asia is rightly proud of its local textile traditions, each of these also bears witness to the centuries of trade in Indian textiles.

NOTES TO TEXT

1. Rouffaer and Ijzerman 1925 I:74.
2. Barbosa 1918–21 II:152–70.
3. Chaudhuri 1978:196–98.
4. Floris 1934:71.
5. *Letters Received* I:30.
6. Moreland 1975:56.
7. Saris 1967:61–62.
8. To help understand Saris' list, I have followed the organization presented in Moreland (1924–25) but have supplemented his explanations with work from other researchers. The most complete published history of terms is in Irwin (1966); Chaudhuri (1978) also lists terms.
9. Moreland 1924–25:231 and Irwin 1966:59.
10. Other calicoes were what Moreland (1924–25:228) would call "stout." These were Saris' dongeryus, or dungarees, used for sail making or for packing materials, and which have come to mean in our vocabulary an overall garment of strong cloth. The cloth was woven on both coasts but enters the trade as dutties or seryas when from Gujarat. Ballachios may also be considered as a stout calico (Raychaudhuri 1962:221), but it seems strange that such a calico would demand the price on Saris' list.
   Calico from the east coast entered the Far East trade in a number of grades by name. Because of its price Saris' sarampouri, or salempore, must surely have been one of the type considered "fine," along with morees and percales, Saris' parcallas (from which we derive the term percale). Percales were sold in lengths of 8 yards by 1 yard, and morees in lengths of 9 yards by 1 yard 8 inches. Salempores were also sold in inferior grades in the eastern trade, but more commonly the cheap textile from India's east coast was called longcloth.
11. Except when containing precious metal, these were not considered luxury goods (Irwin 1966:39 and Moreland 1924–25:234). The cloths were 15 to 25 yards by 1½ yards. Saris' term tancoulous is also muslin—but from Bengal, and one that is rarely seen in the trade (Rouffaer 1900: Appendix III, xv). The Great Potas of Saris' list may have been a muslin headcloth from Bengal (Moreland 1924–25:234) or a dyed calico (Chaudhuri 1978:504).
12. Manrique, *Travels*, cited in Irwin 1966:62.
13. Moreland 1924–25:236.
14. Ibid.
15. Although the name "Guinea cloth" arises from the use of these textiles in the slave trade on the Guinea coast of Africa, the term was still applied in the Asian trade.

16. Matafons were a checkered calico from western India, and chelles were a checkered cloth from the Madras area (Irwin 1966:62, 68). Selas were another inexpensive calico of this sort. Tapseils were patterned on the loom in stripes and came from western India for both the eastern market and African trade. The major distinguishing feature of tapseils was the admixture of silk and cotton.
17. Rouffaer 1900:Appendix III;xi and *Letters Received* I:72.
18. Rouffaer 1900:Appendix III;xii, xiv, xxii fn. 31.
19. *Letters Received* I:72.
20. Varadarajan 1981a says the Gujarati *saras* derives from the Sanskrit *shreyas.*
21. Irwin 1956:42.
22. Rouffaer 1900:Appendix III;xii.
23. Nobuko Kajitani 1982:personal communication.
24. Bühler and Fischer 1979 I:321.
25. *Letters Received* I:72 and Rouffaer 1900:Appendix III; xii.
26. Bühler and Fischer (1979 I:323–24) discuss the many aspects of this terminology.
27. Bühler 1959, Gulati 1951, Bühler and Fischer 1979, and De Bone 1976.
28. Bühler and Fischer 1979 I:263.
29. Cited in Bühler 1959:5. Earlier reference was made to double-ikat telia rumals. It is interesting in relation to this statement that merchants questioned by Mittal said they had exported these textiles to Burma for generations (Mittal 1962:28).
30. Gulati 1951:3, 7.
31. Cited in Bühler and Fischer 1979 I:235.
32. Bühler and Fischer 1979 I:286ff.
33. Ibid.
34. Rouffaer 1900:171.
35. Ramseyer, cited in Bühler and Fischer 1979 I:291.
36. Adams 1969:146.
37. Bühler and Fischer 1979 I:293.
38. Nooy-Palm 1979:83.
39. Ibid.:85.
40. Bühler and Fischer 1979 I:286.
41. Leur 1960:160.
42. Gopal 1975:66.
43. Leur 1960:211.
44. Moreland 1924–25:243.
45. Pires 1944 I:108 cited in Smith 1977:173 fn. 59.
46. Smith 1977:85.
47. Ibid.
48. *Records of Relations* I:139–40.
49. *Records of Relations* II:44, 48, 166.
50. La Loubère 1969:25.
51. Ibid.:27.
52. To some degree the king was able to keep the import of textiles a royal monopoly. This means he also had a role in their dispersal, particularly of the most valued textiles. In addition to courtiers, the paintings of early Thailand clearly depict these Indian textiles in the service of Buddhist monks (Boisselier 1976:196, 211).

53. Moreland 1975:65.
54. Smith 1977:52.
55. Ibid.:53.
56. Ibid.:68–69.
57. Ibid.:105.
58. *Records of Relations* II:166.
59. *Records of Relations* I:81.
60. *Records of Relations* II:104–05.
61. Steinmann 1958:27.
62. For a possible example, see Boisselier 1976:Fig. 92.
63. Ibid.:Figs. 47, 72, 158.
64. Ibid.:Fig. 147.
65. Moreland 1924–25:241.
66. Purchas I:327, cited in Cocks I:xviii.
67. Cocks II:273.
68. Moreland 1924–25:241.
69. Kaempfer 1906:215.
70. Ibid.:214.
71. Yoshioka (1980) illustrates many of these.
72. Ibid.:Figs. 2–4.
73. This explanation is cited in Cort 1982:34.
74. Tomoyuki n.d.:58.
75. The author is indebted to Louise Allison Cort for conversations about this translation.
76. Tomoyuki n.d.:13, 34. A few pages of this notebook were made available by Alan Kennedy.

NOTES TO ILLUSTRATIONS

1. Nobuko Kajitani:personal communication.
2. Bühler 1979 II: nos. 72, 73.
3. Ibid.:292 fn. 53.
4. Tilburg, Netherlands: Tilburg Textile Museum manuscript M241 and MKT 5–3–4–9 [by Snouck Hourgronje].
5. Brennig 1975:9–10.
6. Gopal 1975:61.
7. Bühler and Fischer 1977.
8. Nobuko Kajitani:personal communication.
9. This name refers to a textile with four borders, according to Henry Ginsburg of the British Library. Although his information indicated this type was used on elephants, it may have been used for other purposes as well.
10. Yoshioka 1980:Fig. 119.
11. Henry Ginsburg:personal communication.
12. La Loubère 1969:26.
13. Boisselier 1976:88.
14. Sinor 1966:165 and Seattle Art Museum record 63.151.
15. Louise Allison Cort, May 1982: personal communication.
16. The jar, *mizusashi*, is used for water to rinse the tea bowl and to replenish the kettle during the tea ceremony (Fujioka 1973:136).
17. Bühler and Fischer 1972:Fig. 287.
18. Fujioka 1973:43.
19. Louise Allison Cort, May 1982: personal communication.
20. Joe Earle and Verity Wilson of the Far Eastern Department, Victoria and Albert Museum, London, kindly translated the title pages and introduction of the two *Sarasa benran* in their collection, E.6924–1916 and E.2804–1925. The introduction was written by the sarasa master Kusumi Magozaemon Shuzai, who makes reference to a still earlier work entitled *Sarasa benran.*

Master Dyers to the West

Some 25–30,000 camel loads of cotton textiles were annually escorted across the land routes from India to Persia in the early seventeenth century.[1] A portion remained there, but the remainder was marketed further north or west to Turkey and the other areas of the Levant. Other, equally traditional routes took Indian textiles to the West through the Indian Ocean to the Red Sea and the Persian Gulf. This was the "peddlar" trade of legend that carried the "guddars" and "sallows" to Poland and the fine muslins to North Africa. European traders would call the latter "Barbary shashes," from the contemporary name for North Africa, Barbary, and the Arabic for muslin, *shash.*

When Portuguese ships initiated the sea route to India from Europe in 1498, new factors were introduced that would ultimately lead to even greater dispersal of India's textiles. These would eventually change the fashion of northern Europe, giving rise to new industries and causing the downfall of others.

The Portuguese foresaw little of this potential in the sixteenth century, but they did trade the cheapest calicoes, the so-called Guinea cloths, to the African west coast in exchange for slaves and to new colonies in Brazil for the use of the slaves.[2] Thus, they initiated the triangular trade pattern that was to depend on Indian cottons for nearly two centuries.[3]

With the exception of quilts, which were returned to Portugal, the Portuguese did not attempt to introduce a taste for Indian cottons in Europe. Their immediate efforts in the sixteenth century were directed more toward controlling the existing trade they found in Asian waters.[4]

Critical to this effort were the textiles of western India and the commerce in them by Gujarati merchants through ports such as Cambay, and later, Surat. A sixteenth century visitor to Cambay provides a glimpse of this export trade: ". . . these barkes lade out, as it were, an infinite quantitie of cloth made of Bumbast [cotton] of all sorts, as white stamped and painted, with great quantitie of Indico, dried ginger and conserved, . . . great quantitie of Cotton . . . Turbants made in Diu, great stones. . . ."[5]

Some of this shipping went east, but Gujarati merchants had long based their wealth on their trade advantage to such westerly ports as Aden, Mocha, and Jedda on the Red Sea; Muscat and Gombroon on the Persian Gulf; and a host of lesser ports around the

149   Detail of Figure 150.

175

150 **Wentke** (woman's gown)
Coromandel Coast, 18th century
Cotton; drawn resist, painted
  mordants, dyed
Blue, black
Center back length 145.5 cm, sleeve
  width between cuffs 194 cm
Fries Museum, Leeuwarden, the
  Netherlands 1957–400

*The importation of brightly colored
cottons affected costume in many
parts of Europe, but nowhere more so
than in the Netherlands. In several
northern regions chintz became a
part of traditional costume, and today old pieces are still prized for
wear when regional dress is in order.
It is reputed that wealthy Dutch families buy eighteenth century palampores auctioned in England to cut
into costume elements for use on
these special occasions. Originally
the costume of these regions included
men's lounging robes, women's and
children's gowns, sleeves to be attached to a bodice, gigantic hat
brims, and other elements.*

*The wentke, or woman's gown,
shown here is typical of Hindeloopen,
once an important anchorage for sea
traders. The flowers were outlined in
black, and, after extensive resist was
applied, the fabric was dyed several
shades of blue. Because the pattern
repeats, we can assume a stencil was
initially used to apply the designs.
The garment is lined with plain linen
and has a decorative tape along the
front opening and cuffs.*

*The limited number of colors indi-
cates that this gown was worn by a
woman in mourning. According to
the local custom, the sequence of
costume colors within such a period,
which could last eight years,[1] pro-
gressed from dark blue or black to
dark blue mixed with light blue, then
to white with, little by little, red. In
the final stages, blue almost completely gives way to red.[2]*

*The extensive costume collection
preserved in the Fries Museum at
Leeuwarden shows that these garments were cut from palampore and
yardage specifically made to be tailored. Wealthy families seem to have
stored great quantities of the Indian
textiles for making the costumes long
after the cloth was actually patterned
in India. This practice exemplifies
why costume evidence often does not
help in dating a textile pattern.*

Indian Ocean.[6] The textiles of this trade were calicoes and muslins, but, like the goods for the eastern trade, these too were "tailored" to the market preference. In 1664 the English would report
that cotton cloth for the markets of Persia, Basra, and Mocha would
not sell there unless starched and glazed as smooth as paper.

Cottons for Europe

When the English and the Dutch entered the area in the seventeenth century, they also vied to become traders in this area. The
English in particular needed a share in the commerce of Indian
goods to the West because the Dutch had largely preempted the
more lucrative trade in the Spice Islands and would eventually
monopolize the trade with Japan. The English thus sought to increase their capital by becoming a carrier of Indian products in
Asia and by exporting Indian textiles, already familiar in the Levant, to London for reexport to the eastern Mediterranean.[7] Expanding the areas of transshipment to Europe, Africa, and the New
World, as well as thinking of a home market, was only a small
step. In 1609 the English buyer in India was already recommending
that the company directors buy not only muslins for the North
African trade but also goods that would sell for sheeting; quilts
ready made of white, red, or blue calico; and pintados for quilts
and fine hangings.[8] This buyer, William Finch, proved quite accurate but was somewhat ahead of his time. A steady increase in
the imports of calico to England ensued, from the 14,000 pieces
in 1619 to 120,000 pieces in 1630 (each 12 to 15 yards long).[9] In
England and on the continent, these pieces competed with German, Scotch, and French linens.

The Dutch also had a weaving tradition in linens. Their early
interest in imports of cotton goods was consequently directed toward Guinea cloths for reexport or cottons for inexpensive household needs—towels, tablecloths, rugs, and upholstery.[10] In 1650
their records showed imports numbering 55,128 pieces; a forty-
year history of gross profits ranges from 150 to 240 percent per
season.[11]

In the last half of the seventeenth century there was a dramatic
shift in this trade. Starting in the 1660s, a quickening interest in
cottons gripped the European markets, building into a "boom in
the 1680s."[12] It is worth citing Chaudhuri's work on the details of
this demand: "In 1664 the total quantities of calico imported by
the English Company stood at well over a quarter of a million
pieces and their value accounted for 73 percent of the entire trade
of the Company. In two decades the first figure had climbed to
more than a million and a half pieces, and the relative share of
textiles in total value had also increased to 83 percent."[13]

A major cause of this expansion was the acceptance of the imported cottons as clothing rather than just as household furnishings. This was first experienced, by 1683, in Holland where Indian
cottons were described as "being the ware of gentlewomen...."[14]
So strong was this demand that it brought about a change in the
buying patterns of both the English and Dutch companies, forcing
them to turn from the coarser textiles to more refined products.[15]

151 Fragment (detail)
Coromandel Coast, ca. 1750
Cotton; drawn resist, painted
  mordants, dyed
Red, violet, blue, yellow, green
99 cm x 61 cm
Cooper-Hewitt Museum, The
Smithsonian Institution's National
Museum of Design, New York,
1952-113-1. Pauline Riggs Noyes
Fund

152 Fragment
Coromandel Coast; 18th century
Cotton; drawn resist, painted
  mordant, dyed; partially quilted
Red, purple, blue, yellow, green
56 cm x 90 cm
Indianapolis Museum of Art 33.1247.
  The Eliza M. and Sarah L. Niblack
  Collection

The appearance of endless originality is evoked by the arching branches, leaves, and flowers of these textile fragments. Yet the repeat of a given element can be identified approximately 81 cm apart in Figure 151 and 45 cm apart in Figure 152. To effect the repeat, the artist probably created a stencil. He would draw the design on paper, then pierce the outlines with pins to create small holes, and subsequently dust the stencil with fine charcoal. After this process, the outlines on the textile could be enhanced by additional drawing or could be outlined with the mordant directly. The drawing of resist details and the subsequent painting of the mordants—with the inevitable variation such hand work would lend—endowed the stenciled figures with an original aura.

Such patterns were particularly appropriate for the Dutch market; the fragment in Figure 151 is quite similar to a textile in the Rijksmuseum in Amsterdam (no. 1976–138). That Dutch example carries a 1775 date but is believed to have been made slightly earlier.[3] Here the leaves and petals of flowers and the foliage are filled with a network of details worked with both mordants and fine wax-resist details. Alice Beer has suggested that "the richness and yet delicacy of this pattern recalls that favorite seventeenth-century phrase, 'curious and lively colors.'"[4]

In Figure 152 the design elements are strongly outlined and have a bold quality. Reds and purples are the dominant colors of the flowers except for some smaller blossoms, possibly cornflowers, that are rendered in a startling electric blue. This fragment, created from two pieces joined together, may have been part of a quilt. It is padded and stitched through most of its area and has two small figures, possibly initials, worked in cross stitch. Alternatively, it could have been part of a petticoat.[5]

Although often cited by other writers, the quotations of the time are too delightful not to repeat:

1683, London to India:
You cannot imagine what a great number of the chintzes would sell here, they being the ware of gentlewomen in Holland. Make great provisions of them beforehand; 200,000 of all sorts in a year will not be too much for this market, if the directions be punctually observed in the providing of them. . . .

Send us therefore 100 suits of painted curtains and vallances ready made up of severall sorts and prices, strong, but none too deare, nor any over mean in regard; you know that only the poorest people of England lie without any curtains or vallances and our richest in damask, etc. The vallance to be 1 foot deep and 6½ yds. compass. Curtains to be from 8 to 9 feet deep, the 2 lesser curtains each 1½ yds. wide, the 2 larger curtains to be 3½ yds. wide. The tester and Head-piece proporconable. A Counterpane of the same work to be 3½ yds. wide and 4 yds. long, halfe of them to be quilted and the other halfe not quilted. Each bed to have to it 2 small carpets 1½ yds. wide and 2 yds. long. Each bed to have 12 cushions for chairs of the same work; by the ships you shall have variety of patterns and further directions, but be doing what you can in the meantime. . . ."[16]

1686, London to India:
You may exceed our former orders in Chintz broad of all sorts, whereof some be of grave and cloth colours, with the greatest variety you can invent, they being become the weare of ladyes of the greatest quality, which they wear on the outside of Gowns Mantuoes which they line with velvet and cloth of gold.[17]

1693, London to India:
As much variety as may be, but 50 at least of each work, some purple, and some dark grounds, some red grounds and a few green; but the greatest quantities white grounds, some purple flowered, some red flowers. Note, half the quantity upon stripes, and half upon flowers and some both striped and flowered.[18]

1693, London to Masulipatam. An order for 17,000 piece goods and palampores of very fine painting:
The finest that can be made, done by the neatest hands that can be got upon fine thick cloth such as Sallempores, Moorees, Longcloth . . . as much vanity of works of the Country's invention—nothing like English. Be sure the "Chay" on the paint be the best that can be done. . . .[19]

1699, from a broadside published in London:
It was scarce thought about twenty years since that we should ever see Calicoes, the ornaments of our greatest Gallants (for such they are whether we call them Muslins, Shades or anything else) when they were then rarely used . . . but now few think themselves well dressed till they are made up in Calicoes, both men and women. Calico Shirts, Neckcloths, Cuffs, Pocket-handkerchiefs for the former, Head-Dresses, Night-royls, Hoods, Sleeves, Aprons, Gowns, Petticoats, and what not, for the latter, besides India-Stockings for both Sexes. . . .[20]

The history of the trade in Indian dyed cotton textiles to Europe in the seventeenth century is one of ever increasing quantities and splendor—from mundane toweling and simple Guinea stuffs to household furnishings and, finally, high fashion.

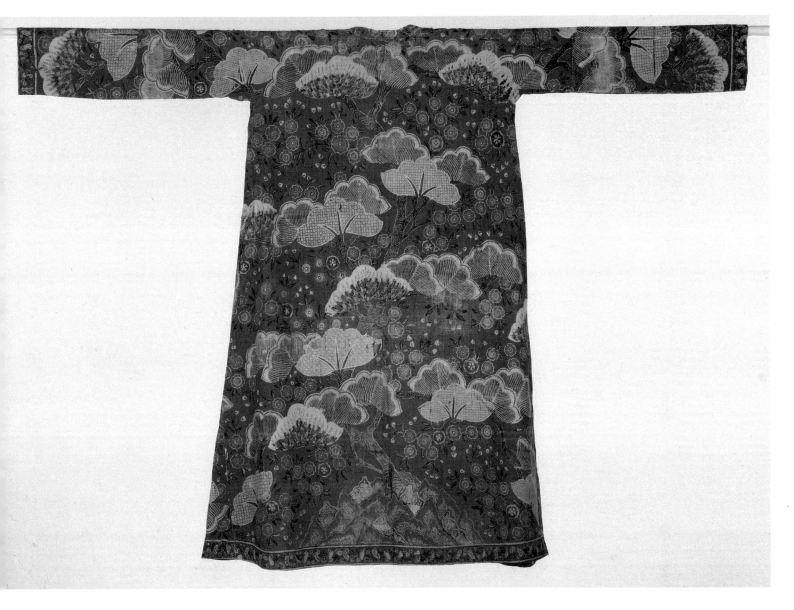

153 **Man's gown**
Coromandel Coast, early 18th century
Cotton; drawn resist, painted
  mordants, dyed
Red, violet, blue, black-violet
Center back length 130 cm, sleeve
  width between cuffs 190 cm
Royal Ontario Museum, Toronto
  959.112

This magnificent morning gown is a brilliant example of the Indian craftsman's skill in patterning for a specific garment. A great flowering tree rises from a rocky mound on the back and "spreads up to the shoulders, down the sleeves, and across the fronts."[6] The tree was designed to fit the garment, as were the narrow borders of the waist, the hem, and the front opening.

The design is of pine trees and plum blossoms, a favored combination (usually together with bamboo) in Japanese symbolism. It is thought that this design and its spatial arrangement is an adaptation of a type of Japanese kimono, and that even the cross-hatching and wavy line worked by an iron mordant on the pine boughs derive from Japanese patterns done by tie-dye work.[7] The original kimono that served as the pattern probably came to the Coromandel Coast through the Dutch, who retained a monopoly on the trade with Japan. Very probably the textile of the gown was created in one of the Dutch enclaves—either Pulicat or the vicinity of Negapatam in the south. It would be the same area that made the palampore of Figure 158, which shows similar plum blossoms and owes an obvious debt to Japanese textile design.

155 *This blossoming tree—part of a pierced stone screen at the tomb of Dada Hari (ca. 1435) in Ahmedabad—was a design familiar to artists in western India. Examples such as* this probably served as inspiration for tree designs on the earliest mordant-worked cotton bedcovers and hangings that were sent to Europe. (Mattiebelle Gittinger, Washington, D.C.)

156 *Many types and styles of trees were rendered on the monuments of Ahmedabad and its environs in the fifteenth century. The examples given here and in Figure 155 illustrate the importance and versatility of this motif that also came to dominance as a textile theme. This carving appears on the Jami Masjid built by Sultan Ahmad II (ca. 1424). (Mattiebelle Gittinger, Washington, D.C.)*

◀ 154 **Palampore** (bedcover) **fragment**
Coromandel Coast, ca. 1700
Cotton; drawn resist, painted
   mordants, dyed
Red, violet, blue, yellow, black
Warp 248.8 cm, weft 124.5 cm
Victoria and Albert Museum, London
   I.S. 119–1950

The sinuous tree hung with exotic blossoms and foliage is one of the most readily recognized patterns in Indian chintz. In the search for the origin of the motif, much weight has been given to European crewel-work embroidery patterns and Chinese painting and embroidery.[8] Clearly the pattern is a hybrid that evolved from several lines and, once given form, continued to change in response to the demands of contemporary fashion. It seems likely that the tree with ornate foliage, a well-established motif in Indian art before the arrival of Western Europeans, acquired a more elaborate assortment of flower heads and greater dominance on the cloth surface through Mughal and European influences.

In this example, the larger diameter of the curving tree trunk, the generous number of flowers and leaves and their large scale, and the careful irregularity of the rocky mound all suggest that the textile belongs to the early eighteenth century. In later examples only a few blossoms are spread over a more open, sinuous tree, and the mound becomes a series of serrated peaks.

This palampore also recalls an important historical note in the record of chintz collecting. It was part of the collection of G. P. Baker, one of the first Englishmen to value and collect the painted cottons of India as artistic works. His *Calico Painting and Printing in the East Indies in the 17th and 18th Centuries, which features his collection, remains an important resource for historians. When the bombing of England in World War II endangered his collection, he stored the textiles in tin boxes in a pit in his garage. Corrosion from the boxes seriously damaged the cottons, and it was only through extensive restoration by the Victoria and Albert Museum, which received the holding, that these remain to us today. The only comparable collection is that made by Harry Wearne, a textile and paper designer, who acquired examples after World War I. The Wearne collection is now at the Royal Ontario Museum in Toronto.[9]*

157

158

157 Palampore (bedcover)
Coromandel Coast, first half of 18th
 century
Cotton; drawn resist, painted
 mordants, dyed
Red, purple, blue, yellow, green, black
Warp 310 cm, weft 220 cm
Fries Museum, Leeuwarden, the
 Netherlands no. 1181D

*This palampore is remarkable for its
vivid colors. Their brilliance gives us
an idea of why the seventeenth and
eighteenth century Europeans were
first stunned by, then enamored with,
the dyed cotton textiles of India. The
rich purple, here forming the background, was a color of fashion and
taste. It is not unusual in Indian textiles now in collections in the Netherlands, and there are cargo invoices
for Philadelphia-bound goods in 1739
and 1742 that stress the desire for
dark purple grounds.[10] The large flowers and foliage that fill the ground
have been finely worked by a wax resist that has left thin white lines and
tiny floral patterns on petals and
leaves. The border and guard stripes
are virtually identical to those of the
textile in Figure 159.*

158 Palampore (bedcover)
Coromandel Coast, first half of 18th
 century
Cotton; drawn resist, painted
 mordants, dyed
Rose, pink, purple, blue, yellow, black
292 cm x 187 cm
Gemeentemuseum de Hidde Nijland
 Stichting, Hindeloopen, the
 Netherlands 131

*With its large center medallion and
corner segments, the basic format of
this palampore resembles that of a
Persian carpet. It is probable that
similar configurations on cotton textiles were used as floor spreads in India and that these patterns were then
adapted for the Western bedcovers
(and possibly table spreads).*
*The filling within this Persian for-
mat, however, originates in entirely
different sources. Here meandering
rose-colored forms drift across a
white, flower-strewn field. The rose
areas are regularly patterned with a
black, undulating line outlined by
white resist work that suggests water;
in contrast, different types of flowers
and foliage fill the white ground.
Birds in a variety of poses enliven the
surface. Designs of this type are
thought to have an origin in Japanese
painted and stenciled cottons of the
Okinawa school.[11] This Japanese influence is also evident in the man's
morning gown of Figure 153, which
carries a flower, thought to be a plum
blossom, that is quite similar to
those on this textile.*

Textiles to Decorate

The notable items among the furnishings were the bed hangings,
quilts, and wall hangings. Wall hangings seem to have been sent
to England early in the seventeenth century. According to the research of Irwin and Brett,[21] in the time of their use there were
three different types: designs in which human figures predominated, a large vertical flower cluster framed with borders similar
to the Indian tent hangings, Figure 70, and the overall patterning
of floral scrolls. In time, chintz hangings became a part of coor-
dinated sets that decorated entire rooms; a set would include hangings, curtains, carpets, canopy, and valance.[22]

As shown in the 1683 order from London, chintz bed hangings
were ready-made in India and sent to Europe. Before this, at least
by 1623, cottons patterned in India had certainly been used as bed
hangings[23] and curtains that hung from and enclosed the large
English four-poster beds for both warmth and privacy.

The "painted" and embroidered quilts that had attracted the
admiration of the first European voyagers to India are found in the
early import lists, but they give way by 1687 to the more popular
palampore.[24] This word enters our language from the Hindi and
Persian word *palang posh*, "bed cover,"[25] and is used to designate
a single chintz panel. The designs on these resembled the quilts
and had as their format a center field containing a central medallion with related corner quadrants, a format that recalls certain
Persian carpets.

By the second half of the seventeenth century the taste expressed on the part of the London office, presumably reflecting
their buyers' preferences, selected and gave guidance for the making of palampore with "branched hangings." By the turn of the
century, it has been suggested, this became the flowery tree, or
"tree of life," we associate with Indian chintz. Irwin at one time
proposed that ultimately this was a hybrid principally inspired by
Persian miniatures, English crewel embroidery patterns, and European chinoiserie.[26] Certainly the huge blossoming flowers that
wreath the curving tree limbs on these palampore suggest a European contribution. In parts of western India where many of the
early quilts and hangings were "painted," however, there existed
a long and important tradition of tree motifs. These remain visible,
now as then, in the pierced stone screens and carved stone reliefs
of early fifteenth century tombs and mosques of Ahmedabad, Figures 155 and 156.[27] Even at that time, the designs are mature artistic expressions reflecting a still more ancient past. That the
tradition endured can be seen in the beautiful stone screens of the
Sidi Sayyid mosque carved at the beginning of the sixteenth century. This was not an isolated occurrence, for Percy Brown says
similar motifs were created at the same time in Bengal.[28] It is much
more probable that the earliest mordant-painted Indian quilts that
went to Europe, of which there is only literary evidence, carried
designs related to these screens, and that these quilts provided the
models that were later adjusted by the English company to suit
the European market. Recorded, too, is that the company asked
for the central placing of a single form and the rendering of the

designs on a white rather than red or green ground. It is possible that the earlier palampore had one or more trees oriented upright on each of the four sides of the cloth. This format would be desirable if the cloth were to be used on a bed or as a floor spread, but fabric to be hung as a drapery or bed curtain would require a single design orientation.

In the course of the eighteenth century this strong, vigorous tree with its voluptuous flowers is transformed through designs found on French and Chinese textiles (as well as on Chinese wallpapers) to a thin, angular tree on a stylized mound or to a sinuous plant with smaller blossoms.[29] The broad borders that frame the center field change from luxuriously blossoming vines to routinely patterned swags.

The motif of a single dominant tree that developed through the eighteenth century did not eclipse other styles of hangings and palampore. The painted cottons structured with a centered medallion and corner details, as well as those with uninterrupted floral patterning, continued in the eighteenth century. In the medallion type, however, large mixed floral bouquets, in vases or tied with trailing ribbons, might now appear in the center and corners. According to Irwin and Brett, the extensive crosshatching and washes or shading that characterize some of these indicate they derived from European engravings. Brett has even identified the English work *The Twelve Months of Flowers*, a set of engravings from 1730, as the inspiration for the "bouquets" used in certain palampore.[30]

There were several variations of the palampore format, one of which has been called the coat-of-arms, or heraldic, chintz.[31] In place of the center medallion and corner segments there appear family or city coats-of-arms. These may be on a plain or flower-strewn ground. The very earliest we know of the creation of a coat-of-arms on cloth for a European was the sample sent in 1613 or 1614 by the Dutch company director on the Coromandel Coast to his superior in Java.[32] The majority of these, however, were made in the first half of the eighteenth century for families in the Netherlands,[33] although a few with English and French heraldic devices are known. Examples of this type also exist that have an armorial device with blank shields. These were presumably to be completed in Europe by painting or embroidering details of the specific crest of a buyer.

Cotton for Costume

In time some of the palampore and hangings were cut to make garments. Indeed, some of the earliest surviving garments from the Netherlands seem to have been tailored from these furnishings.[34] India also sent to Europe patterned yardage and textiles painted in a manner characteristic of a specific garment—for example, patterning to suit the border of a petticoat. The Dutch initiated the use of chintz in high fashion, although as early as 1661 chintz morning gowns were used by men in England.[35] As the "Indian craze" took hold in northern Europe in the 1680s and continued into the eighteenth century, the designs available in

160   Detail of Figure 159.

◄ 159   **Fragment** (part of palampore
[bedcover] or hanging)
Coromandel Coast, first half 18th
  century
Cotton; drawn resist, painted
  mordants, dyed
Red, purple, brown, blue, green
289 cm x 137 cm (includes border
  added)
Cooper-Hewitt Museum, The
  Smithsonian Institution's National
  Museum of Design, New York
  1959-146-1. Au Panier Fleuri Fund

This fragment is composed of two
different textiles, a center field and a
border sewn on the left and bottom
margins. Each of the pieces was probably made originally for the Dutch
market, but that they were meant to
be joined is doubtful. More probably
the border completed a bedcover similar to that in Figure 157, which has
virtually identical borders and guard
stripes.

In the center field of this example,
design elements—a wind-bent tree
and long-legged wading birds perched
on rocks or near a pool—have been
grouped and repeated in stepped intervals on a brilliant red ground. In
all, there are three basic patterns
used as repeats. In one, the birds are
beneath a pine tree, which is rendered in a Japanese style. In a second, a bird flies toward a pool lined
with waterweeds in which another
bird nests. The third segment of the
pattern is created by stylized rocks. It
is thought that these designs were inspired by Japanese painted and sten-

ciled cottons from Okinawa.[12]

Comparison of the fine details
within the repeated arrangements reveals that, although a pattern (probably a stencil) dictated the shapes, the
dyer with his brush and resist pen
created the details. He probably had
the aid of a finished textile or
painted guide for these shapes, but
not a given line to follow.

These small filler patterns, or
closely related ones, also seem to
have been used on textiles traded to
Indonesia. In the north-coast Javanese batiks, at least, we find them
favored as design elements serving a
similar function as filler to larger
forms. Certain artistic conventions
used to designate rocks in this Indian
textile also seem to have been taken
into particular Javanese batik patterns. These points are only minor
details for comparison, but there is
on the whole an extensive correspondence between the textiles of the
Coromandel Coast and Java that remains to be examined.

chintz patterns also broadened. Irwin and Brett believe that much of this increased vocabulary of textile design was the result of flowered silks and printed cottons and linens being sent from Europe to be copied by Indian painters and dyers.[36] What can be seen in the evidence left today is often a fanciful amalgamation of motifs from East and West.[37]

It was natural for these fashionable Indian chintz to find a trade from England to the American colonies. This started at least by the late seventeenth century,[38] and, by the eighteenth century, records show that some cottons were traded along most of the American coast. A Philadelphia Quaker merchant, placing an order in London in 1739, requested:

> 100 pieces purple (each 18 yards) Small Sprigg & Spots, the darker the purple and the fuller the stamp, the better. Light purples and them that have a great deal of white in 'em, are not liked. The last was a handsome parcel in general; From what I have said don't send black & white . . . ."[39]

By 1700, men (particularly in the southern colonies) had adopted a patterned cotton dressing gown called a nightgown, Indian robe, or *banyan* that was worn beyond the confines of the house and was judged to be "shocking clothes for gentlemen" by visitors to the area.[40]

The Reaction to Indian Cottons

After the Revolution, American ships traded for pepper directly with North Sumatra. This region had served for more than two centuries as an entrepot for Indian textiles desired in the Asian trade, and some textiles surely returned to the Americas by this trade. The esteem given the Indian textiles is shown by the number that remain in museums and historic houses and also by evidence of the first textile printing and blocking done in the Americas, which imitated Indian palampore in important ways.[41] In absolute quantities, however, the trade of fancy piece goods to the limited population in the Americas was scarcely significant in comparison with the trade to Europe.

The great influx of Indian cottons into England, France, the Netherlands, and Switzerland was not greeted with unanimous pleasure. Particularly in the first two countries, where sizable wool or silk industries (or both) felt threatened, workers and their supporters clamored for laws forbidding the import of Eastern textiles. A prohibition was enacted by France in 1686 that seems to have been somewhat effective. An English law passed in 1700 that forbade the import of chintz was ineffective because chintz was allowed entry for reexport purposes; means of evading the law were therefore numerous. A subsequent law in 1720 tried to solve the problem by banning the use of chintz in wearing apparel and household furnishings, but this restriction was also largely ignored. In the Netherlands the overlapping commercial interests between the owners of the V.O.C. and the cloth producers forestalled such laws, and here, as in England, Indian cottons remained in fashion throughout the eighteenth century.

India's position as supplier of high-quality cotton textiles was eventually doomed by a combination of complex factors. Indigo and cotton plantations were founded in the New World. The Industrial Revolution in Britain gave rise to new machines that could spin and weave. Chemists in Europe were inspired to create new dyes; inventors devised new printing processes, and, finally, a short-sighted English colonial policy favored development of a home industry. All combined to eclipse India's preeminence as supplier to the world of brilliantly patterned cotton textiles. At one time this had created a virtual floral paradise for the West, highly glazed sashes for the Middle East, muted prayer spreads for Persia, and a host of variation for the East—from small, meticulously patterned textiles to bold geometric forms. The heritage from these centuries has now been subsumed into the national and ethnic design vocabularies of peoples around the world. It was the major contributing strain in what we label "English chintz," "Javanese batiks," and the like. It is a rich source that contemporary designers and—now, more than ever—the Indians themselves reach back to examine for inspiration as India once more strives to become a major supplier of quality cotton textiles to world markets.

NOTES TO TEXT

1. Steensgaard 1974:410.
2. Moreland 1975:55.
3. Chaudhuri 1978:277.
4. Gopal 1975:9ff.
5. Purchas X:90, Caesar Frederici cited in Gopal 1975:17.
6. Gopal 1975:22ff.
7. Chaudhuri 1978:12.
8. Finch, cited in Moreland 1975:125.
9. Moreland 1975:126–27.
10. Glamann 1958:133. Guinea cloth was 30 to 40 yards long.
11. Ibid.:137.
12. Chaudhuri 1978:282 and Glamann 1958:143.
13. Chaudhuri 1978:292.
14. Slomann 1953:115.
15. Glamann 1958:141–42, 145.
16. Cited in Baker 1921:33.
17. Ibid.
18. Ibid.
19. Ibid.
20. J. Cary, *A Discourse Concerning the East India Trade*, 1699, p. 4, cited in Slomann 1953:104 fn. 1.
21. Irwin and Brett 1970:24.
22. Ibid.:22.
23. Ibid.:25.
24. Ibid.:27.
25. Yule and Burnell 1979:662.
26. Irwin and Brett 1970:16ff. In December 1980, Irwin indicated to the author that he no longer entirely agreed with his earlier argument.
27. Some of the artistic conventions expressed in the tree on the palampore may be seen in the trees in the border of the Devasano Pado Bhandar manuscript of 1475. Here the tree trunks are filled with erratic circles and wavy, sinuous lines just as on the textiles (Khandalavala and Chandra 1969:Fig. 88).

28. Brown 1942:58.
29. Irwin and Brett 1970:Pls. 43–49.
30. Brett 1955:40–53.
31. Hartkamp-Jonxis 1980:7 and Irwin and Brett 1970:Pl. 70.
32. Raychaudhuri 1962:145.
33. Hartkamp-Jonxis 1980:7, 8.
34. Irwin and Brett 1970:33.
35. Ibid.:30.
36. Ibid.:33.
37. Examples are presented in Jonxis 1970:37ff.
38. Beer 1970:35.
39. John Reynell 1739:letter. This excerpt was brought to my attention through the original research of Leanna Lee-Whitman, Curatorial Assistant, INA Corporation Museum, Philadelphia.
40. Pettit 1970:91.
41. Ibid.:168, 173.

NOTES TO ILLUSTRATIONS

1. Wille-Engelsma 1979:3.
2. Ibid.
3. C.A. Burger, Curator, Rijksmuseum, Amsterdam, March 1982:personal communication.
4. Beer 1970:85.
5. Peggy Gilfoy, Curator, Indianapolis Museum of Art, April 1982:personal communication.
6. Brett 1960:42.
7. Ibid.:45.
8. Irwin and Brett 1970:16ff.
9. Irwin and Brett 1970:vii.
10. Leanna Lee-Whitman, Curatorial Assistant, INA Corporation Museum, Philadelphia, April 1982:personal communication.
11. Irwin and Brett 1970:105.
12. Irwin and Brett 1970:105 and Beer 1970:77.

Pictorial Supplement

While most contemporary dyers use petroleum-based dyes, they continue to follow many ancient procedures recognizable from the eighteenth century descriptions. The following photographs illustrate a few of today's scenes.

161   *A washer beats a cloth on a flat stone at the river's edge while other textile lengths, anchored to stones, soak in the running water behind him. All newly purchased cloth, called grey cloth, is bleached with dung and soaked in water to remove traces of sizing as a preparation for dyeing. (Photographs by Mattiebelle Gittinger unless otherwise noted.)*

162   *Textiles are further prepared for dyeing by repeated soaking in a myrabolan solution, which gives the textile an ocher color.*

163   *Black outlines are stamped on the cloth.*

164 *A mordant is stamped within and around the outlines, which will give a red ground to the textile when it is dyed.*

165 *In some areas, such as Deesa in northern Gujarat, mud is stamped on parts of the design to act as a resist in a subsequent dye bath.*

167 *To enhance a textile after dyeing, an adhesive may be stamped on the surface and "gold dust" pounced through a bag as shown here. (Courtesy of Carol Westfall, Montclair, New Jersey.)*

166 *Recently worked textiles are "cured" on the broad riverbanks at each stage in the dyeing.*

168 A relatively simple design may require four or more stamps to create the desired effect.
a. One block creates the outline, usually stamped in black.
b. One block is used to stamp the background color.
c. One block fills the flowers and buds with a color.
d. Another block fills the leaves and flowers.
e. All four blocks coincide to create a pleasing composition.

a

b

c

d

e

169 Instead of stamping, designs may be drawn on the cloth with the kalam. The ball of fibers, such as hair, wrapped around the core acts as a reservoir to hold the dye, mordant, or wax. Gentle pressure squeezes the liquid to the drawing point. (Courtesy of Carol Westfall, Montclair, New Jersey.)

170

171

172

173

In the following abbreviated sequence, Mohammad Siddik of Dhamadkha, near Bhuj, demonstrates the procedure for decorating a textile with wax resist.

170   A flat, slightly moist bed of sand is prepared as the work surface before beginning the resist work.

171   The prepared cloth is stretched on the sand, and the margins and center field are stamped with molten wax. The wax penetrates to the reverse of the cloth, thus acting as a resist on both faces.

172   The textile is dyed and a second layer of wax stamped to reserve certain red and white areas.

173   A final blue dye bath completes the coloring. The wax will be melted off and the textile washed, then cured in the sun.

In Ahmedabad a few families of printers and dyers still create traditional religious screens called *matano candarvo* with depictions of the mother goddess. Formerly an itinerant community, these Vaghris now live near the central post office and use the nearby broad sidewalk as their work space to draw, stamp, and mordant-paint their hangings.

174 *Stamps are used to create the black outlines of the figures.*

175 *Intervals between the black outlines are filled by a mordant for red. Here a child applies the mordant with a brush created from the frayed end of a stick.*

176 *This textile, originating in the nineteenth century, is one of the oldest matano candarvo remaining. It is in the collection of the Museum für Volkerkunde, Vienna. (Courtesy of Museum für Völkerkunde, Vienna.)*

177 *An assortment of matano candarvo define a sacred space around a shrine to the mother goddess as offerings are presented. (Courtesy of Eberhard Fischer, Zurich.)*

174

175

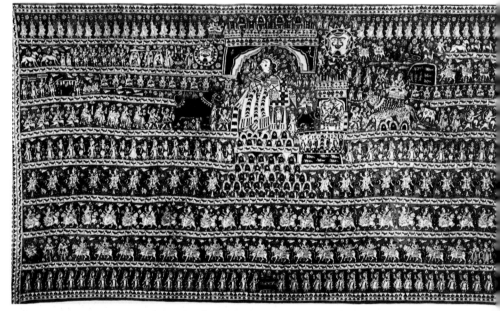

176

177

Glossary

Abra	Principal face of a curtain.
Al, also **ail**	The name in western India for the root of the plant genus *Morinda.* The plant, especially the roots, carries the red dye agent alizarin.
Alizarin	Orange or red crystalline compound prepared from madder and related plants. Acts as a red dye agent.
Bandhana, also **bandhani,** also **bandh**	Process of tying off areas of a textile or yarns to reserve them from a dye solution. Compare with ikat; see also plangi.
Batik	Resist-dye process in which wax is applied to cloth surface. When dyed, patterns are reserved in the color of the foundation. For more than one color, sequences of waxing and dyeing are used.
Buta, also **buti**	Small decorative motif usually associated with the Mughal period. Sometimes the shape is described as a cone or mango.
Chakram	Tamil for disk, symbol, and weapon of the Hindu god Vishnu. Also called *sudarsana* or *vajra-nabha.*
Chay	Plant, *Oldenlandia umbellata,* of the Kistna River delta, Ceylon, and parts of south India; known for the red dye contained in the roots.
Chhatri	Kiosk, or small pavilion, on roof of a building.
Chintz	Mordant-worked and dyed cotton textile; from the Indian *chitta,* "spotted cloth." In English has come to mean a highly glazed, floral printed cotton used in household furnishings.
Chippa, also **chhippa**	One who prints cloth.
Chit, also **chhit,** also **chitte**	Term in the seventeenth and eighteen century textile trade to designate mordant-worked and dyed cotton textiles. From the Indian *chitta,* "spotted cloth."
Choli	Tightly tailored blouse worn in India.
Chunari	Rajasthani word for *bandhana.* See bandhana.
Dargah	Muslim shrine or tomb of note.
Dhoti	Man's wrapper. Although both *dhoti* and *lungi* are worn about the hips, the *dhoti* is longer and is pulled through the legs.
Dupatta	Shawl worn over head and shoulder. May be appropriate for men and women, depending on the custom of the region.
Gajasinha	Mythological animal with the body of a lion and the trunk of an elephant.
Ghaghara, also **ghaghra**	Woman's skirt common in north and northwest India.
Gopura	Storied, monumental gateway of south Indian temple, palace, or city.
Halda	The tumeric plant, *Curcuma domestica.* The plant has a rhizome that carries a yellow coloring agent used as a fugitive dye.
Hamsa	Goose. Early textile pattern represented in murals, miniatures, and textile fragments found in Fostat in Egypt. It is the vehicle of the Hindu god Brahma.

Ikat	"String" or "band," from the Indonesian *mengikat*, "to tie" or "to bind." Term applied to resist-dye process in which designs are reserved in warp or weft yarns by tying off small bundles of yarns with palm leaf strips or similar material to prevent penetration of dye. Resists are cut away, or new ones are added for each color, or both. After dyeing, all resists are cut away, leaving pattern yarns ready for weaving. Process may be applied either to warp or weft yarns, or, as on Bali, to both. Latter process is called "double ikat."
Jama	Man's tight-fitting gown or coat.
Kain	Indonesian term for a length of cloth used as a hip wrapper.
Kalamkari	Worked with a pen, or *kalam*. Refers to textiles with hand-applied rather than stamped mordants.
Khanjar	Type of Indian dagger.
Lungi	Man's straight hip wrapper.
Manjeet, also munjeet	Plant, *Rubia munjista*, of the madder family.
Mordant	Chemical that serves to fix a dye in or on a substance by combining with the dye to form an insoluble compound.
Mudra	Explicatory hand gestures seen in Indian dance, sculpture, painting, and the like.
Odhani	Woman's long (ca. 300 cm) shawl worn over the head and shoulders. One end may be tucked into the skirt waistband. Common in north and northwest India.
Palampore, also palempore	From *palang-posh*, "bedcover."
Pallava, also pallav, also palla	Decorative ends of an odhani or patka; also used to designate the decorative end of a sari.
Pan	Refreshment of chopped areca nut, lime paste, and various spices, all wrapped in betel leaf.
Patka	Waistband or girdle tied in front.
Patola (pl.), **patolu**(s)	Double-ikat textile. Important in western India and in trade to Indonesia.
Peshwa	From the Persian, "leader" or "guide." Chancellor.
Pichwai, also pichhavai	Hanging for a shrine of Vallabhacharya sect of the Hindu god Vishnu.
Pintado	From the Portuguese *pinta*, "spot or fleck." Used in trade records of the seventeenth and eighteenth century to designate a mordant-worked and dyed textile.
Plangi	From the Indonesian word for rainbow. A resist-dye process in which small areas of textile are bound off by cord or string to reserve the area from dye. Patterns are generally built up from small circular forms. Name probably originates in colorful nature of these textiles. Compare with ikat; see also bandhana.
Pounce	To transfer a pattern by dusting fine charcoal through a perforated pattern or stencil.
Purdah	Rules of seclusion observed by some upper-class Indian women.
Qanat, also kanat	Portable screen, also tent wall.
Rumal	Small cloth square.
Sangu	Tamil for conch, symbol of the Hindu god Vishnu. Also called *panchajanya*.
Sapan, also sappan	Small tree, *Caesalpinia sappan*, yielding a red dye that is fugitive on cotton; also called "brazilwood."
Saranguy	Dye derived from the roots of *Morinda citrifolia*, or the closely related *M. tinctoria*.
Sarasa, also sarassa, also serassah	Specific type of textile or garment included in the seventeenth and eighteenth century trade lists to Asia. Today the term designates mordant-worked and dyed cotton textile.

Sikhara	Towering roof of Hindu temple sanctuary.
Surahi	Persian vessel for drink.
Tapis	Woman's sarong. Used here to designate a length of cotton textile worn as a hip wrapper in Southeast Asia.
Tiruchurnam	Middle stroke, usually red, in the three-pronged sign traced on the image of the Hindu god Vishnu and on the bodies of his followers.
Tumeric, also **turmeric**	Plant, *Curcuma domestica,* known as halda. The rhizome produces a fugitive yellow dye.
Tumpal	Triangular form, usually used as a motif in a row at fringed end of a textile.
Warp	Parallel elements that run longitudinally in loom or fabric.
Weft	Traverse elements in fabric that cross and interwork with warp.
Yalam	Moulding that terminates in yali heads.
Yali	Portrayal of an animal with the body of a lion and the trunk of an elephant, used as an architectural decoration and, occasionally, on textiles.

Bibliography

Abu'l-Fazl
1975   *The A'in-i Akbari.* Trans. H. Blochmann. 2nd ed. Original translation
          1927. Lahore: Qausain.

Adams, Marie Jeanne
1969   *System and Meaning in East Sumba Textile Design: A Study in Tradi-
          tional Indonesian Art.* New Haven: Yale University Press.

Agrawala, V. S.
1959   "References to textiles in Bana's Harshacharita." *Journal of Indian
          Textile History* IV:65–68.

Arasaratnam, S.
1967   "The Dutch East India Company and its Coromandel trade," *Bijdragen
          tot de Taal-, Land- en Volkenkunde* 123:325–46.

Atil, Esin
1978   *The Brush of the Masters: Drawings from Iran and India.* Washington,
          D.C.: Smithsonian Institution, Freer Gallery of Art.

Baker, G. P.
1921   *Calico Painting and Printing in the East Indies in the XVIIth and
          XVIIIth Centuries.* London: E. Arnold.

Barbosa, Duarte
1918–21   *The Book of Barbosa: An Account of the Countries Bordering on the
          Indian Ocean and Their Inhabitants, Written by Duarte Barbosa, and
          Completed about the Year 1518 A.D.* Trans. M. Longworth Dames. 2
          vols. London: Hakluyt Society.

Barrett, Douglas
1958   *Painting of the Deccan, XVI–XVII Century.* London: Faber and Faber.

Barrett, Douglas, and Basil Gray
1978   *Indian Painting.* New York: Skira. Rizzoli.

Beach, Milo C.
1978   *The Grand Mogul: Imperial Painting in India: 1600–1660.* Williams-
          town, Mass.: Clark Art Institute.
1981   *The Imperial Image: Paintings for the Mughal Court.* Washington,
          D.C.: Smithsonian Institution, Freer Gallery of Art.

Beer, Alice Baldwin
1970   *Trade Goods. A Study of Indian Chintz.* Washington, D.C.: Smithson-
          ian Institution.

Birdwood, George C. M.
1880   *The Industrial Arts of India.* London: Chapman and Hall.

Boisselier, Jean
1976   *Thai Painting.* Tokyo: Kodansha International.

Born, Wolfgang
1946   "An Indo-Portuguese painting of the late sixteenth century." *Gazette
          des Beaux-Arts* 30:165–78.

Breck, Joseph
1928   "Four seventeenth-century pintadoes." *Metropolitan Museum Studies*
        I:3–15.

Brennig, Joseph Jerome
1975   *The textile trade of seventeenth-century Northern Coromandel: a
        study of a pre-modern Asian export industry.* Ph.D. dissertation, Uni-
        versity of Wisconsin. Ann Arbor, Mich.: University Microfilms.

Brett, Katharine B.
1955   "An English source of Indian chintz design." *Journal of Indian Textile
        History* I:40–53.
1957   "The flowering tree in Indian chintz." *Journal of Indian Textile His-
        tory* III:45–57.
1959   "Variants of the flowering tree in Indian chintz." *Antiques* LXXV (3):
        278–81.
1960   "The Japanese style in Indian chintz design." *Journal of Indian Textile
        History* V:42–50.

Brown, Percy
1942   *Indian Architecture (The Islamic Period).* Bombay: D. B. Taraporevale
        Sons.

Brunello, Franco
1973   *The Art of Dyeing.* Venice: Neri Pozza Editore.

Bry, Johann Israel de, and Johann Theodor de Bry
1606   *Indiae Orientalis* (Parts II, VII, and VIII). Frankfort.

Bühler, Alfred
1941   "Turkey red dyeing in South and South East Asia." *Ciba Review*
        39:1423–26.
1948   "Primitive dyeing methods." *Ciba Review* 68:2485–2507.
1959   "Patola influences in Southeast Asia." *Journal of Indian Textile His-
        tory* IV:4–46.
1972   *Ikat Batik Plangi.* Basel: Pharos-Verlag Hansrudolf Schwab AG.

Bühler, Alfred, and Eberhard Fischer
1977   *Clamp Resist Dyeing of Fabrics.* Ahmedabad: Calico Museum of Tex-
        tiles.
1979   *The Patola of Gujarat.* 2 vols. Basel: Krebs AG.

Bussagli, Mario, and Calembus Sivaramamurti
1978   *5000 Years of the Art of India.* New York: Harry N. Abrams.

Census of India 1961.
1961   II, part VII-A(1). *Selected Crafts of Andhra Pradesh.* Andhra Pradesh:
        Superintendent of Census Operations.
1961   V, part VII-A. *Selected Crafts of Gujarat.* Gujarat: Superintendent of
        Census Operations.

Chandra, Moti
1973   *Costume Textiles, Cosmetics, and Coiffure in Ancient and Medieval
        India.* Delhi: Indian Archaelogical Society.

Chandra, Moti, and U. P. Shah
1975   *New Documents of Jaina Painting.* Bombay: Shri Mahavira Jaina Vid-
        yalaya Publications.

Chattopadhyay, Kamaladevi
1980   "Handcrafts." In *Splendours of Tamil Nadu,* pp. 125–33. Bombay:
        Marg Publications.

Chaudhuri, K. N.
1978   *The Trading World of Asia and the English East India Company 1660–
        1670.* Cambridge: Cambridge University Press.

Chisholm, R. F.
1876   "Tiroomal Niak's Palace, Madura." In *Sessional Papers of the Royal
        Institute of British Architects 1875–76,* pp. 159–78. London: Institute
        of British Architects.

Cocks, Richard
1615   *Diary of Richard Cocks Cape-Merchant in the English Factory in Ja-
        pan 1615–1622.* 2 vols. Ed. Edward M. Thompson. New York: Burt
        Franklin.

Coomaraswamy, A. K.
1927   "A Hamsa-laksana sari." *Bulletin of Museum of Fine Arts, Boston*
        25:1927.

Cort, Louise Allison
1982   "Gen'ya's devil bucket." *Chanoyu Quarterly,* no. 30:31ff.

Culin, Stewart
1918   "The story of the painted curtain." *Good Furniture Magazine* (Septem-
        ber):133–47.

Cunnington, C. Willet, and Phillis Cunnington
1972a   *Handbook of English Costume in the Sixteenth Century.* London:
        Faber and Faber.
1972b   *Handbook of English Costume in the Seventeenth Century.* London:
        Faber and Faber.

Dam, Pieter van
1932   *Beschryvinge van het Oostindische Compagnie.* The Hague: Martinus
        Nijhoff.

Davenport, Millia
1948   *The Book of Costume.* 2 vols. New York: Crown Publishers.

De Bone, Mary Golden
1976   "Patolu and its techniques." *Textile Museum Journal* IV(3): 49–62.

Devakunjari, D.
1970   *Hampi.* New Delhi: Archaeological Survey of India.

Early Travels in India 1583–1619
1968   Ed. William Foster. New Delhi: S. Chand and Co.

English Factories in India, 1618–1669
1906–27 13 vols. Ed. William Foster. Oxford: Clarendon Press.

Fischer, Eberhard
1980   *Orissa.* Zurich: Museum Rietberg.
1981   *Textiles for the Mother Goddess in India.* Zurich: Museum Rietberg.

Floris, Peter
1934   *Peter Floris, His Voyage to the East in the Globe, 1611–1615.* Ed. W.
        H. Moreland. London: Hakluyt Society.

Forbes, R. J.
1956   *Studies in Ancient Technology.* Vol. IV. Leiden: E. J. Brill.

Fujioka, Ryoichi
1973   *Tea Ceremony Utensils.* Arts of Japan no. 3. Trans. and adapted by
        Louise Allison Cort. New York: Weatherhill.

Gangoly, O. C.
1919   "The story of a cotton printed fabric from Orissa." *The Journal of the
        Bihar and Orissa Research Society* V, Pt. III:325–30.

Gittinger, Mattiebelle
1979   *Splendid Symbols.* Washington, D.C.: The Textile Museum.

Glamann, Kristof
1958   *Dutch-Asiatic Trade 1620–1740.* The Hague: Martinus Nijhoff.

Goodrich, L. Carrington
1942-43 "Cotton in China." *Isis* 34(94, part 5):408–10.

Gopal, Surendra
1975   *Commerce and Crafts in Gujarat, 16th and 17th Centuries.* New
        Delhi: People's Publishing House.

Gopala Rao, Amancharla
1969   *Lepakshi.* Hyderabad: Andhra Pradesh Lalit Kala Akademi.

Gulati, A. N.
1951   *The Patolu of Gujarat.* Bombay: Museums Association of India.

Hadaway, W. S.
1917   *Cotton Painting and Printing in the Madras Presidency.* Madras: Madras Presidency.

Hartkamp-Jonxis, Ebeltje
1980   "Voor-Indische sitsen voor Groninger families." *Vereniging van Vrienden van het Groninger Museum, Bulletin* 6:4–8.

Havart, Daniel
1693   *Op-en Ondergang van Coromandel.* 3 vols. Amsterdam: Jan ten Hoorn.

Heras, Henry
1927   *The Aravidu Dynasty of Vijayanagara.* Vol. I. Madras: B. G. Paul and Co.

Hourgronje, Snouck
1899   Tilburg, The Netherlands. Textile Museum Library Manuscript M241. MT 5–3–4–9 Correspondence 15 November 1899 and 28 June 1900. "Extract brief van den heer Snouck Hourgronje an den heer Rouffaer uit Kotta-Radja 15 November 1899."

Irwin, John
1955   "Indian textile trade in the seventeenth century, (1) western India." *Journal of Indian Textile History* I:5–33.

1956   "Indian textile trade in the seventeenth century, (2) Coromandel Coast." *Journal of Indian Textile History* II:24–42.

1959a   "Golconda cotton paintings of the early seventeenth century." *Lalit Kala* 5:8–48.

1959b   "Indian textile trade in the seventeenth century, (4) foreign influence." *Journal of Indian Textile History* IV:57–64.

1959c   "The etymology of chintz and pintado." *Journal of Indian Textile History* IV:77.

Irwin, John, and Katharine B. Brett
1970   *Origins of Chintz.* London: Her Majesty's Stationery Office.

Irwin, John, and Margaret Hall
1971   *Indian Painted and Printed Fabrics.* Ahmedabad: Calico Museum of Textiles.

Irwin, John, and Paul R. Schwartz
1966   *Studies in Indo-European Textile History.* Ahmedabad: Calico Museum of Textiles.

Jain, Jyotindra
1980   "The painted scrolls of the Baroda picture showmen of Gujarat." *The Journal of the National Centre for the Performing Arts* IX(3):3–23.

Jayakar, Pupul
1955   "A neglected group of Indian ikat fabrics." *Indian Journal of Textile History* I:55–59.

Jonxis, Ebeltje
1970   "Some Coromandel chintzes." *Bulletin of the Needle and Bobbin Club* 53(1, 2):37–57.

Jouveau-Dubreuil, G.
1978   *Iconography of Southern India.* Trans. A. C. Martin. Delhi: Bharatiya Publishing House.

Kaempfer, Engelbert
1906   *The History of Japan.* 2 vols. Glasgow: James Machose and Sons.

Kahlenberg, M. H.
1972   "A study of the development and use of the Mughal patka (sash) with reference to the Los Angeles County Museum of Art collection." In *Aspects of Indian Art.* Ed. Pratapaditya Pal. Leiden: E. J. Brill.

Kamma, F. C.
1970   "A spontaneous 'capitalist' revolution in the Western Vogelkop area of West Irian." In *Anniversary Contributions to Anthropology: Twelve Essays.* Published on the Occasion of the 40th Anniversary of the Leiden Ethnological Society. Leiden: W.D.O.

Khandalavala, Karl J., and Moti Chandra
1969   *New Documents of Indian Painting—A Reappraisal.* Bombay: Prince of Wales Museum of Western India.

Kirtikar, K. R.
1918   *Indian Medicinal Plants.* Allahabad: Sudhindra Nath Basu.

Kramrisch, Stella
1937   *A Survey of Paintings in the Deccan.* London: India Society.

La Loubère, Simon de
1969   *The Kingdom of Siam.* Oxford in Asia Historical Reprints. London: Oxford University Press.

Lach, Donald F.
1965   *Asia in the Making of Europe.* Vol. I. Chicago: University of Chicago Press.
1970   *Asia in the Making of Europe.* Vol. II. Chicago: University of Chicago Press.

Letters Received by the East Indian Company from Its Servants in the East, 1603–1708.
1896–1902   Ed. F. C. Danvers and William Foster. London: Samson Low Marston & Co.

Leur, J. C. van
1960   *Indonesian Trade and Society.* 2nd ed. Bandung, Indonesia: Sumur Bandung.

Linschoten, J. H.
1970   *The Voyage of John Huyghen van Linschoten to the East Indies.* Vols. I and II. Reprint of 1885 edition for Hakluyt Society. Original English translation 1598. Ed. A. C. Burnell and P. A. Tiele. New York: Burt Franklin.

Mehta, R. N.
1957   "Picchavais: temple hangings of the Vallabhacarya sect." *Journal of Indian Textile History* III:4–14.

Mittal, Jagdish
1962   "Telia rumals of Pochampali and Chjirals." *Marg* XV(4):26–29.

Moreland, W. H.
1975   *From Akbar to Aurangzeb.* Reprint of 1923 London edition. New York: AMS Press.
1924–25   "Indian exports of cotton goods in the seventeenth century." *Indian Journal of Economics* V(3):225–45.

Mundy, Peter
1914–19   *The Travels of Peter Mundy, 1634–1638.* London: Hakluyt Society.

Nagaswamy, R.
1980   "Tamil paintings." In *Splendours of Tamil Nadu,* pp. 103–24. Bombay: Marg Publications.

Naqvi, Hameeda Khatoon
1967   "Dyeing of cotton goods in the Mughal Hindustan (1556–1803)." *Journal of Indian Textile History* VII:45–56.
1968   *Mughal Hindustan: Cities and Industries.* Karachi: National Book Foundation.

Natural Dyes of India
1980   All India Handicrafts Board, Government of India. Bangalore: Regional Design and Technical Development Centre.

Nelson, James Henry
1868   *Madura Country.* Madras: William Thomas.

Nooy-Palm, Hetty
1979   "The role of the sacred cloths in the mythology and ritual of the
            Sa'adan-Toraja of Sulawesi, Indonesia." In *Indonesian Textiles.*
            Irene Emery Roundtable on Museum Textiles 1979 Proceedings. Ed.
            Mattiebelle Gittinger, pp. 81–85. Washington, D. C.: The Textile Mu-
            seum.

Pelsaert, Francisco
1925   *Jahangir's India.* The Remonstrantie of Francisco Pelsaert. Trans. W.
            H. Moreland and P. Geyl. Cambridge: Heiffer & Sons.

Pettit, Florence H.
1970   *America's Printed and Painted Fabrics 1600–1900.* New York: Has-
            tings House.

Pfister, R.
1938   *Les Toiles Imprimées de Fostat et l'Hindoustan.* Paris: Les Editions
            d'Art et d'Historie.

Pires, Tomé
1944   *The Suma Oriental of Tomé Pires; an Account of the East from the
            Red Sea to Japan, Written in Malacca and India 1512–1515; and the
            Book of Francisco Rodrigues, Rutter of a Voyage in the Red Sea.* 2
            vols. Ed. and trans. Armando Cortesao. London: Hakluyt Society.

Plinius Secundus, C.
1857   *The Natural History of Pliny.* VI. Trans. John Bostock and H. T. Riley.
            London: Henry G. Bohn.

Pyrard de Laval, F.
1887–89   *The Voyage of François Pyrard of Laval.* 2 vols. Trans. A. Gray. Lon-
            don: Hakluyt Society.

Rawson, C.
1915   *A Dictionary of Dyes, Mordants, Etc.* London: Charles Griffin and Co.

Raychaudhuri, Tapan
1962   *Jan Company in Coromandel, 1605–1690.* The Hague: Martinus
            Nijhoff.

Reade, Brian
1951   *The Dominance of Spain, 1550–1660.* Costume of the Western World
            Series. London: Harrap.

Records of Relations between Siam and Foreign Countries, 1607–1700.
1915   5 vols. Copied from papers preserved in the India Office, London. Bang-
            kok: National Library.

Relations of Golconda
1931   Ed. W. H. Moreland. London: Hakluyt Society.

Reynolds, Graham
1951   *Elizabethan and Jacobean, 1558–1625.* Costume of the Western World
            Series. London: Harrap.

Rouffaer, G. P., and H. H. Juynboll
1900   *Die Indische Batikkunst und ihre Geschichte.* Haarlem: von H. Klein-
            mann and Co.

Rouffaer, G. P., and J. W. Ijzerman
1915   *De Eerste Schipvaart der Nederlanders naar Oost-Indische onder Cor-
            nelis de Houtman 1595–1597.* 3 vols. The Hague: Martinus Nijhoff.

Saris, John
1967   *The Voyage of Captain John Saris to Japan, 1613.* Ed. Ernest M. Satow.
            Original edition 1900. London: Hakluyt Society.

Schaefer, G.
1941   "The cultivation of madder." *Ciba Review* 39:1398–1416.

Schwartz, Paul R.
1956   "French documents on Indian cotton painting: (1) the Beaulieu ms., c.
            1734." *Journal of Indian Textile History* II:5–23.

1957 "French documents on Indian cotton painting, II, new light on old material." *Journal of Indian Textile History,* III:15–44.

1966 See Irwin and Schwartz 1966.

1969 *Printing on Cotton at Ahmedabad, India in 1678.* Ahmedabad: Calico Museum of Textiles.

Sewell, Robert
1900 *A Forgotten Empire.* London: Swan Sonnenschein and Co.

Shah, Rajdeep
1977–78 "Block Printing in Ahmedabad." Research paper. Ahmedabad: National Institute of Design.

Shah, U. P.
1976 *More Documents of Jaina Paintings and Gujarati Paintings of Sixteenth and Later Centuries.* Ahmedabad: L. D. Institute of Indology.

Sherwani, H. K., and P. M. Joshi, eds.
1973–74 *History of Medieval Deccan (1295–1724).* Vols. I and II. Hyderabad: Government of Andhra Pradesh.

Simkin, C. G. F.
1968 *The Traditional Trade of Asia.* London: Oxford University Press.

Singh, Chandramani
1979 *Textiles and Costumes from the Maharaja Sawai Man Singh II Museum.* Jaipur: Museum Trust, City Palace.

Sinor, Denis
1966 "Foreigner-barbarian-monster." In *East-West in Art.* Ed. Theodore Bowie, pp. 154–73. Bloomington: Indiana University Press.

Skelton, Robert
1972 "A decorative motif in Mughal art." In *Aspects of Indian Art.* Ed. Pratapaditya Pal. Leiden: E. J. Brill.

1982 *The Indian Heritage. Court Life and Arts under Moghul Rule.* London: Victoria and Albert Museum.

Slesin, Suzanne
1982 "Chintz flowers in grand revival," *The New York Times* (June 10):C1,8.

Slomann, Vilhelm
1953 *Bizarre Designs in Silk.* Copenhagen: Ejnar Munksgaard.

Smith, George Vinal
1977 *The Dutch in Seventeenth Century Thailand.* Special Report no. 16. DeKalb: Northern Illinois University Center for Southeast Asian Studies.

Sonday, Milton, and Nobuko Kajitani
1970 "A type of Mughal sash." *Textile Museum Journal* III(1):45–54.

Splendours of the Vijayanagara Empire: Hampi
1981 Bombay: Marg Publications.

Steensgaard, Niels
1974 *The Asian Trade Revolution of the Seventeenth Century.* Chicago: University of Chicago Press.

Steinmann, Alfred
1958 *Batik. A Survey of Batik Design.* Leigh-on-Sea, England: F. Lewis.

Stone, George Cameron
1934 *A Glossary of the Construction, Decoration, and Use of Arms and Armor.* Portland, Me.: Southworth Press.

Tachard, Gui
1755 *Voyage de Gui Tachard à Siam.* In *Histoire Générale des Voyages,* vol. 12. Ed. A. F. Prévost. Based on 1688 edition. The Hague: Chez Pierre de Hondt.

Talwar, Kay, and Kalyan Krishna
1979 *Indian Pigment Paintings on Cloth.* Ahmedabad: Calico Museum of Textiles.

Tavernier, Jean-Baptiste
1925   *Travels in India by Jean-Baptiste Tavernier.* 2 vols. Trans. V. Ball. 2nd ed. Ed. William Crooke. London: Oxford University Press.

Terpstra, H.
1915   "De Nederlanders in Voor-Indie bij de stichting van het Fort Geldria te Paliacatta." *De Indische Gids* I:331–60.

Thiagarajan, K.
1966   *Meenakshi Temple, Madurai.* Madura: The Meenakshi Sundareswarar Temple Renovation Committee.

Thienen, Frithjof van
1951   *The Great Age of Holland, 1600–1660.* Costume of the Western World Series. London: Harrap.

Tomoyuki, Yamanobe
n.d.   "Meibutsu-gire." Unpublished typescript. Tokyo: The National Museum.

Turner, Ralph L.
1962   *Comparative Dictionary of the Indo-Aryan Language.* IV. London: Oxford University Press.

Varadarajan, Lotika
1981   *South Indian Traditions of Kalamkari.* Ahmedabad: National Institute of Design, in press.
1981a   "Traditional trade textiles of Gujarat." Unpublished manuscript.

Vetterli, W. A.
1951   "History of indigo." *Ciba Review* 55:3066–71.

Warmington, E. H.
1974   *The Commerce between the Roman Empire and India.* Original publication 1928. Delhi: Vikas Publishing House Pvt. Ltd.

Watson, Andrew M.
1977   "The Rise and Spread of Old World Cotton." In *Studies in Textile History.* Ed. Veronika Gervers, pp. 355–68. Toronto: Royal Ontario Museum.

Welch, Stuart Cary
1976   *Indian Drawings and Painted Sketches, 16th through 19th Centuries.* New York: Asia Society.

Whitcomb, Donald S., and Janet H. Johnston
1978   *Quseir Al-Qadim 1978 Preliminary Report.* Cairo: American Research Center in Egypt, Inc.
1980   *Quseir Al-Qadim 1980 Reports.* Cairo: American Research Center in Egypt, Inc.

Wille-Engelsma, Sytske, and Gert Elzinaga
1979   *Het Hindeloopen van Hendrik Lap.* Leeuwarden, The Netherlands: Fries Museum.

Wolters, O. W.
1967   *Early Indonesian Commerce.* Ithaca: Cornell University Press.

Yazdani, G.
1930   *Ajanta.* Part IV. London: Oxford University Press.

Yoshioka, Tsuneo, and Yoshimoto Shinobu
1980   *Sarasa of the World.* Kyoto: Kyoto Shoin Co.

Yule, Henry, and A. C. Burnell
1979   *Hobson-Jobson, a Glossary of Anglo-Indian Words and Phrases.* Ed. William Crooke. 3rd ed. Original edition 1903. New Delhi: Munshiram Manoharlal.

Zimmer, Heinrich
1964   *The Art of Indian Asia.* 2 vols. New York: Bollingen Foundation.